Robert Lowie and The Crow

The Sun Dance of the Crow Indians

and

The Religion of the Crow Indians

Primary Sources in Native North America

ANTHROPOLOGICAL PAPERS

OF THE

American Museum of Natural History.

Vol. XVI, Part I.

————

THE SUN DANCE OF THE CROW INDIANS.

BY

ROBERT H. LOWIE.

————

NEW YORK:
Published by Order of the Trustees.
1915.

THE SUN DANCE OF THE CROW.

By Robert H. Lowie.

CONTENTS.

ILLUSTRATIONS.

TEXT FIGURES.

PREFACE.

The last Crow sun dance dates back to about forty years ago, for with the old warfare disappeared the sole *raison d'être* of the performance from the Crow point of view. The notes presented in this paper are therefore not at all based on personal observation. Moreover, as none of the main performers survived to the time when I began my inquiries in 1907, the following account is based on the statements of mere eye-witnesses and participants who played a minor part. Within the limitations thus imposed, the data seem satisfactory. I recorded independent descriptions of the entire ceremony by Gray-bull, Muskrat, Bear-gets-up, the Fire-weasel couple, Bear-crane, and others; and the accounts given in 1910 by the two informants heading this list were checked by having them repeat their narratives from beginning to end in the following summer. Ralph Saco (Bighorn District), Henry Russel (Pryor), Robert Yellowtail (Lodge Grass), and James Carpenter (Lodge Grass) are the interpreters who assisted me during this work. I am under special obligations to James Carpenter, who spared no pains in ascertaining additional facts from various native authorities and gave me the benefit of the information thus obtained by his own efforts.

I am acquainted with only two published accounts of the Crow sun dance. The earlier description by Clark in *The Indian Sign Language* (pp. 135–136) is very brief but gives a correct notion of the fundamental features. Curtis' far more detailed account in *The North American Indian* (IV, pp. 67ff.) deserves high praise. On all essential points it stands corroborated by subsequent investigation.

May, 1915.

INTRODUCTION.

The Crow *acki'cirùa*, which corresponds to the sun dance of other Plains tribes, was not a periodical ceremony. It was pledged only whenever a mourner was especially eager to avenge the killing of a close relative by a hostile tribe. In order to attain this end, the mourner or "whistler" (*ak'ō'oce*), as he was called, had to obtain the vision of a vanquished enemy, implying a promise that he immediately set out to see fulfilled. The requisite vision was secured through a sacred effigy known as the *marē' wirɛxbā'k'e*, offering (?) doll, which forms the most important object in the ceremony. The owner of the doll (*ak'bā+ē'ɛxtsia* = charmer?) accordingly acted as master of ceremonies; and he and the whistler must be regarded as the only performers theoretically essential to the ceremony.

That the central idea in the performance was indeed the desire for revenge, is proved by the fact that the ceremony closed with the supernatural revelation sought. In an exceptional instance referred to by many informants even the vision proved unnecessary: one of the enemy had been caught and killed in camp on the first night of the ceremony proper, and this immediately put a stop to the proceedings. The native interpretation of this case is that the whistler was unusually fortunate in thus having the period of his suffering terminated at the very start.

The basic conception thus outlined is so different from what is currently associated with the words "sun dance" that it may seem unwarrantable to apply the term to the Crow ceremony. Here, however, we must draw a distinction between the esoteric and the exoteric aspects of the dance. From the whistler's and doll owner's point of view, the *acki'cirùa* was indeed solely or primarily a means to revenge; but for the tribe at large it was a tremendous spectacle, an occasion for general social and individual religious activity. Many of the exoteric features bear a resemblance to corresponding elements of alien sun dances that is quite convincing as to their having sprung from the same source. There can be no doubt that these spectacular external features are the ones that have in the past led writers to attach the convenient label "sun dance" to a number of Plains Indian ceremonies. Accordingly, the extension of the term to the Crow *acki'cirùa* is unexceptionable so long as we mean merely that some of the elements of the Crow ceremony are historically connected with elements of other "sun dances." Beyond this nothing is implied. For example, it is not at all clear that the Crow ceremony had very much to do with the sun.

The native name, *acki'cirùa* was said to refer to a miniature lodge such as is used by children when playing. According to several interpretations, to be sure, the significance of the term in this connection is that the lodge erected was regarded as a miniature representation of the sun's lodge. This interpretation, however, was by no means unanimous. Sharp-horn, for example, denied any connection with the sun, and several informants thought that the customary English rendering of *acki'cirùa* had been suggested by the name of a corresponding ceremony in some other tribe, such as the Dakota.

The historical relations of the Crow sun dance to that of other tribes will, of course, be clearer after the descriptive section of this paper. For a psychological understanding a word on its relation to Crow culture generally seems necessary.

The Crow sun dance being, from the main performer's point of view, nothing but a quest for revenge, we must inquire how it compares with other Crow attempts to wreak vengeance on the enemy. Now, we find that among the Crow *all* movements against hostile tribes were based on dreams or visions. These the visionary accepted as a promise of achievement that was to be made real either by himself or by the leader who had sought his aid. In the latter case the visionary equipped his disciple with some or all of his mysterious powers and objects, and the two regarded each other as "son" and "father" respectively. In the sun dance this same relationship obtained between the whistler and the doll owner, and as in the preparations for a normal war party the "son" tried to attain his end through his "father's" medicine. The only difference is that in the sun dance it was not the medicineman but the disciple that experienced a revelation, but this is hardly significant since the war captains themselves might have secondary visions specifying the exact conditions under which enemies were to be killed. The particular medicines employed in war parties varied with the visionary's revelations. From this point of view, the sun dance might be characterized as that form of war medicine ritual in which the aim was attained through the magic powers of a doll. But this would constitute a difference only in detail, not in principle, since it is not necessarily greater than that between two ordinary war medicines. Considering the method of securing a vision, we also encounter familiar features. Mortification of the flesh was the common way to arouse the compassion of the supernatural powers, who were thus induced to grant the supplicant a vision with promise of success and well-being. Here again there is nothing distinctive in the whistler's procedure: at bottom he did nothing but what any mourner in quest of revenge might do without undertaking a sun dance.

We might therefore picture the Crow sun dance as composed of two fundamentally independent and but loosely interrelated procedures. On the one hand, there is a complex of social activities shared with other tribes, and therefore possibly of foreign origin; on the other hand, an individual's quest for supernatural aid against the enemy,— a thing likewise in no way peculiar to the Crow when taken by itself, but peculiar to them as the core of the sun dance celebration. On the one hand, we see the aged warriors recounting or acting out their deeds and the entire male population waging mock-warfare against the symbolic tree; lovers philander freely amidst the license of the period; and the virtuous are rewarded with the honor of special duties in the ceremony. But apart from the din of camp activity the whistler, assisted by the doll owner, prepares for the dance in the lodge, his mind fixed only on the consummation of his purpose.

Yet, though this picture would not be wholly wrong, it is probably no more than a rationalistic simplification of the facts. It is, indeed, likely that to the onlooker the sun dance was merely a spectacular performance on the grandest scale within the tribal comprehension. But it is hardly conceivable that the feelings of the whistler should have remained unaffected by such a display of tribal activity. This activity he could indeed wilfully disregard, but its effects could not be wiped from his consciousness. And in so far as the knowledge of it entered into and modified his consciousness the sun dance ceased to be even for him a purely personal religious quest, and his psychological attitude was transformed from that of religious exaltation to that union of social and religious factors known as ceremonialism.[1]

THE VOW.

As stated in the Introduction, there was only one reason for the performance of a sun dance. A man who had lost a child or younger brother — more rarely an elder brother — killed by the enemy, might decide to show the excess of his grief by undergoing the hardest form of mourning, which would at the same time lead to a vision of retaliation, to be followed by a fulfillment of the promise involved in the vision. Such a man would not express his intentions immediately. For a while he would fast on the prairies and mourn, no one as yet knowing what he was about. After some time he would hear a herald announcing to the camp that the people were to

---

[1] Cf. my articles on "The Crow Sun Dance" (*Journal of American Folk-Lore,* **XXVII**, 1914, pp. 94–96) and "Ceremonialism" (*American Anthropologist,* **XII**, 1914, pp. 602–631).

hunt buffalo and get meat for themselves. When he heard this proclamation, the mourner would call the first person who came near him and ask him to send for the chief. The chief came to look at the mourner, who was emaciated and would not look at the chief. "On this hunt," the mourner would say, "I want you to have the hunters keep all the tongues, do not let the children eat any; I want them all." The chief went back and issued an order through the herald who cried: "Save all tongues, he is going to cut ankles!" The pledger's name was not mentioned. Then the people knew what was going to happen. The mourner no longer stayed away after telling the chief, but returned to camp the same night.

Other informants say that the man who wished to make a sun dance, when having his hair cut for mourning, would say to the haircutter, "Leave a little hair on my head, so that I shall be able to tie a feather to it." The haircutter spread the news about camp, and thus all the people learned of the mourner's pledge.

Since it was purely optional with a mourner to pledge the sun dance, it was performed at irregular intervals. And as it involved unusual hardship, there were relatively few mourners who made the vow. Old-dog estimated the number of sun dances he had witnessed at no less than thirty, and Bear-gets-up said he had seen twenty, but these estimates are at variance with those of the oldest informants, who counted no more than thirteen.[1] From comparing different statements I have arrived at the conclusion that during the interval between 1830 and 1874 sun dances were not more frequent than once every three or four years. On the whole, the River Crow and Mountain Crow seem to have had distinct performances, but there is evidence that the two bands sometimes joined for a common ceremony.

THE COLLECTION OF BUFFALO TONGUES.

As stated in the preceding section, the mourner requested the chief to have all the buffalo tongues saved. He required the tongues both in order to compensate those who performed certain special services and also because he was expected to entertain the people at noon during the entire course of the ceremony. In an exceptional instance noted by Bear-gets-up, Big-shade, as whistler, could not get a vision until the sixth day. Accordingly, the supply of tongues was completely exhausted before the close of

---

[1] Young-crane, a River Crow about eighty years of age, enumerated six, and Strikes-both-ways, the oldest Crow living in 1911, recollected only five.

the dance, and he was obliged to feast his guests with $b\bar{a}'rice'$, a kind of dried meat.

When the people set out on the hunt, the mourner was far ahead of them, though always afoot. He wore nothing but moccasins and a buffalo robe. Sometimes the people were lucky enough to find buffalo very soon, at other times it would take them many days. When they finally got to a herd, the young men were requested to kill the game and take only the tongues, Thus, a large number of tongues was secured.

The essential point in what followed was that the tongues obtained were collected, arranged in sets, and re-distributed among prominent warriors who were to have them sliced and dried. As to the details the accounts vary.

According to Muskrat, two men, one of whom had had his locks cut, started out with pack-horses from opposite sides of the camp circle, each accompanied by one attendant. The attendants would peep into every lodge on their way and collect the tongues, which had already been prepared for them. When the two parties met, they crossed each other's paths, turned about, talked, and marched along a diameter of the camp circle to a tent, furnished only with spreads, on which the tongues were unloaded, while two old men were singing songs of joy. The mourner had summoned his relatives to this lodge, where the tongues were strung together in tens, five on each side, and packed on the same horses that had brought them. Then the collectors retraced their steps and unloaded one set of tongues at every war captain's lodge, where the captains' wives laid them on their best blankets. Finally, the two parties again went back along the same diametrical path and unsaddled their horses, which closed this part of the proceedings.

According to Big-snake, there were eight men who gathered the tongues, two of them leading the horses and the rest actually getting the tongues from the people. When they had done collecting, they decided on the bravest men, who would number about twenty, and redistributed the tongues in sets as described above. Gray-bull says that the tongue-gathering party embraced five or six men who had accompanied the mourned-for man on the fatal war party.[1] After the collection, the men went outside the circle and stood there chatting for a while. When re-approaching the camp, they called out aloud the names of distinguished warriors, bidding them prepare by spreading robes. During this procession songs of joy were sung, and as the famous men's dwellings were passed the collectors dropped tongues on robes laid outside the lodges in obedience to their request.

---

[1] This is confirmed by Fire-weasel's wife.

Bear-crane's version does not specifically refer to comrades of the slain man. It makes the mourner borrow five or six horses from as many men, who led them behind the doll owner, who in turn followed the mourner on this tongue-gathering procession. The doll owner's face was painted black to symbolize in customary Crow fashion the killing of an enemy and thus express a hope for the realization of this event. He sang a glad song and shook a rattle; he also gave the mourner his straight-pipe, facing toward the camp.

A single hunt did not always suffice to secure the desired number of tongues, which some informants set at one thousand. Indeed, according to Gray-bull four successive hunts were customary, after all of which the method of procedure was identical except that the first and third time tongues were redistributed among strikers of coups, while after the second and fourth collections the tongues were given to the men who had stolen enemies' horses. Bear-crane says that it was optional with the mourner to demand a second hunt. After the first collection his opinion was asked for, and after some deliberations he would say that another hunt was, or was not, necessary. In the former case, a herald was ordered to make a corresponding announcement. Big-snake seems to think that four hunts were proper, but that it depended on circumstances whether there were two or four.

THE DOLL AND THE DOLL OWNER.

As the desired vision was secured only through a sacred doll, the mourner was obliged to enlist the services of one of the men who owned such dolls. This seems to have taken place after the collection, but before the redistribution, of the tongues. The mourner decided which doll owner to choose for master of ceremonies, and approached him with a filled straight-pipe, asking him to smoke. The medicineman accepted the office with the pipe, thereby adopting the mourner as his son. Sometimes the "son" would try to buy the doll bundle outright from his ceremonial father, but it happened very rarely that an owner consented to sell, and then only for a high price.

Bear-crane knew of six men who had owned distinct dolls, Lone-tree of five, while Young Crane named four owners: Wrinkled-face (Pretty-enemy's deceased husband); Braided-tail; I+ā′kac; and Wandering-old-man. Even apart from spurious effigies made on the basis of a merely pretended revelation (see p. 49), these dolls were not of equal efficacy. According to all Lodge Grass informants and most others, the doll owned by Wrinkled-face took precedence not only of the rest, but of all other Crow medicines whatsoever.

The last-mentioned doll was not supposed to be handled by a woman. When an elderly Indian learned that Pretty-enemy (Wrinkled-face's widow) had unwrapped it for me, he prophesied that she herself, or some of her relatives, would die in consequence. Whether a like taboo extended to the other dolls, I do not know; the contrary is indicated in one account.

The only purpose originally served by the medicine dolls apart from the sun dance confirms the view that this ceremony was essentially a preparation for warlike achievement. Gray-bull says that the doll bundle was sometimes opened before a party set out on the warpath. The doll was then addressed in prayer, and occasionally a feather from the bundle was taken along. Birds-all-over-the-ground gave more specific information. A man going on the warpath sometimes came to a doll owner and paid him some property in order to get good luck. In such a case the owner unwrapped the doll, made a smaller imitation of it, tied the latter to a little willow hoop, and smoked it with sweetgrass incense from a charcoal fire. He also put a string over the buyer's neck (for suspension of the doll?). If the warrior struck a horse in the next battle, he gave the doll owner a horse and returned the doll to him. After he had done this four times, however, he merely gave the owner a horse, and kept the doll for himself. This method of procedure tallies exactly with that followed by a young man desirous of obtaining a reputation and approaching a tribesman renowned for his war medicines.[1] More recently old men were wont to visit Pretty-enemy, requested to see the doll, unwrapped it, and presumably addressed it in supplication.

The origin of medicine dolls is thus accounted for by Birds-all-over-the-ground.

Andícicòpc was the first discoverer of a medicine doll. He was very poor, having lost his parents while a boy. The Indians were moving toward the site of Billings. Andícicòpc went to the highest peak there, where he fasted for two days and two nights. On the third morning a little bird came to the foot of the place where he was resting, and said to him, "Look towards the west, across Mt. I'EXUXPEC." He looked and beheld seven men and one woman who was standing in front of them. Several of the men were beating drums painted with the representation of a skunk. The woman wore an elk-hide blanket and was holding a doll before her face. They began to sing. Andícicòpc could hear them plainly, and learned the songs. For a moment Andícicòpc looked round, and when he had turned back again the singers had drawn nearer, standing now on the top of a high hill. After a while he looked away again, and when he turned back, they were moving on the top of a bluff between the sites of Park City and Absaroka. Again he looked away, and did not see

---

[1] This series, vol. 9, *Social Life of the Crow Indians*, p. 232.

them again until he heard a noise at the foot of his bed, where the seven men and the woman suddenly appeared. The woman stood in front, holding the doll in both hands. One of the men addressed the others: "We live so far away, and have come so far to see this boy; we are tired." The woman in the elk-hide robe was the moon. They sang again. The doll was tied up in a buckskin envelope. At the end of the first song, the head of the doll suddenly popped out of its own accord. A second song was sung. The moon shook the doll at the boy, and stepped back. Then the doll came out of its cover far enough to expose its arms. At the end of the third song, it exposed its waist. After the fourth song, the woman stepped forward and then back again. The doll came out completely in the guise of a screech-owl, and sat down on the moon's hand. The boy was at this time lying straight on his back. The screech-owl flew about, and then perched on Andícicòpc's breast. Suddenly one of the men loaded and cocked a breechloader, then he stepped toward the boy and sang a song. The woman said to the screech-owl, "Now, little screech-owl, this man is going to shoot you, you must make your medicine." It stood up on its feet, and began to flap its wings. The man drew closer, and shot at the owl, which entered his breast and began to hoot inside. Andícicòpc looked towards the northeast. In the valley he saw a sun dance lodge. The seven men and moon got up, singing and beating their drums. They moved towards the lodge, making four stops on the way and singing a song each time. After the end of the fourth song, they entered the lodge. Andícicòpc looked through the lodge and saw the doll attached to a cedar tree on the north side of the lodge. At the foot of the tree he saw the whistler lying flat on his back. The seven men sang four songs again. Moon went to the whistler, and seized him by both hands. At each song she raised him slightly, then put him back to his former position, but the fourth time she pulled him up completely. Moon then stepped up to the doll and gave it to the whistler, who held it in both hands. After a short time he put it back in its place. They sang and danced, facing the medicine doll. Thus the doll was discovered, and whenever anyone wished to have a sun dance he requested the visionary to direct the ceremony. The doll represents the moon-woman, and the lodge the sun's lodge.[1]

Sharp-horn gave the following fragmentary data with regard to I+ā′-kac's doll and his own (see p. 15).

The sun dance was started by a Crow named I+ā′kac. One day he went up to the highest part of the mountains near Yellowstone Park. There he fasted and abstained from drink for five or six days. Finally he saw the sun dance and the doll in it. The lodge was very large, and was painted with four black streaks extending from top to bottom. When he returned, he was very lean and weak, and his lips were sore. He told the people that if an enemy came to the lodge at night they must kill him. One day an enemy was found sitting in the lodge unarmed. The Crow killed and scalped him, and then danced and rejoiced over his death. When a person wanted to have a sun dance on account of a relative's death, he came to I+ā′kac. I+ā′kac painted his everyday lodge to represent the sun dance lodge: the upper half was painted black, and four streaks ran down to the ground, one on either side of the door, and the others more to the east and west, respectively.

---

[1] Bear-gets-up said the doll owner had a vision of the sun. This is interesting in view of other statements that the ceremony was not at all connected with the sun (p. 8).

The doll described on p. 15 ff. was revealed to Sharp-horn's brother, who went up a mountain after one of his brothers had been killed by the enemy. After four days he heard the beating of drums inside the mountain. Some-one was calling out aloud: "Everyone, come in! They are going to have a sun dance here!" Someone came out, and took the visionary inside, where he saw the dance. Thus he became a medicineman and afterwards made a doll in accordance with what he had seen in his vision. He bequeathed it to Sharp-horn, and if there were still enemies in existence my informant would still feel entitled to make a sun dance.

Another informant [1] furnished the following statements with regard to Bear-from-above's doll.

This doll was discovered by an old woman, no one knows where or how. She made and kept it all her life, and told people that this doll had a big lodge. Being a woman, however, she could not erect a lodge. The doll entered her body and she took it out only just before her death. She made four dolls in all, which were in-herited by her son. When he died, one of the dolls came into the possession of Bear-from-above's father, a brother of the former owner. Then it was inherited by Bear-from-above, who kept it until his wife's death, when he buried it with the corpse. Probably the old woman who discovered the doll was the only one that ever saw all of it. In later times, when they wished to look at the doll, they first took cedar leaves and made incense over a charcoal fire, and then unwrapped the doll, but so as not to expose anything but the head and shoulders. The face looked like that of a doll baby; it was painted yellowish and red. Bear-from-above, being a doll owner, might have conducted a sun dance, but he never did so. He placed it on the outside of his tipi, and no one touched it; there it remained so long as the Crow camped in the same locality. When Bear-from-above had dreamt to that effect, he took the doll down on the following morning, smoked it with cedar-leaf incense, spread a blanket and laid the doll on it, unwrapped it as described above, and finally replaced it. Only on such occasions did he unwrap the doll. The two owners preceding Bear-from-above had conducted sun dance ceremonies.

Of the doll figured in Fig. 1 Muskrat said that it was revealed to Little-son when he was mourning for a brother's death. Little-son passed it on to his brother, and he to Akékuc. It was inherited by Akékuc's brother, and through his death it passed into the possession of his wife, Pretty-enemy.

I have seen two dolls, the one owned by Sharp-horn, and another which I purchased of Pretty-enemy.

At Pryor, Sharp-horn showed me a buckskin doll. It was smaller than Pretty-enemy's, being probably not more than five inches in length, and seemed to be of much more recent origin. The body was triangular, taper-ing toward the bottom. A belt encircled the waist, and on the breast there was a rectangular cross of greenish-blue beads, two rows to each arm, which

---

[1] I am not sure whether this was Bear-from-above himself.

represented the morningstar. The neck was completely covered with a strip of weaselskin. The head was painted with small circles for eyes, and a mouth; the place of the nose was taken by the lower half of the vertical

Fig. 1 (50.1–4011a). Sun Dance Doll.

arm of a morningstar design precisely similar to that noted on the breast, except for its lesser size. The entire figure was almost covered out of sight with a profusion of owl feathers. Some shells and strips of skin were attached to the back. Near the center of a twisted string serving for suspension, there was attached a little bag stuffed with tobacco. This bag was constricted into two fairly spherical halves, the upper and smaller of which was decorated with blue beads and from its form might have been taken for a head, though Sharp-horn did not know that it was meant for one. Sharp-horn said that the doll was stuffed with parts of herbs and roots, as well as with tobacco seeds. The bundle from which the doll was taken also contained a large globular buffalo-hide rattle. The outside of the rectangular bag containing the doll was painted on one side with the design in Fig. 2.

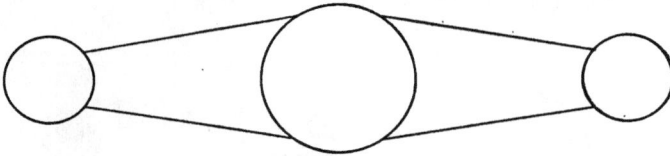

Fig. 2.   Decoration on Sharp-horn's Doll Bag.

The lateral figures, according to Sharp-horn, represented persons. He did not know the meaning of the central circle; Plenty-coups suggested that it might represent a lodge.

The doll purchased for the Museum (Fig. 1) formed part of a bundle, all of which was enclosed in a rectangular rawhide bag (Fig. 3). A duplicate

Fig. 3 (50.1–4011c). Doll Envelope, which contained the doll in Fig. 1, and all the objects shown in Figs. 4, 5, 7, 8.

of lesser value was said to have been buried with the owner's husband. Owing to the fact that Pretty-enemy, being a woman, had never even unwrapped the bundle prior to the negotiations with me, her information as to the contents of the bag was very unsatisfactory, and since the fact of the purchase was to be kept secret her statements could not be supplemented by directly questioning others. The doll was only used on two occasions,— by some braves who unwrapped it and prayed to it before setting out on a war party, and in the sun dance, where it became a living person for those gazing at it. The lower part of the doll is covered by a piece of buffalo skin with the hairy side on the inside. Eyes and mouth are crudely marked in black; on the body, front and back, were a number of rectangular crosses (already partly faded in 1910) which represented the morningstar. The head is topped with a profusion of plumes. Pretty-enemy did not know what kind of stuffing there was, but Birds-all-over-the-ground made the general statement that sun dance dolls were stuffed with sweetgrass and white pine needles, and had their hair parted like women.

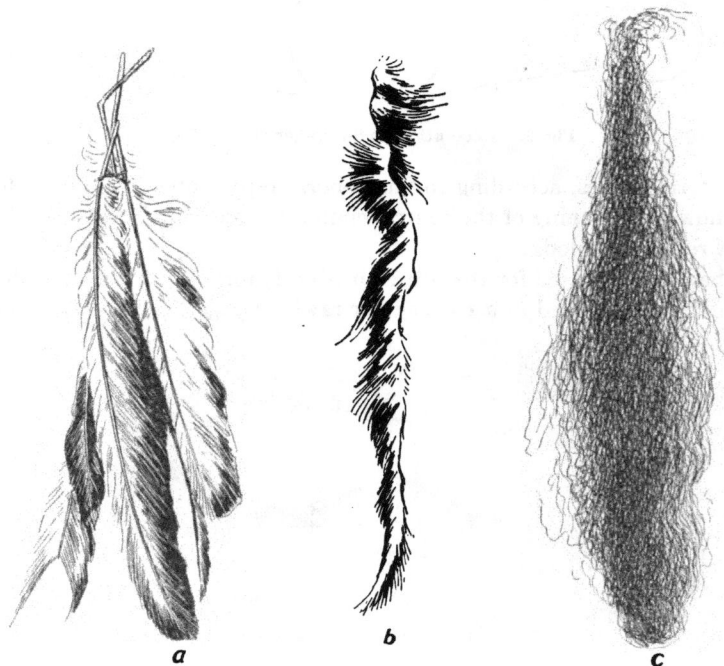

Fig. 4 *abc* (50.1–4011k, n, l). Feathers, Skunkskin, and Hair forming Part of Contents of the Doll Envelope shown in Fig. 3.

Three strips of skunkskin (Fig. 4b) in the bundle undoubtedly represent the anklets and necklace referred to in accounts of the ceremony, the latter being placed round the pledger's neck to make him go mad (see p. 48). Of the two rawhide effigies (Fig. 5b, c), one was said to have been attached to the whistler's hair. The remaining articles include two beaded plaques (Fig. 7), fairly large bunches of feathers (Figs. 4a, 8b), hair (Fig. 4c), and an awl (Fig. 5a) mounted in a wrapped handle.

THE PRELIMINARY LODGE.

The precise relative order of the events following the (last) tongue hunt is not certain; it may be that the contradictory statements obtained reflect actual transposition of proceedings at different performances. Thus, it would appear from some accounts that after the tongue hunt, the site of the ceremony was selected, that then the entire camp set out toward it, making the trip in four stages, and that on each of the four nights of the journey a preparatory ceremony took place in the whistler's lodge. But Gray-bull makes the four preparatory ceremonies precede the journey to the

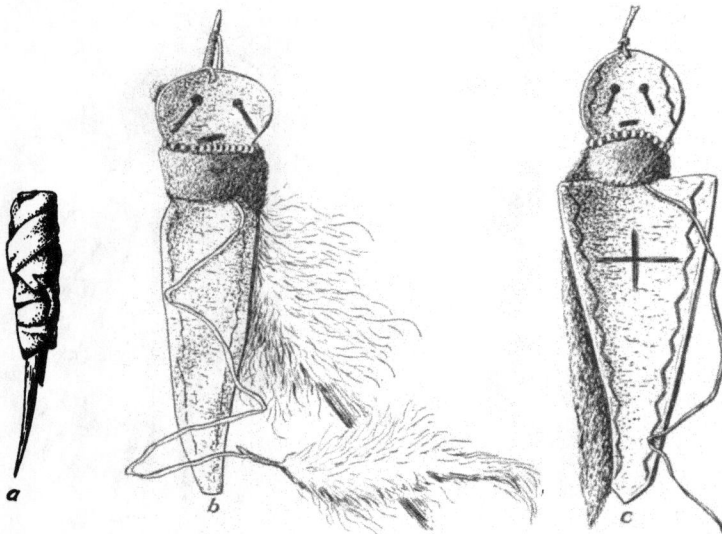

Fig. 5 *a* (50.1–4011f), *b* (50.1–4011g), *c* (50.1–4011h). **Awl and Rawhide Effigies from Doll Envelope.**

site; and Bear-crane puts the first performance in the preliminary lodge even before the *selection* of the site. The following account is based on Bear-crane's narrative.

After the hunt the whistler's tipi was carpeted with ground-cedar and a bed of small-leaved sagebrush was prepared in the rear. As soon as the lodge was ready, the whistler entered from the left side and went to the bed, followed by the doll owner, who seated himself on his right. Old men came in uninvited and sat down on the mourner's left without approaching close to him.   They would ask how many days he intended to dance and he might reply, "I'll dance a night and a day till the sun goes down," or specify some other time.[1]   Then he would say, "Sing for me tonight, and I will dance for you."   The doll owner deliberated for a while and then answered

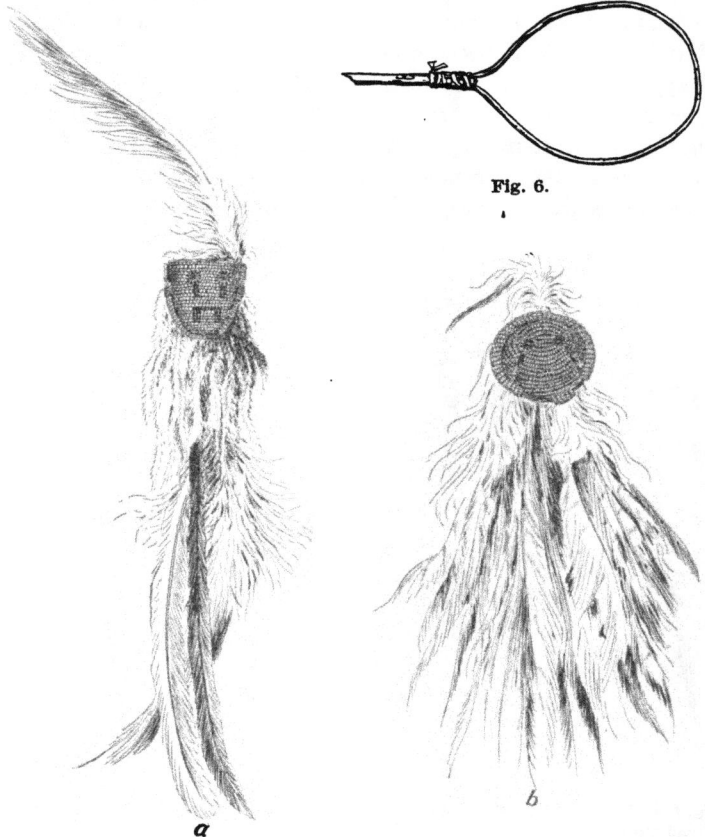

Fig. 6.

Fig. 6 (50.1–3938).   Model of Hoop, within which the Doll was suspended.   The real hoop was edged with feathers.
  Fig. 7 *ab* (50.1–4011 e, d).   Beaded Plaques with Feather Ornamentation, from Envelope shown in Fig. 3.

that he would.   Then any of the old visitors might leave or stay according as they wished.

The doll owner went to his own lodge to ask his wife whether she knew

---

[1] But the termination of the ceremony was always dependent on the circumstances indicated on p. 49.

of any tanned deerskin. She went out and got one. Then her husband bade her take it to some virtuous woman, who accepted it, shouldered it, and took it to the doll owner's lodge. There the doll owner smoked it with ground-cedar incense, smoked himself, and also the chaste woman's body and hands. The medicineman smoked a knife, pretended three times to cut the skin, and the fourth time actually cut it. Then the virtuous woman sewed a kilt of it, with seams on the sides. Takes-the-dead did the

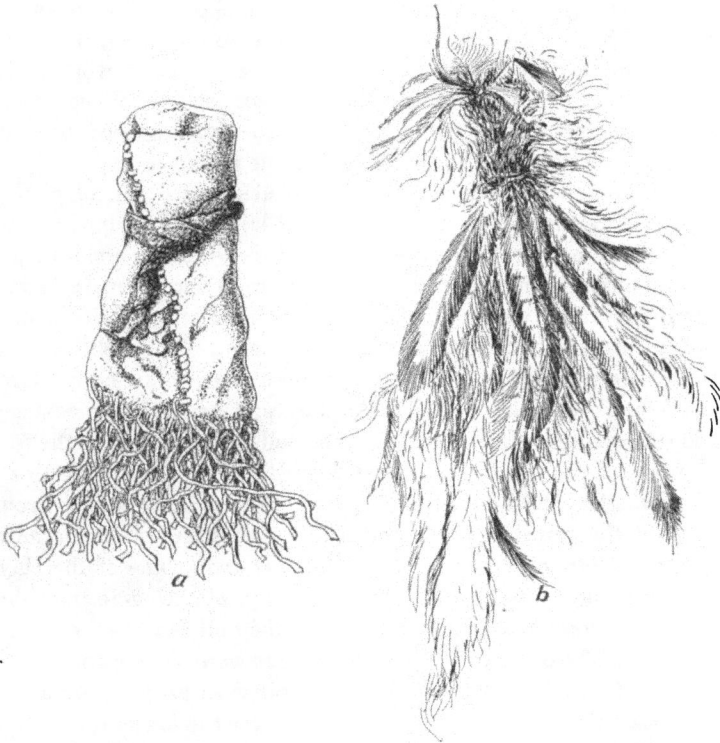

Fig. 8 *a b* (50.1–4011j, l). Folded Buckskin and Bunch of Feathers from Doll Envelope.

sewing when a young woman; she used buckskin thread instead of sinew and made four feints at sewing before she actually began. When done, the woman went home. The medicineman smoked the garment, wrapped it up, and put it away. Next he asked his wife to get a robe that had never been worn. She went out and brought it to her husband, who smoked it and put it away.

Then the medicineman said, "I will go over to see my son and find out whether he has any medicine and whether he can get any." Returning to the whistler's tipi, he sat down in his customary place, smoking a pipe without saying anything till the whistler finally asked him what was up. Then the doll owner bade him try to get eagle tail-feathers. The doll owner returned at once to his own lodge, while the whistler got the feathers only' from his relatives, who gave them gratis because of their pity for the whistler. A man was dispatched to present the tail to the doll owner, who bade the messenger summon a certain other man, for during the ceremony the doll owner had dictatorial powers. The messenger looked for the person named and delivered his message. When the second man appeared, the medicineman bade him tell five or six women renowned as good workers to cut branches and leaves for the tongue lodge (dë'ĕce asu'a). When this structure was completed, a herald proclaimed that the tongues distributed among distinguished warriors were to be brought to the tongue lodge.

Among the articles prepared for the whistler was a pair of plain moccasins, sewed by the wife of a man who had killed and scalped an enemy. The moccasins were blackened with charcoal to symbolize the killing of an enemy, and buffalo hair was sewed on them to represent an enemy's scalp.

When everything was ready for the first preliminary performance, the best singers were called in, including two women. The doll owner came in with his wife, who sat by him. He brought a cup of white clay. Ground-cedar, a whistle, a rattle, two feather plumes, a skunk-hide necklace, the kilt, and the robe were all brought in. The doll owner went near the whistler and brought all the articles enumerated within easy reach. No one went near the whistler, the doll owner, and the doll owner's wife. From the beginning of the sun dance preparations the whistler was not allowed to come near any other woman. The doll owner took some of the clay and sang the first song as yet sung in the ceremony, at the same time shaking the rattle. As soon as the people heard it, they all ran over to watch the performance. The doors of the whistler's lodge were wide open.

In front of the doll owner's seat was a pit with burning buffalo chips. His wife took a little ground-cedar and put it over the fire so that it burned. She sang with her husband, and smoked some ground-cedar after every song. They sang four times, alternating two distinct songs. After the fourth song, the doll owner slowly lifted the kilt, as if it were something delicate, smoked it, and put it down. The same four songs with the accompanying actions were repeated, then the medicineman took the whistler by his thumbs and raised him gently. A crier inside the lodge bade all the people keep still and listen. The whistler wore nothing but a clout. While being lifted, the whistler put his left foot over the chips to smoke it. Then he stepped into the kilt with his left foot. The doll owner's wife gently raised the kilt into position, tied it with a leather cord serving as a belt, and tucked in the part of the kilt above the belt.   The doll owner looked over the whistler, regarding his emaciated form.   The singers put down their pipes and got ready to sing.   Then the doll owner called for the best drum. When it had been picked out, the drummer rose, and taking care not to pass the whistler, went round by the door to hand the drum to the doll owner. The latter's wife cast more ground-cedar on the buffalo chips and turned the drum back and forth over the fire, while her husband sang.   The drum was returned to the drummer, who retraced his steps to resume his seat. The medicineman smoked his rattle, and sang three times in a low voice, but the fourth time he sang out aloud, and was then joined by all the singers. Now he was ready to paint the whistler.   At the first song he smoked his own hands, holding them close to the whistler's head and slowly lowering them to the ground by the end of the song, keeping time with the singing. He acted similarly during the second song, and also during the third, but when that ended he dipped his hand in the white clay.   At the fourth song he put clay on the whistler from head to foot.   Next he went round and similarly painted the whistler's back, then his left and right side, down to the ground.   Then his wife took a sagebrush, mixed it with white clay, and now actually [1] painted the whistler with white clay all over his body.   The same song was continually repeated.   After the woman had done, her husband made a cross on the whistler's breast and another on his back, both representing the morningstar.   Then, beginning at the space below the mourner's eyes he marked with his fingers a lightning design down his face to represent the whistler's tears, and also put a lightning mark on his forehead to represent the mode of painting used by the sun.   The doll owner now took the skunk-hide, made a slit in the middle, smoked it with cedar, painted it with white clay, and put it first round the whistler's right side, then round his neck, and finally round his left side.   As no one was allowed to go in front of the whistler, the doll owner himself, in putting the skunk-hide on him, passed back of him.   Then he tied a plume to the top of his ward's head, and repainted with white clay the spot where paint might have been rubbed off during the process of tying.   Standing back, he took a long square look at the mourner.   Then he got a plume for the little finger of the right hand, painted it with clay, tied it on the whistler's finger, stepped back, and looked at him again for a long time.   In the same way he tied a plume to the little finger of his "son's" left hand.   During these proceedings the drummers continued singing.

Next the medicineman's wife threw cedar into the fire and smoked the

---

[1] This word indicates that her husband merely pretended to paint the mourner.

moccasins previously prepared on both the inside and outside. She first put the left moccasin, then the right, on the whistler's feet, for he himself assumed a passive attitude at this stage. Her husband took the robe, smoked it, and at the end of each of three songs feigned to put down the robe, actually laying it down the fourth time. Taking the whistler by the arm, he made him sit down, and put the flaps of the robe round his "son," who did not so much as touch the garment, the woman adjusting the robe for him. Taking the whistle, the doll owner smoked it with cedar incense, put clay on it, and knelt down before the whistler. Putting the whistle into his own mouth, he danced in kneeling posture, blowing his whistle and facing the whistler. This occupied the time consumed by four songs. After dancing through this period, the medicineman took the whistle from his own mouth and pretended to put it into the whistler's, which was open, ready to receive it. This was done three times, the whistle being moved closer each time, until at the fourth time the whistler took the whistle into his mouth and began forthwith to dance as his instructor had done before, to the drummer's accompaniment, who sang four songs. The whistler then took the whistle out of his mouth and shook it. The doll owner took it from him, then the whistler bent forward and the doll owner placed the whistle round his neck.

The singers ceased to sing, and smoked four times, emptying their pipe. It was now time for prominent men to enter. Four warriors came in from the left, and four from the right. All of them were equipped as though for a war expedition on foot. Wolfskins were carried as scout badges. The warriors had a rope, and each had a bundle of moccasins tied to his belt. They were not allowed to carry guns. At this time the eagle tail-feathers were still in the doll owner's tipi. The warriors remained standing after their entrance. The drummers waited for the two women singers to sing this song: —

hī′ra	wacúE	rāwi′ewà,	bāsúE	hirě′rEk'.
Woman-friend,	my song	sing,	my house	is here!

Then the drummers all took up the song, while the warriors clapped their mouths and shouted. The eight warriors flirted with the women. When the song had been sung four times, the warriors closest to the whistler on his left and right side said: —

ku'′ kahé,	karīrī′at'bak'	dúxiwarē`k·.
Well to begin that	just like this I did	when I went on warpath.

Then each told how he had brought horses from the enemy, achieving undisputed honors. The drum was beaten after every sentence. When each of the eight warriors had told of his deeds, they went out. The drummers had another smoke, then sang again. The medicineman went through the motions of touching the whistler three times, before he finally took off the plume from his head and laid it down. His wife threw cedar on the fire, then her husband smoked the plume and laid it down. After three feigned motions he took off the skunkskin and laid it down. Next he removed the plumes from the little fingers, the whistle, and last of all the moccasins, for the kilt was not taken off. The singing continued. Then the medicineman said, "Bring in his quilts." Sagebrush and cedar were brought in two bundles, and the doll owner made a pillow of cedar, and a bed of the scented sagebrush. Taking hold of the whistler, he seated him, then gently threw him on his back and put his arms down, with the palms up. Taking the robe, he acted three times as if about to cover the whistler and the fourth time actually covered him. The whistler was obliged to remain thus on his back all night, with his feet toward the fireplace. The doll owner said: "Bring in the buffalo bull." The people then brought in a skull with the horns. The medicineman put the skull close to the whistler's head, making it face the same way as the whistler.

All singers then went out except the doll owner and his wife, who talked to each other and decided where would be the best site for the sun dance lodge, saying, "We'll move over there." The place might be about three miles away.

When their mind was made up, the man bade his wife summon the crier, who was told to notify the camp. Then the couple decided which society was to act as police, whether the Big Dogs or Muddy Hands, etc. The crier notified the camp and told the police to go early and put a wood pile on the site of the lodge. A pile of wood was raised to the height of about fifteen feet. The tongue lodge had been put up in the meantime; it belonged to the whistler. It was very close to the preparatory lodge.

The next morning the police were waiting at the site. The people came in, and the police made them form a circle round the site. The whistler's lodge (ak'ō'oce asu'ᴇ) was moved together with the tongue lodge, which was in the form of a shade-lodge. Both were placed a little distance in from the circumference, toward the center. The whistler's lodge faced the wood pile.

Now the performance in the preparatory lodge was repeated on three nights.

THE BULL HUNT.

Before the sun dance lodge could be erected it was necessary to select and fell the lodge poles and to obtain two buffalo bull hides for tying the tops of the poles. Statements vary as to which event preceded the other. Following Bear-crane, I will first give an account of the bull hunt.

After the fourth night in the preparatory lodge, the doll owner began to think. No one was allowed to go out. People did not know where the buffalo were. The doll owner tried to find out. He thought to himself, "Where can a bull be?" Then, when he had made up his mind, he thought of the best marksman and the best butcher in the tribe. Finally, he would say, "Over yonder will be found a buffalo bull. Call So-and-so for marksman and So-and-so for butcher." Of course the medicineman had got an inspiration from some supernatural source. Then some man went out and summoned the men named. They might be far off, but came in neverthe-less. "Look here!" said the doll owner to the hunter. "Yes!" "Look here! Tomorrow at dawn you shall rise, select a fast horse to take you out and another fast hunting horse, take two arrows from your quiver and go out. With one arrow you must kill a buffalo bull, and with the second arrow you must kill another. Kill a bull six, seven, eight, nine, or ten years old, but not one younger than six years." No common marksman was allowed to go out, for there were a number of taboos to be observed that severely taxed the skill of the best sharpshooter. The bull had to be killed before sunrise, without the use of a gun, and he had to be killed with the first shot. More-over, the arrow must not pass clean through his body, for there was to be but a single hole in the hide. Sharp-horn, who had himself served as marks-man on the bull hunt, said that if the arrow went clean through the body, he at once discarded the bull he had shot and looked for another.

The butcher also received his instructions. To him the doll owner said: "Make your knife as sharp as possible. Have one horse to ride, and one to pack on. Do not eat any part of the bull, not even the smallest particle. Do not taste of it, for it belongs to the sun, and the sun will watch, looking down at you all the time." Both the sharpshooter and the butcher received two plumes and a string. To the former the doll owner said: "When you shoot the first buffalo, let him die. When you shoot the second, you must tie one plume to his tail and the other between his horns, before he falls to the ground." The butcher was instructed to deal in the same way with the first bull shot. This part of the undertaking was, of course, exceedingly dangerous, and though Bear-crane said that no bull ever tried to hook the

butcher or marksman, another informant who had actually participated in
these expeditions spoke of having been repeatedly put to flight by the
wounded buffalo.

The hunting party set out and executed their commission in accordance
with the instruction received. As soon as a bull had expired, the butcher
cut him up with the utmost dispatch, though with great care. The head
was severed and discarded except for the nasal cartilage and tongue. The
four feet and the backbone were also left behind. All the remaining parts
of the body were taken back to camp, the hide being thrown over the sharpshooter's horse, and all the meat on the pack-horse. On the return trip the
marksman surrendered his knives and weapons to the butcher so as not to
carry anything sharp, and rode in front of his companion.[1]

While the bull-hunters were gone, the doll owner tried to think of the
best two [2] scouts in camp. All men in the tipi being ready to act as his
servants, some were selected to call the scouts, who immediately appeared
in obedience to the summons. The doll owner told them to prepare wolf-
hide sashes,[3] take white clay, and go out to watch for the bull-hunters.
They were to act like real scouts on a war party. As soon as they saw the
returning bull-hunters they were to paint themselves with the white clay,
and come back to camp, howling like wolves.

On one occasion one of the scouts fell asleep and the other did not notice
the returning party till they were quite close. The hunters said: "Look
at those sleepy wolves." Then the scouts saw them and rushed back to
camp with the utmost dispatch. Every one was amused at this incident.

When the scouts caught sight of the hunters they ran back to camp
howling like coyotes or wolves. According to Gray-bull, they went straight
to a four-post shade-lodge erected in the center of the camp for the deposition of the meat to be brought in later by the hunting party. Then there
was a big stir, the people came out, and sang songs (according to Old-dog,
in praise of the returning hunters). They took away the scouts' guns, and
asked them whether they had seen anything. The scouts replied that they
had seen an enemy who had no weapons and could easily be killed. Then
all rejoiced and shouted. According to Gray-bull, the scouts coming back
exclaimed: "The men who went out have killed some person, and are
bringing the scalp and good horses!" In another version by the same
informant the scouts are made to announce: *ĕ'k·ōn barĕ ra'sastsïs'e-taherïa*

---

[1] Bear-gets-up said there were two bull-hunting parties, each comprising a sharpshooter
and a butcher. They went in opposite directions and each tried to get back to camp before
the rival party.

[2] Gray-bull speaks of three or four such men. Red-eye said the scouts were men who
had fought the enemy without suffering injury.

[3] The customary badge of scouts.

kā'mnem dū'ok'. hā'ma+u! (Over there not disturbing our alertness (?) some Piegan came. Wipe them out!) Red-eye says that, when the scouts appeared at the edge of the camp, the people rushed toward them, trying to count coup on them, and take their weapons. One would say, "Here I strike an enemy"; another, "Here I take a bow"; and so forth.

In preparation for the reception of the bull-hunters the flaps of the whistler's tipi were thrown up, and the whistler faced toward the incoming party. Nearly the entire camp were lined up, but left a free passageway. The doll owner had ground-cedar spread on the ground. He put on a cedar crown, blackened his face, took his rattle and slowly approached the hunters, who stood still in the center of the camp, where they packed all the meat on one horse. It was necessary that all guns, arrows, and knives should be removed from the place where the hunters and doll owner met. When the doll owner had got there, the hunter reported: "You sent me out to those two people. I got them without trouble, all their heads, etc. They are here, and you can do with them as you please." Then the doll owner, singing a song of rejoicing, led the hunter and butcher toward the whistler's tipi. No dog was allowed to get in front of him. Before the whistler's tipi two plots had been strewn with cedar. After four stops they got to the cedar plots. There three or four lucky warriors gently lifted the hunter and butcher from their horses, so that they stepped on the cedar carpet. They were made to sit on robes. The scouts who had reported their approach were seated among the crowd. The meat and hide were unloaded and spread out on the cedar leaves. Then the people examined the buffalo to see whether any part of it were lacking, and if it was all there, a crier bade the old men and women come and sit in a ring outside the lodge. The people said: "We'll eat. It is well. It is well that there is only one hole in the hide." Two lucky chiefs were selected, each to cut up the inside of one of the two buffalo, and two others sliced the meat, which was distributed among all the people there. Gray-bull says that the entrails and marrow bones were given to the old men, and the meat to the old women. One man took the first hide by the neck end, another by the tail, hairy side down, and carried it to the whistler's tipi. There the second hide was placed on top of the first with its hairy side up. According to Gray-bull, each hide was spread out, and water was poured on it. Then it was carefully folded and put away, leaving as much water on it as possible. A big lump of pounded charcoal was laid with it.

Sharp-horn's personal reminiscences indicate some variation from the proceedings as recounted above. When he came back from the bull-hunt, a certain medicineman (apparently not the doll owner) was waiting for him with blackened face, wearing a headband of cedar leaves, and holding a rawhide rattle in his hand.   No sooner had he caught sight of Sharp-horn than he began to sing sacred songs.   When my informant got nearer, the medicineman seized his bridle-rein, and conducted him to the whistler's lodge.   The whistler had painted his entire body with white clay, and was wearing a bone whistle round his neck.   Sharp-horn remained on horseback until one of his own paternal uncles came and helped him dismount.   The same uncle bade him enter the lodge, where he found the whistler and Iā′kac, the doll owner.   Iā′kac asked Sharp-horn, what he had done. Sharp-horn replied, "I saw two enemies moving away from me.   They did not see me.   I ran toward them and killed one; the other ran away." Thereupon he was requested to smoke from a pipe, and then went home. One corner of the lodge was carpeted with ground-cedar, and over it the buffalo hide was spread.   The meat was put on the skin.   In the opposite corner the meat and skin obtained by another hunter were treated in the same way.   The old people then came and stayed outside the lodge, where the meat was distributed among them.   They feasted there, sang and enjoyed themselves, and finally went home with whatever meat was left. The skin of the buffalo remained in the lodge all day.   Old men came in and smoked with the whistler and doll owner in the course of the day.

Muskrat has the whistler himself going out to meet the hunters and bring them to his lodge.   He asked them, who had killed the buffalo with the first arrow, helped the marksman dismount, and had all the parts of the buffalo brought to the lodge, where they were deposited on skins. Muskrat, as cook, sat down in front of the whistler's lodge.   The head end of the skin, which rested on ground-cedar, was turned northward, while the head itself was made to face south.   One person inside made an offering. Then old people were invited to come there.   Muskrat took a knife, cut up the buffalo meat into so many parts, and distributed these among the old people.   Even the guts were divided in this way.   Then the old people were sent home.

THE LODGE POLES.

After the proceedings just described the doll owner said, "Tomorrow we shall cut the lodge poles."   One of the men announced this to the people and bade them rise as early as possible on the following day.   A lucky warrior, or otherwise one of the policemen, was dispatched to select the best trees for lodge poles, and returned to report.   The first tree (corresponding to the center tree of other tribes) was generally a cottonwood, the rest cottonwood or pine trees according to the doll owner's vision. Early the next morning the crier roused the people, bidding the young men fetch their horses and telling the young women to paint and dress up in their best clothes. So all put on their best finery, and the men used their finest trappings, such as mountain-lion skins for saddlecloths.

Now the tail-feathers and the tongues collected for the ceremony were to be used. The doll owner bent a willow into a hoop (Fig. 6), and made a network of twelve willow sticks in the hoop, topping each with an eagle feather painted black. In the center of the hoop the doll itself was suspended, representing the sun's face. The doll owner held up the doll in the hoop and stood beside the whistler, who faced the doll owner's wife. The doll owner said to his wife: "I am holding this doll. Sing your song of joy, and then put the tongues in a kettle, and when you come back we shall all start." The woman sang the song four times, and then went to put the tongues into the kettle. She sent for fresh willows and had them sharpened and painted black. A real scalp was tied to the fork she used in cooking.

When the woman got back, the people set out to cut lodge poles. The whistler walked way ahead with the doll, behind him the doll owner and his wife, next the singers and the police, then four women who were carrying as many of the newly cooked tongues as possible. One of the policemen went ahead toward the trees selected: "It's here, come over here." Then they went to the spot, where the whistler stood still and faced eastward. The four women put down their tongues and made a small shade, under which the doll was put. The whistler sat under the doll, both he and the doll facing eastward. No one was allowed to come within a certain distance from the tree. Half of the police stayed in the rear of the camp. There was always someone on the watch. There was a big stir in the camp. The police made everyone go, except the very old men and women and the sick, who were not compelled to go if unwilling. Then the police in the rear notified the other policemen in front, and a crier proclaimed to the whole camp that all were here and were to keep still.

It was now necessary to select an absolutely virtuous woman for the office of tree-notcher,— one who had been married in the most honorable manner, that is, by purchase, and who had always remained faithful to her husband. Chastity was also a prerequisite for the office of firewood-carrier to be mentioned below (p. 35), but in this latter case it was not necessary that the woman should have been purchased by her husband. According to Bíricé-rútsic (Takes-the-dead), even eligible women would decline to serve as tree-notcher because anyone who had filled the position thereby forfeited the right to re-marry if her husband died. It was for this reason probably that my informant herself had at first declined to serve, saying, "Not yet, I shall wait till I am an older woman." She remained virtuous, however, though she was often courted by young men, and in order to avoid their advances she refrained from dressing in an attractive way, so finally they let her alone. At one time her son (grandson?), No-horse, was almost dead, and then she vowed that if he recovered and she were asked again she would consent to serve as tree-notcher. He was restored to health, and she carried out her vow, praying at the same time that her husband might live for a long time. Thereafter she was greatly respected and received the first share in the distribution of food.

Takes-the-dead says that the whistler himself, painted white, and leading the doll owner and men volunteering to fast during the sun dance, chose the virtuous woman. According to Bear-crane, the doll owner ordered the police to bring her, but first of all the four tongue-bearers opened their bags, selected the best tongue, and gave it to the police. One of these took it and, followed by his associates, went to a woman reported to be of irreproachable character, and handed her the tongue. If, in spite of her reputation, she was not perfectly chaste, she would openly confess her deficiency, being afraid to deceive the people, for her acceptance bore the character of an oath, and deception would bring bad luck on the camp. The formula of refusal on the ground of unchastity was: "*masa'pĕ hupïk·*" ("My moccasin has a hole in it"). According to Curtis' narrator, a woman who consented to fill the office was led through the camp and the young men were expected to challenge her oath if they truthfully could. This informant mentioned a particular case where a woman who had been challenged was at once ignominiously dismissed and ever after taunted by her joking-relatives with reference to her public disgrace.[1]

The tree-notcher who accepted the office handed the tongue to her husband, who rejoiced over the honor conferred on his wife. She was taken to the whistler, who had remained under the shade with the doll owner and his wife.

The doll owner next sent the police for a berdache. The berdaches were hiding, but at last one was discovered and brought to the spot amidst the laughter of the crowd. Being ashamed, he would cover his face. He was made to stand next to the tree-notcher with an ax in his hand.

The berdache received a tongue as his fee.

A crier next announced that one thing remained to be done,— the selection of a captive (*dä'tse*), apparently of the tribe that had killed the whistler's relative and thus occasioned the sun dance. This captive seems

---

[1] Curtis, op. cit., 69.

from Crane-bear's account to have been a woman.[1] She also received a tongue in compensation for her services; but if she had a child, the child got the fee instead of the mother. The herald now announced that everything was ready and that all the people should come close to the tree.

The captive greased her hands and blackened them with charcoal. The virtuous woman was holding a stone maul or ax and the prong of an elk antler, chipped into a fine awl-like point and blackened at the top. She faced west, the captive east, the berdache north. The doll owner and his wife stood behind the virtuous woman, the man having a rattle in his hand and holding the tree-notcher by the shoulders. The doll owner began to sing and shake his rattle. At the close of his song he pushed the tree-notcher a little and she touched the tree with the prong and pretended to drive it in with the maul (or ax). While pointing her prong at the tree, she would think to herself, "I'll stick this in his eye," meaning the enemy. At the same time the captive and berdache also made corresponding motions of pretense. The people who had gathered around hallooed. The second song was sung by the doll owner amidst growing excitement on the part of the bystanders, the men getting ready to discharge their guns at the tree. At the close of the song the woman again pretended to drive in her wedge. A third song was sung with similar concluding actions on the part of the tree-notcher. At the close of the fourth song the tree-notcher actually tapped the horn without driving it in, the berdache touched the tree with his ax, and the captive painted a black [2] ring round it by rubbing his blackened hands round the trunk. Gray-bull said that the captive was expected to address the tree as follows: "May the poor Indians have a good war the next time, may they kill a Dakota and take captives!" As soon as the captive had done her work, she and the tree-notcher stepped back and the berdache began to chop down the tree. All the people began to shout and shoot at the tree, regarding it as an enemy.[3] The young men shot at its limbs and struck it with their coup sticks. After felling the tree, the berdache hid in the crowd, being ashamed. According to Bear-crane, this first tree was not used in the construction of the sun dance lodge, but was allowed to remain where it fell. The performance in connection with the tree was called *ī'tsia ō'waxùa*, "pole-notching," while the chaste woman was designated as *ak"ī'tsi+ōwaxè*, *ak'* being a prefix denoting the actor; *ī'tsia* is the term applied to one of the first four poles put up in the erection of a lodge.

---

[1] This does not appear from other versions to have been necessarily the case.

[2] Some said the ring was red, but the majority expressed the opinion stated in the text. Black, it was explained, always symbolized the killing of an enemy and was thus appropriate for the occasion.

[3] Old-dog said it represented the enemy who was to be killed as a result of the ceremony.

Twenty poles had been selected for the lodge. The young women rode double with their sweethearts, chopped the trees and dragged the logs toward camp, where they were placed together in a row.

The police went round to count the trees chopped down, and when twenty had been cut they gave orders to cease and bade all the people go to the flat. The police kept watch on the outside of the crowd to prevent the people from getting away, for now twenty young warriors were to be selected to sit on the logs, and as this involved an obligation on the first four chosen [1] never to retreat from the enemy, the young men tried to run away and hide in avoidance of the dangerous honor. The police — or, in other versions, the whistler's relatives — rode fast horses in pursuit of the young men. When seized, the fugitives cried out four times and sometimes resisted capture, so that they had to be pulled by the hair and brought in by main force. In the meantime the whistler was seated with doll and hoop, awaiting the pursuers' return; he was painted white all over his body and wore a robe. When the horsemen came back with the captives, the whistler, walking slowly because of his weakness, approached them, carrying his hoops, with which he touched the captives. This act at once broke their resistance and made them utter a cry of distress and sit down each on the edge of one of the logs. Each captive received a tongue. According to Red-eye, the whistler put white clay on the young men's faces and with the doll brushed their bodies from head to foot. A crier announced "So-and-so has been touched by the sun's feathers." After the first four who were "made to die" [2] had been selected — the first one, according to Bear-crane, by the whistler, the other three by the police —, sixteen men were chosen by the police because of their wealth. Though they cried out, "I am poor," they were forcibly seized and made to straddle the remaining logs without being touched by the whistler. The relatives of all the captives brought robes, beadwork, horses, and other property, and deposited them before the young men straddling the logs. Instead of actually bringing a horse, a little stick was laid down to symbolize such a gift; sometimes as many as fifty horses were thus pledged. All this property was appropriated by the doll owner, but after reserving the bulk of it for himself he distributed the rest among those who aided in the performance of the dance. [3]

Muskrat sets the number of poles, and accordingly of captured warriors, at ten, and adds some details. Each of the warriors had a relative raise the pole before he sat down on it. When all were seated, a herald announced

---

[1] From other accounts, the duty was incumbent on all the twenty men.

[2] The same term, *ce'kᵘuk'*, is applied to them and to the officers of military societies with corresponding duties.

[3] But compare p. 38.

that they were ready. Then girls came running, and tied strings round the poles, each girl then sitting down behind the corresponding warrior. This indicated that she was to ride behind him, when he should drag the pole to the site of the Lodge.[1] There the ten poles were arranged like the spokes of a wheel, the place of the hub being taken by a free circular area.

Gray-bull said that a man captured by the police in order to sit on one of the logs would lift the end of the pole. If he said, "My pole is heavy for me, I will sit down," this meant his willingness to serve the whistler. If he lifted it with ease, he was absolved from duty, and a substitute was obtained. When the girls had taken their places on the horses' backs behind the young men, a young woman whose brother sat on one of the first four logs would ask her sweetheart to haul her brother's pole before the others. A rope was attached to the logs, and they were dragged to the site. The first man to untie a log had the privilege of leading the others in an expedition for willows to shade the sun dance lodge.

All started as though for a race. The girls cut the willow twigs, then the young men approached them, made them ride double, and dragged the willows to camp. They went out twice for willows, then different societies, such as the Foxes and Lumpwoods, went round on opposite sides of the camp and wherever they met they laid the willows in a ring round the lodge poles. Then it was about evening, and everyone went home. During the night the societies met and sang in front of different lodges, accompanied by a few young women.

The tongues were returned to the tongue lodge, and the whistler returned to his tipi. People were careful not to pass him from the side whence the wind blew; they were also afraid of menstruating women. The whistler had not eaten or drunk for six (?) days and nights now and was not even able to expectorate and barely able to look about. The doll owner had also abstained largely, though not entirely, from food since the beginning of the ceremony, so he was also lean by this time. People came in and out of the whistler's tipi. Only the whistler and the doll owner were allowed to smoke a straight pipe, indeed the former was not permitted to touch any other, though the doll owner might do so when outside. The doll owner instructed the whistler, but in so low a tone of voice that no one else could hear what he said. The visitors dropped out one by one till only the whistler and the doll owner couple remained. The woman had her husband announce that the lodge was to be erected on the next day. Her husband planted a cedar

---

[1] A Reno informant, on the other hand, said that the men sitting on the logs were not required to help drag the poles. One-horn said that the first four poles were taken straightway to the site in front of the woodpile, the others being placed symmetrically on each side of them.

behind the buffalo skull, tied the doll hoop to the tree, and secured another buffalo skull,— the two skulls representing those of the two bulls killed and butchered by the sharpshooters' parties. Finally the doll owner took off his son's ceremonial raiment, smoked him, and retired with his wife.

ERECTION OF THE LODGE.

At dawn the crier told the people to rise since the lodge was to be erected. The people rose and got ready. At breakfast the young men saddled their horses, and all the young women assembled in one place. The young men rode horses and invited partners from among the young women to ride behind them. Then they went to the timber and got firewood, partners assisting each other. They tied together what wood they had. The police, after a consultation among themselves, went among the women to look for a leader. If the one they sought was there, they would go to her camp and hand her one tongue. They asked her whether she had ever had a paramour. If not, she accepted the tongue and gave it to her husband. Then she was brought to the assembled party of young men and women, was put on horseback and took a bundle of brushwood, which she put in front of her saddle. Then the police went among the renowned young men, selected one and gave him a tongue, as a token that he was to lead the chaste woman. Then all went to the camp in single file. The leader was called *ak'birĭtbasā́ane* (the one who goes first for firewood). They circled round the inside of the camp, then went straight to the site of the lodge and deposited the brushwood; there was a big pile of it. The members of this party then scattered to their respective homes and for a time did as they pleased.[1]

Muskrat's version is slightly different. The girls, according to her, dressed up as neatly as possible, and sat down in a circle, each keeping before her some wood. The young men approached singing, and stopped in front of the girls. They said nothing for a while, then each drew closer, and asked some girl to ride with him. The wood was tied to the front of the saddle, and they mounted, the girls riding in front and the man behind. They went through the camp looking for an absolutely virtuous woman to lead the procession. If a young man was able to say of a candidate for the honor, "She has a hole in her moccasin," some other girl had to be chosen.

---

[1] According to others, the clay expedition (p. 42) preceded that for firewood, but the order given in the text is that given by Crane-bear, Muskrat, and Fire-weasel's wife.

One informant said that if an unchaste woman attempted to lead, someone would shout, "You are crazy! You have done so-and-so!" When a proper leader had been chosen, she and her following set out to collect brushwood, and piled it up outside the lodge. Both this leader and the young man who got the clay received a cooked tongue. Red-eye said that the virtuous woman walked afoot during this expedition, leading the horse of the bravest warrior.

Then the men were told to prepare some outer tipi poles (those regulating the smoke-vent). All the young men got some, paired them off, and tied each pair together. Three of the poles for the sun dance lodge were joined and laid on top of the pile at the site and the remaining poles were laid down, as were the willows.

The doll owner prepared ground-cedar and smoked the two buffalo hides brought by the hunting party. The first hide was laid in line with one lodge pole. The ground was chipped, and on it was laid the first hide. Then the whistler was brought to sit on the ground-cedar in front of the tipi. The doll owner painted him with charcoal, and then painted with the same substance the fleshy side of one of the hides. The second hide had to be handled with care. He turned the hide outside where it had been hit by the arrow and first painted part of the hide down to the back, then carefully took up the other half of the hide. Before painting the buffalo hides, the shaman sang four times. One of the whistler's female relatives brought a sharp knife, a whetstone, and a hoe; these she handed to the doll owner, who sharpened the knife. The doll owner had his chin, forehead and cheeks blackened; he wore a cedar crown and moccasins like those worn by the whistler. The blackening of the hide symbolized vengeance on the enemy. People flocked round to look on while the police were joining and tying the first three poles with a bundle of willows.

The shaman gave the knife to his wife. A man renowned for horse-stealing was sent out to cut willows and brought them in. These willows were about two feet long. Two other men, renowned horse-stealers, were picked out to tell of their deeds, and began to make the sticks sharp-pointed. The woman painted the willows with charcoal. The knife is likewise blackened. She sang four times, then began to cut the buffalo hide. Ground cedar had already been put wherever the shaman had to step. He motioned toward the four quarters, then he cut one foreleg. Then he made four motions and cut the hind leg. He did the same with the other side of the first hide, and repeated the same performance with the second. After learning how many pins there were for fastening the hides, he began to make perforations along the edge equal to one-half the number of sticks prepared for this purpose and did the same with the other skin. The hides were taken up by two parties of renowned men respectively and rubbed under one of the lodge poles without being made to touch the ground. The heads of both hides were made to face east. The willowstick pins were run through the peripheral holes to unite the two hides. Other hides were soaked in water and cut into strips at this time to be tied to the lodge poles so that voluntary self-torturers might suspend themselves therefrom.

The three or four main poles of the lodge [1] were raised at one end so as to rest on the woodpile heaped up to mark the site, and their point of intersection was wrapped with willows. Then the ends of the poles were pushed through the perforations of the hides, which were twisted so that the poles could be run through several times; and the sharpened pegs were run through the hides so as to hold them together. Together with a wrapping of willow-sticks and ground-cedar, these hides represented an eyrie. The next step was for the police to get some man who had a bird [2] for his medicine and bid him hasten to sit in the nest.

The bird man wrapped himself in a robe pinned with a wing-feather, painted his face according to his vision, tied his medicine objects to the back of his head, took an eagle feather fan in each hand, and began to whistle bird-fashion in his lodge. He approached the site, making four stops on the way. No one, not even a dog, was permitted to pass in front of him by the police. If he heard a dog bark, he would go right back to his lodge. He continued to imitate the actions of a bird. At every halting place he sang a song. He walked toward the pole against which the hides had been rubbed, and when he got there he again began to sing. At the end of the fourth song he walked up the pole, flapping his "wings," and sat or knelt down in the nest. Then all the people shouted and raised the main poles with the aid of the coupled tipi-poles that had been prepared. The main poles were lifted a short distance, perhaps a foot, then they were lowered again. The bird man whistled. The poles were lifted and lowered three times, and the fourth time they were raised to the proper height. At this point, one witness states, the bird man stood up and faced successively toward the west, north, east, and south. Holes were dug and the butt-ends of the poles were made to rest in them. The man in the nest continued to impersonate a big bird, pretending to fly and to raise the big poles as they were being hoisted into position. The remaining lodge poles were lifted by the same device of coupled tipi poles as if to push the nestling down, but

---

[1] Fire-weasel's wife, Muskrat, and Crane-bear give the number as three, One-horn, Gray-bull, and Sharp-horn as four.

[2] Crane-bear specifies that it was a spotted eagle. When the Crow speak of a "bird" in this connection, they usually mean an eagle. Muskrat was the only informant who said that the man's medicine was the sun.

he managed to get out of the way, and with a rope thrown to him he succeeded in tying together the main and additional poles. The willows and brush collected by the parties of young men and women were now employed in the construction of a cover. The willows were tied between poles from the ground to the height of a person's breast, where a space was left free to permit looking in. Thence the covering was continued to the top. On a windy day the lower part of the screen was supplanted with sheeting. Sometimes rawhide was used to cover the upper space. Muskrat said the sun dance was sometimes held in the winter, in which case the willow railing

Fig. 9. Frame of Crow Tobacco Adoption Lodge, resembling in structure that of the Crow Sun Dance Lodge.

was constructed as usual, but the upper part of the lodge was covered with buffalo hides. According to Gray-bull, however, the ceremony took place only in the summer.

The woodpile marking the site was removed, and the bird man slid to the ground as fast as possible and ran home. According to Gray-bull, he was entitled to all the gifts deposited by the log-straddlers' relatives, while others say he received only four choice articles from the lot.[1] On descending

---

[1] However, compare the statement on p. 33, that the doll owner appropriated all these goods.

to the ground the bird man announced a consolatory vision in the whistler's behalf, such as: "I have seen a person killed. A short distance off in the prairie I saw a person lying down dead already."

In view of the type of sun dance lodge found among the Dakota and other Plains tribes, it is necessary to emphasize the difference between them and the Crow structure. The latter was unanimously declared to resemble the tobacco adoption lodge (Fig. 9), except that it was larger, having twenty instead of ten poles. It is further worthy of note that the general plan of structure of, say, the Arapaho sun dance lodge is not unknown to the Crow, for they use a somewhat similarly constructed shade lodge in the summer (Fig. 10). The distinctive type of sun dance lodge used by the Crow is all

Fig. 10.   Frame of Crow Shade Lodge, resembling Structure of Sun Dance Lodge of other Tribes.

the more remarkable. A model constructed by Red-eye (from Pryor) is illustrated in Fig. 11.

The time had now arrived for the *birā'retarisùa,* No-fire dance, also called "Animal Dance." Crane-bear said this performance had been instituted by the morningstar, who had asked the sun to sanction its intro-duction. The police gave notice to the people, who came scurrying to the screen and got ready to look on.

The No-Fire dance consisted of the entrance of war leaders with their respective followers for the purpose of possibly seeing a vision in the as yet not quite completed structure. The war parties took turns, each being headed by a scout, while the captain, carrying a pipe with a scalp tied to it, came last. These performers had prepared during the last part of the lodge-raising procedure and now came out of the captains' tipis, to the singing and drumming of musicians seated within the lodge. The young women

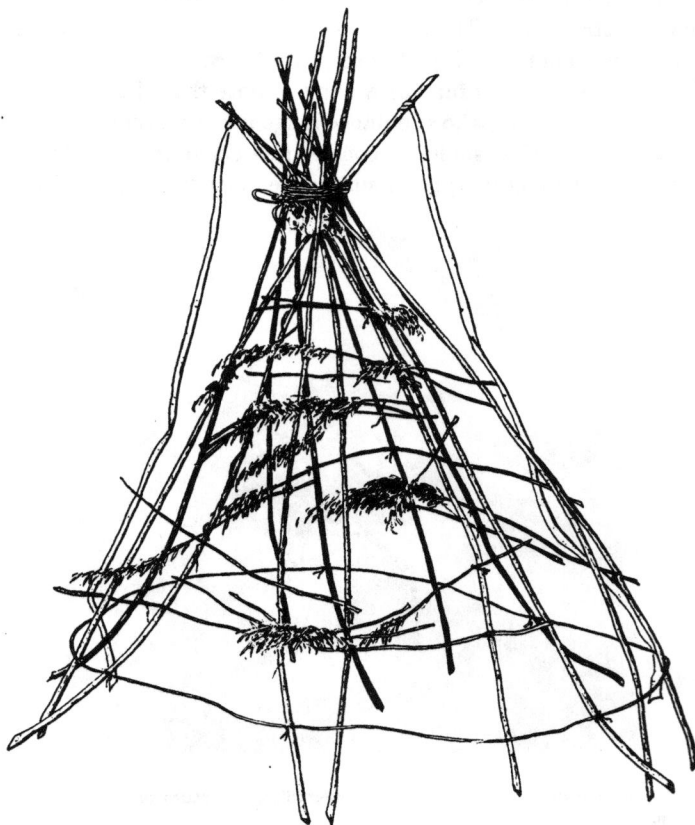

Fig. 11 (50.1–4012). Model of Crow Sun Dance Lodge, made by Red-eye. The nest and the ropes for the self-torturers are represented.

clapped their hands to their mouths, and the people shouted, "The war leaders are ready to come now!" Then the captains and warriors ran to the lodge, making four stops; some dragging ropes, others carrying whips, and all acting as though in a fight. The first party entered, swung about to the right, circled round, and then faced the door (i. e., east). While making their circuit they were looking up at the nest in quest of a vision. Then the captain might announce that he saw nothing, or perchance he might proclaim that he had seen a Sioux killed, whereupon he and his men made their exit on the side so as to avoid collision with the second group of war-riors at the main entrance. They hurried to their tipi to change clothes and rush back to the lodge to watch the next party perform. Possibly as many as ten war parties made their successive appearance in the lodge, all repeating practically the same procedure, which consumed several hours altogether. Finally, the people went home and the singers adjourned to the whistler's lodge, where they sang throughout the evening. No one was allowed to enter the sun dance lodge. A herald went through the camp announcing that the people must rise early the next day since one more thing remained to be done. That night the whistler was already almost dead with exhaustion though he had undergone but a small part of the suffering that was to fall to his lot.

A characteristic story of a war captain's vision was told by Lone-tree, who had previously experienced revelations from the Dipper and the bald-headed eagle: —

As I was sitting in front of my tent, watching the people build the (sun dance) lodge, the widow of the slain Crow for whom the ceremony was undertaken came crying through the camp and looking for me. When she saw me, she laid her hand on my head. I was considered the best medicineman. She begged me to help her and come in to make medicine for her. My medicine was the bald-headed eagle. I promised to do the best I could, and bade my wife summon six men, for with them I should make seven, and there are seven stars in the Dipper (í'g·e sá'puɛ = seven stars). The men came clad in buffalo robes. We all painted our faces yellow, and put red paint below our eyes and on the forehead. We carried ground-cedar branches in our hands and a shell on the braid in the back of our hair to represent the bright-ness of the Dipper. I wore a whistle and carried a bald-headed eagle, of which I had reddened the nose. When we were ready, I got up, and we smoked outside my tent. Then we walked a short distance, halted and smoked, then proceeded again until at the fourth stop we came to the lodge. The singers were in there waiting, and a crowd had gathered outside, but the whistler was not yet there. My party went in, and I entered last of all. We came in on the left side. I stood there and began to whistle near the fire, looking up toward the sky. I sang the bald-headed eagle song: when doing this I was wont to close my eyes and could then see everything about me. While whistling, I beheld a body hanging, head foremost, from the intersection of the poles, with blood all over the body. I ceased whistling, looked up again, and saw nothing. The widow was standing outside waiting for me. I told her what I had seen in my vision, and she thanked me. Since there was so much blood I thought that it represented three enemies. Four days later three enemies were killed.

Muskrat told of another instance, when a captain walked backward instead of forward, stopped, whistled, and looked at the nest. The singers called to the party to stop as their captain had seen something. Then the captain, standing in the center, said: "I saw a man lying down, I saw his yellow foot. There are many medicinemen here, but not one of you has seen him." That same night a Piegan was killed by the Crow.

The day after the war captains' performance the crier announced again that the young people were to get white clay. Then all the young women dressed and assembled in one spot, the police looking into every lodge to see that the female inmates joined the gathering. The young men also went there, and selected partners with whom to ride double. The police took a tongue and began looking for a virtuous young man to act as leader of the expedition. It must be a man who had never taken liberties with any woman but his own wife, in particular, one who was not *ak'bǐ'arùsace* [1] and had never played with his sisters-in-law. Anyone who had transgressed these rules of sexual decorum would decline office, saying, "I made a hole in my moccasin." If a pretender attempted to serve, some one of his sisters-in-law would cry out: "You played with me!" "You touched my breasts!" "isa'pe' it'bū'retk', bitǎ' xīᴇre! (His moccasin is soleless, cast him aside!)

At last a suitable man was found, and he led the procession to a spot where there was good clay. He picked up some of it before any of his following, but before so doing he said, "Because I never did such and such a thing, I wish you to kill an enemy and have a good time." Then he put the clay into a cloth, all the rest following suit. On the return trip the virtuous man went afoot, leading the horse of the best-looking woman round the camp so that everyone might see them. He and the rider got a tongue each. Finally he laid the clay down in a big pile by the place where the whistler's bed was to be arranged, i. e., in the rear of the lodge. The police came in, and a man who had been with a party that made a captive told of the deed, whereupon the police chipped and smoothed the rectangular site of the whistler's bed, where the clay was then put on in the form of a little ridge.

THE WHISTLER'S ENTRANCE.

In the meantime a crier had gone out to summon good singers to take drums and go to the whistler's tipi. While the police were fixing the clay, these musicians were with the whistler. The cedar tree was carried out of the whistler's tipi to the sun dance lodge by two men, two others carried the buffalo skulls one apiece, and the doll owner and his wife followed in the

---

[1] *ak*, one who; *bǐ'a*, woman; *rùsace*, kneads (?). The term is applied to one who sneaks to a lodge at night, lifts the cover where a woman is lying, and takes certain liberties with her. See *Social Life of the Crow*, p. 221.

rear. The doll owner adjusted the cedar and the skulls in their proper
position in the lodge, and sprinkled charcoal on the fireplace, while his wife
brought in some fat from a buffalo's neck and painted the bottom of the
cedar with greased charcoal. The whistler, who had already been painted
up with the same ceremony as on the first preparatory day, remained in his
tipi. He wore a skunkskin necklace and skunkskin anklets; a plume was
tied to the solitary lock of hair on his head, and another to each of his little
fingers. Gray-bull says that the whistler wore a buckskin shirt sewed by
the leader of the firewood expedition, while others speak of his wearing
nothing but a deerskin round his waist or buckskin knee-leggings.

As soon as the doll owner and his wife had returned, they and the musicians commenced to sing and the whistler began to dance, blowing an
eagle-bone whistle suspended from his neck, and holding the hoop enclosing
the doll. The people were lined up in two long rows to watch his exit, but
left a passageway for the procession. The whistler took a few steps towards
the door. At the close of the first song he thrust his hoop outside and pretended to go out, but stepped back. At the close of the second song he
put the hoop outside so as to expose a little more of the feathers, but also
his head and bust. At the close of the fourth song he came outside, and
walked a short distance, followed by the singers. Then he halted and
danced, looking at the doll. He proceeded toward the lodge, making four
stops altogether before he reached the entrance. Then he went in, putting
the feathers in front of him and walked up to the cedar, followed by the
doll owner couple. The husband took the hoop and tied it to the cedar,
which was behind the bed, like the buffalo skull. The doll was arranged so
as to be on a level with the whistler's face when he stood up. The musicians
entered on the right side and formed a circle. When the whistler had entered, all the spectators ran to the lodge to watch the performance from the
outside. The men allowed the women to get ahead and lean against the
railing, then came up and hugged them from behind.

In a rectangular space in the center of the lodge a fire was built and
maintained by the fire-tenders (*ak'birā'aptse*), who were members of the
slain Crow's war party. Some say they sat on the right side of the door
for one entering, but Fire-weasel's wife, whose statement is supported by
Crane-bear's diagram, says they sat on the left. On each side of the fire
a pole was stuck into the ground, and from a crosspiece connecting them
kettles were suspended. The women acting as cooks wore ground-cedar
head-bands and carried forks painted with charcoal and decorated with
scalps at the upper end.[1] They brought in tongues and cooked them. In

---

[1] Red-eye says the forks were painted with black stripes.

the meantime the musicians were resting and smoking. The cooks were to prepare tongues every day of the ceremony.[1] Either on the night of the whistler's entrance or on the following day, young men distinguished for their war record took long poles, sharpened at one end, and painted yellow rings around them at different levels. These poles they stuck into the lodge, pointing them at the cook. If a man was really a noted warrior, those inside impaled a tongue on the stick; the warrior took it outside and presented it to his sweetheart. Another informant said that the warrior's sticks were painted red. When the young men stuck in their poles, someone first inquired, "Who is that?" If the person was not a pretender, he received a tongue. An especially eminent man, according to Bear-gets-up, would get two tongues.

During the cooking of the tongues on the first night of the whistler's entrance renowned men had their wives painted red and themselves painted according to their medicines. The women carried bundles of spoils secured by their husbands from the enemy. The distinguished men had the privilege of coming in from either side, but the first one entered on the right side. Their wives deposited guns and bows in front of their husbands and pointing toward the door. According to one version, one of the warriors would represent his exploits in battle, selecting four or five men to impersonate his own party and several others to play the part of the enemy. Then he ran round the lodge, pretending to kill four or five enemies. Other captains followed suit. However, according to Red-eye, the warriors merely *recited* their deeds. He says that they were supposed to walk toward the left when in the lodge. One man transgressed the rule on one occasion, but another took a branch, slapped the offender's face with the leaves, and said, "You are going the wrong way, people are going in the opposite direction."[2]

About this time those who desired to torture themselves in order to obtain visions suspended themselves by the breast or shoulder from the twenty poles of the lodge. Their bodies were daubed white all over. Sometimes there were two ropes hanging from each pole, and a correspondingly greater number of would-be visionaries. Those who did not find room to suspend themselves from the poles fixed forked posts with ropes outside the lodge and underwent the same mode of torture. Medicinemen or other famous tribesmen would assist these young men in their preparations on account of their power to get visions for them. A noted warrior would tell of his own deeds. Then he would say, "This man wishes to do

---

[1] Fire-weasel's wife said that a certain woman who also acted as cook in the tobacco dance served in the same capacity during the sun dance.

[2] Crane-bear puts the warriors' pantomime at a somewhat later time (see below).

what I did," and pierce his breast for him.   Some tortured themselves by
dragging through the camp as many as seven buffalo skulls attached to a
skewer piercing their backs until the skulls tore loose.   The self-torturers
would begin with mortification of their bodies in the morning and release
themselves at night.   Then they would retire to little four-pole structures
covered with leaves and brush, outside the lodge.   According to Fire-
weasel's wife, they would finally proclaim their visions, saying, for example,
"I shall strike a coup with a coup stick in the next battle," "I am going to
steal a bay horse," etc.

The whistler never tortured himself beyond fasting and not drinking
any water, the period of his complete abstention beginning with his entrance.
In this he was joined not only by the self-torturers, but also by the fire-
tenders and, according to Muskrat, by a party of twenty young men, who
stayed behind a willow screen erected near the door.   Some informants set
the number of fire-tenders at ten or more and seem to suggest that this
office was filled by the members of the war party that sustained the loss of
the whistler's relative.

As soon as the renowned men had come into the lodge and the tongues
were cooked, the musicians sang their first song: "bìmāpéciwe, dā′ciri
k·ōk'. birɛ′xe k'andit'ā′rarawa." ("Water weeds are your lodge poles.
The drum (obj.) beat ye!")   The doll owner took a whistle and began to
dance.   At the close of the song he put the whistle into the whistler's
mouth, and the whistler himself then began to dance on the clay bed,
making the dirt fly and continually gazing at the doll.   At the first drum-
beat the self-torturers, both inside and outside, began to run round their
poles.

The first song was sung four times.   Then a renowned man went to the
door and mimicked his deeds against the enemy, went back to his place, and
told about his deed in words.   After he had sat down, the song was sung
again eight times.   Then a second man rose and told of his deeds, and so on
until all had told theirs.   The first night the number of renowned men was
only about six; there certainly were not so many as ten.   Eight songs were
continued for all the deed-tellers.   When all deeds had been told, the doll
owner beat a rattle and sang a song, which was taken up by the musicians.
Standing behind the whistler, he removed his robe, slowly untying the belt,
and laid it down, with the hairy side up.   After motioning four times with
his hands, he removed the whistle from the whistler's mouth, untied his
skunkskin necklace, and laid both on the robe.   The drums were beating,
and the singing continued all the time.   Next the doll owner removed the
plume from the whistler's head, took off the left moccasin and laid it down by
the robe, then removed and placed the right moccasin on the same side,

both toes facing the door.[1] The whistle, necklace, and plume were then picked up and tied to the doll, as was the owner's rattle to the cedar.

While being undressed, the whistler continued to stand facing the doll. The plumes were taken from his little fingers, then he was seized by the right arm and made to face the door. The doll owner took him by the thumbs, made him lie down on his bed, and covered him with a robe up to the neck. As soon as the whistler caught sight of the doll, he began again to gaze at it. At the foot of the bed a hole was dug in the ground, charcoal was put in, and ground-cedar leaves were smoked there.

Now the whistler went to sleep, and all the people went away. No one except the fasters were permitted to come near the lodge. The fasters' beds, patterned on the whistler's, were made by their relatives, of ground-cedar and scented sagebrush. The doll owner couple went home and called a crier, whom they ordered to rouse the camp before dawn.

THE CONSUMMATION OF THE CEREMONY.

Early before dawn the crier proclaimed: "Our friend has been lying on his back for a long time. Get up and eat!"[2] All the young people of both sexes now began to paint and dress in their best clothes. The musicians ate their breakfast and proceeded directly to the lodge, where they began to sing. The doll owner was as yet at home, bathing, resting, or combing his wife. The people were waiting for him to prepare the whistler. When he was ready, he walked slowly toward the lodge, stopped and looked round for a while, and finally slowly took a seat with his wife amidst the beating of drums. The people made a rush as soon as they noticed the doll owner's exit because they wished to watch his performance. White clay, scented sagebrush, and cedar leaves had been prepared; the clay was soaked in water and the woman laid it before her husband, who began to smoke. His wife used a buffalo shoulderblade to scoop buffalo chips into the pit at the foot of the whistler's bed. The large fire in the center had gone out, but had been renewed by a fire-tender before the doll owner's entrance that day. Now the woman built a fire in the pit, throwing in

---

[1] This seems inconsistent with a statement by the same informant, that the whistler wore no moccasins while dancing, and that the moccasins are put on his feet before he goes to sleep.

[2] In another version the old people are made to rouse the doll owner, saying, "Your comrade has been lying down for a long time." (*dĭ'rapä̀'tse kàraxapä' cī'Ek'.*)

cedar leaves for incense, while her husband was smoking a straight-pipe.[1] The doll owner put some ground-cedar branches below the whistler's feet. To the singing (of the musicians?) he smoked his hand and pretended to remove his ward's robe three times. The fourth time he actually took off the robe, smoked it, and let it lie as on the previous day. After laying down the robe, he removed the right moccasin, smoked it, removed the left moccasin, and laid both down as before.[2]

While the doll owner was preparing the whistler, the other fasters might do as they pleased, sit up or lie down. Those who had not torn loose might be still running round, while some who had dragged buffalo skulls attached to their backs began to come into camp.

The doll owner raised the whistler to his feet, holding him by his thumbs. The whistler tried to limber his legs, nearly fell from weakness, but was supported by the doll owner. He stepped on the ground-cedar and was then turned round to face the white clay prepared in a cup.

The singers continued to sing. The doll owner made three motions, and the fourth time put his hand into the cup. Then he made three motions toward the whistler's person, and the fourth time touched him from the top of his head down to his feet, then on the sides and back of his body as before. Dipping his hands into the clay, he daubed it all over the whistler's body. Standing back a little, he painted any spot that was not yet daubed. He made a cross on the front and back of the whistler's body. He made three motions for the head-plume, the fourth time he smoked it and put the plume and skunkskin on the whistler. Then he smoked and tied the plumes for the little fingers. Taking the whistle, he daubed it, took it into his own mouth, and danced alongside of the whistler, who did not dance at this time. Taking the whistle out of his own mouth he put it into the whistler's. Then the drumming stopped. The whistler stood still. Yells of excitement were heard: "He is going to start to dance!" Famous men who had painted up for the occasion now came in; their number was not fixed.

The doll owner sat down and smoked. On the right-hand side for one facing the rear there was a crowd, while on the left there were only a few relatives. When ready the musicians sang a song, the whistler only moving the upper part of his body and his hands. Women joined in the singing. They repeated the first song sung in the preparatory tipi. The renowned men on the right side began to have a sham battle against the warriors on the left side, one party representing the Crow, the other the enemy. Two

---

[1] It seems that this pipe had been deposited by the whistler's side. The whistler himself was not allowed to smoke after entering the lodge.

[2] This confirms the version that the whistler danced in his bare feet and had his moccasins put on when going to bed (see p. 46).

women in charge of the tongues began to cook. They wore ground-cedar crowns and a kilt made of the skin of a spring calf (*nā'xape*) with the hair side out.

At the first song the whistler only danced slowly, at the second a little faster, in the third words were sung and the whistler's heels began to move. The words were:—

"irā'ricirìɛ k'arahū'k'." ("What you dance for, has come.") This sentence is past in form, but prophetic in meaning.

When the fourth song was started, the whistler danced as hard as possible. He did not blow his whistle purposely, but his panting produced an automatic blowing of the whistle. The singers went on till they were tired out, then they stopped drumming and the sham battle also ceased. Three or four of the warriors told about their deeds, then they started in again. The drummers beat the drum for every sentence uttered by the deed-reciters. During the sham fight shots were fired by the mock fighters without regard to the whistler, and after their performance their fathers' clansmen sang songs of joy and received gifts of horses.

The drum only stopped four times during the day. Between the second and third, or third and fourth stops the whistler's relatives brought in robes, etc., as gifts for the doll owner and piled them up, horses being of course kept outside.

After the third song they smoked. Then came the fourth song. The whistler was expected to dance as long as the musicians continued to sing. When he was very tired, the men singers would stop, wishing to give him a rest, but the women wanted to exhaust him and sang the first song over again. Thus they forced him to go on dancing. This song was repeated twenty times. At the end of this period of singing the dancer was completely tired out. He went crazy.[1] He imagined that the doll was directly between his eyes, went out of his head, and fell back panting. The people cried: "Leave him alone! Don't touch him!" The shaman waited to see on which side the whistler was to fall and then whirled his rattle over him till the panting subsided. In the meantime the other fasters were lying down. The doll owner dragged the whistler to his bed.

In the foregoing account (as in most other versions) the assumption is made that the whistler saw a vision the day after his entrance. This, of course, was not uniformly the case. According to Crane-bear, Big-shadow fasted as long as ten days before he received the desired revelation, but Bear-gets-up says it took only six, and One-horn gave three days and two nights as the longest period of fasting he could remember. On the other

---

[1] One informant used the ordinary word for "demented" (*warā'axe*) in this connection; another the word for "intoxicated" (*kā'xutsēk·*).

hand, a whistler tutored by Iā'kac did not have to wait for a vision because a Piegan who had entered the camp was killed on the first night of the sun dance proper (see p. 7).[1] In the absence of such unusual occurrences the whistler was under obligations to wait for a supernatural communication and was not expected to terminate the ceremony arbitrarily. This is illustrated by the story of White-spot-on-his-neck. This Crow had only danced for one night, when he became exhausted and famished from the excessive heat, tore off his sun dance paraphernalia, and rushed for water though he had not yet received a vision. This was simply due to the fact that he had not danced for a long-enough time, for the doll then used was the famous one that had never failed, which afterwards passed into the hands of Pretty-enemy and was ultimately purchased by the present writer. Accordingly, it was unjustifiable for the whistler to stop the dance. The next day the Crow moved towards the Bighorn. All had forebodings of evil. Then the Sioux came upon them, and White-spot-on-his-neck, who was chief, lost eleven young men and one woman, the loss being imputed to his actions at the sun dance.

Misfortune was also invited when a spurious doll was used, a doll, that is to say, of which the manufacture was based on a pretended revelation. In one such case, witnessed by Gray-bull and referred to by other informants, all the guns taken from the enemy had been placed in a ring. They were all supposed to be uncharged, but suddenly one gun went off. The bullet first grazed the buffalo skull, then it struck and killed the whistler's wife. From this the Indians inferred that the doll was not genuine.

Some whistlers had their vision while falling, others would go home and get a vision that very night,[2] one man had a vision both in the lodge and afterwards at home. The whistler did not announce his vision directly, but would say, " I think it will be well, and I shall have revenge." Most of the whistlers told of what they had seen just before starting out on the campaign of vengeance, some (though this happened rarely) made the announcement after the enemy had been killed in retaliation.

For reasons stated, no first-hand account of the vision could be obtained. During the dance the onlookers watched both the whistler and the doll. Whenever the warriors lied about their exploits, the doll winked its eyes. "We looked at the doll," said Bear-gets-up, "and as we looked at it, it changed." When a whistler saw a lot of his enemies killed in a vision, it was the doll that showed them to him as he was dancing back and forth in

---

[1] This was considered the greatest thing that ever happened, and Iā'kac accordingly ranked as the foremost of doll owners. (Crane-bear.)

[2] This seems inconsistent with the view that the ceremony terminates only with the vision.

front of it.   Some saw the entire body of an enemy in front of the doll, with his scalp removed from his head.   According to one informant, the whistler prayed to the doll, saying, "I am poor, I put up the lodge in order to kill an enemy soon."   The dancer's trance seems to have resulted automatically in some instances, while in others special treatment by the doll owner was required.   In the latter case the doll owner was approached by some of the whistler's relatives and paid to put him into the desired condition; sometimes they felt that it would be more beneficial to prolong the period of fasting and would defer this step.   In attempting to induce the vision, the owner took a rattle, approached the doll, made incense of cedar leaves, and made the whistler smoke himself with it.   Then he ordered him to look at the doll, while he himself took a seat at the foot of the pole to which the doll was suspended.   He shook the post and looked at the whistler, who began to dance, riveting his eyes on the doll, while the owner began to chant his songs. After a while, the dancer saw the doll painting its face black, and promising that he should kill an enemy at such a season of the year and under such circumstances.   Suddenly, the whistler ceased to dance, and fell down in a swoon, his eyes still fixed on the doll.

When the immediate object of the sun dance,— the whistler's vision — had been attained, each person inside the lodge received a tongue, and all went homeward, including the fasters.   The doll owner smoked until all were gone, then laid down the pipe, removed all the whistler's paraphernalia, and smoked each article in turn.   He smoked the whistler's robe, and put it on him, whereupon the whistler went home, sometimes supported by some relatives on account of his weakness.   The gifts offered to the owner were taken to his lodge, where he distributed them.   The owner took the doll from the hoop and carried it to his lodge.   Later some relative of the whistler's came in, took the hoop, and offered it to the sun in some exposed place, such as the top of the lodge poles.   The lodge was left standing to fall a prey to the elements.

If the self-torturers had broken loose before the time of the whistler's vision, they waited till the close of the dance before touching their ropes. Those who were still hanging were released by their respective medicinemen, who first recited one of their own deeds.   Little boys would take down the ropes, and their owners took them home.

With the close of the ceremony ended the doll owner's dictatorial power. The camp chief resumed his normal functions, and the people moved toward the enemy to see the promise of the vision fulfilled.

ANTHROPOLOGICAL PAPERS

OF

THE AMERICAN MUSEUM OF NATURAL HISTORY

VOL. XXV, PART II·

THE RELIGION OF THE CROW INDIANS

BY

ROBERT H. LOWIE

NEW YORK
PUBLISHED BY ORDER OF THE TRUSTEES
1922

THE RELIGION OF THE CROW INDIANS.

By Robert H. Lowie.

CONTENTS.

LIST OF ILLUSTRATIONS.

Text Figures.

PREFACE.

Religious beliefs penetrate practically every phase of Crow culture, and accordingly considerable information on this topic is sprinkled through a number of previous publications dealing with this tribe, notably those devoted to the description of ceremonial activities. In the present paper, I attempt to expound those Crow conceptions that would naturally be looked for under the caption of "Religion" and in the interests of clearness, I have sometimes drawn on material already in print.

How fruitful comparative researches in this field are likely to be, is suggested by a preliminary essay on the guardian spirit and vision concept of the area, by Mrs. Ruth Benedict, which is to appear in the "American Anthropologist" and which I have had the pleasure of reading in typescript. Naturally comparison cannot logically stop at the more or less artificial boundaries involved in the delimitation of culture areas. The student of the Plains is led imperceptibly to consider conditions in the Woodland area as well, and it would be odd if the undoubted ceremonial connections between the Plains and the Southwest were wholly unaccompanied by corresponding resemblances in the subjective counterpart of ritual. However, though keenly interested in comparative investigations of this type, I have in the present paper confined myself almost entirely to offering some additional raw data to my colleagues.

The material was not gathered during a single visit specially devoted to the subject here dealt with, but at various times during my Crow field-trips, ranging from 1907 to 1916. Probably more information was obtained from Gray-bull than from any one other native authority, and the sum-total of the statements attributed to him furnishes a fair conception of the religious attitude of a Crow Indian ranking high, though not among the very highest, in public esteem and entering fully into the religious life of his people without functioning as a religious leader. In that sense his career is more typical than that of personalities like Medicine-crow, Big-ox, or Lone-tree, from and about whom, however, I have secured as much information as I could.

ROBERT H. LOWIE.

January, 1922.

SUPERNATURAL BEINGS.

The Siouan term that has become best known as an equivalent of the Algonkian *manito* is the Dakota *waką*. Variants of this stem, such as *wakanda, wakandagi, maką*, have been reported from Southern Siouan tribes. I know of no phonetic equivalent in Crow. On the other hand, J. O. Dorsey records another Omaha word for mysterious, viz. *qube*, which is clearly related to the Winnebago *qopine*, Mandan *xǫpini*[1], Hidatsa *xupí* or *maxupí*, Crow *maxpé* or *maxpá*. The initial *ma* in Hidatsa and Crow is simply the generic nominal prefix, leaving *xp* as the consonantal complex to be used for comparative purposes. The occurrence of Biloxi *xi* with the identical connotation is at least suggestive.[2] Whether it represents a reduced Siouan stem or a radical form, is a question to be decided by linguistic specialists. That the Biloxi form should recall the Northern Siouan languages rather than those of the Omaha group, is not remarkable since this tallies with Swanton's observations on the language generally.

It remains to elucidate the Crow concept by some concrete examples of the application of its linguistic correlate. So far as I know, the Crow never refer to the Supreme Being by a term corresponding to the Dakota Wakǫ́-tañka (Great Mystery). The concept of God with which they have been familiarized by missionaries is rendered *ak'-bítǝt-diǝ*, He-who-everything-made; and the aboriginal notion that most closely resembles that of Christianity is covered by terms not involving the stem *maxpé* at all, viz., by the words *Isá'kawuǝtè* (Old-Man-Coyote) and *Áx'acè* (Sun). This, of course, does not mean that Old-Man-Coyote and the Sun are not regarded as *maxpé*; I am convinced that they are. However, it indicates that the Crow are charier of using the term than the Dakota. They apply it, so far as I can see, not to designate particular individualized supernatural beings, but to convey the idea that a person or object is possessed of those qualities transcending the ordinary which are summarized by the generic word *maxpé*. This, then, is an abstract notion to which concrete experiences are or are not assimilated. The man who superintended the driving of deer into a corral is thus described in a text: *ak'diǝ batsé rǝk maxpí'-tseruk*, "The one who did it was a *maxpí* man, it is said." In a myth a woman who has transformed herself into a bear is pursuing her sister and brothers. A magical obstacle is created to delay her. But: *maxpí-racen ik' uctsí'-tseruk*, "She was *maxpá*,

---

[1] I also recorded a Mandan stem *máxana*.
[2] J. O. Dorsey, "A Study of Siouan Cults" (*Eleventh Annual Report, Bureau of American Ethnology*, Washington, 1894), 366 f.; J. O. Dorsey and John R. Swanton, "A Dictionary of the Biloxi and Ofo Languages" (*Bulletin 47, Bureau of American Ethnology*, Washington, 1912), 221.

that is why she got out, it is said." Old-Woman's-Grandchild, the hero who conquers all sorts of monsters, is of course *maxpé*; his adoptive grandmother, who is often identified with the witch Hícictawìɔ, is specifically described as "also *maxpí*" (*ku maxpí͏ᵃrǝk‘*).

The stem appears nominally without the prefix in the form *xapíri(ǝ)* e.g., *xapíri-ice*, medicine-case. The suffix I interpret as the stem *díǝ*, to make, to cause. Generally possessive pronouns are prefixed and the medial *p* becomes a sonant. Thus, we get such combinations as, *naxpitsɛ iǝxbíriǝc*, the bear is his medicine; *biǝxbíriǝc dúta*, take that medicine of mine. This noun designates any tangible object regarded with special veneration, e.g., the feather derived from a vision and insuring safety in battle.

Altogether the Crow concepts correspond to the Hidatsa equivalents, *xupí*, *maxupí*, as defined by Matthews, who writes them *hopá*, *mahopá*. The former means "to be mysterious; sacred, to have curative powers, to possess charm, incomprehensible, spiritual. Same as Dakota *wakan*, but signifies also the power of curing diseases." The noun is rendered "medicine, charm, spell."[1]

Of recent years the question has been broached whether the manitou concept may not be completely merged in that of animism. That is to say, the sacredness of *maxpé* persons or objects is ascribed solely to the connection they have had with spirits.[2] Thus, Dr. Radin quite categorically states that the Winnebago and Ojibway apply their respective terms for 'mysterious' invariably "to definite spirits, not necessarily definite in shape,"; and he evidently regards this statement as of universal validity, at least in North America. A peculiarly shaped object, he argues, receives offerings because it *belongs* to a spirit or is a spirit's dwelling-place; an arrow possesses specific virtues because it is a spirit transformed or a spirit's abode; and so forth.

This point of view does not appear to me to be borne out by the Crow data. It is true that in Crow *theory* almost all 'medicine' objects are derived from a vision, that is to say, from a spiritual visitant. But this spirit is frequently not 'definite' in any ordinary sense of the term. That is, it is not one of a series of supernatural beings definitely conceived by the Indian before his vision, but merely a personified cause of the visionary's subjective experiences. This is why the Crow who has

---

[1]Washington Matthews, "Ethnography and Philology of the Hidatsa Indians" (*Miscellaneous Publications, United States Geological and Geographical Survey*, no. 7, Washington, 1877), 47 seq., 149, 184.
[2]Paul Radin, "Religion of the North American Indians" (*Journal of American Folk-Lore*, vol. 27, 1914), 344–351.

prayed for a blessing to the Sun may receive a revelation from a quite different being. For the same reason he differentiates between dream experiences of two different types,—the ordinary dreams without religious significance, and the dreams that are reckoned the full equivalent of visions. Evidently the difference can only rest on a difference in subjective reaction; one experience thrills and thereby convinces the beholder that he is in communication with the supernatural, the other does not.

Secondly, the application of the term *maxpé* suggests that it is primarily an expression of power transcending the ordinary. The bear-woman of the myth is *maxpé* because she has power to transform herself into a bear, to extricate herself from difficult positions, etc. There is no other way to account for such activities than to assume that she has some of that supernatural attribute by which such results are effected. But there is no suggestion that she ever acquired her powers from a definite spirit. This, however, merely brings us to the question, "What is a spirit?" And the only *empirical* answer possible seems to be that the *maxpé* power is the generic principle of which spirits are the personified concrete manifestations. What makes it possible to group together so heterogeneous an assemblage of beings as the Sun, the Thunderbird, the mythical Dwarf, and a hundred and one others who may appear in visions is that they possess *maxpé* power and are able to transfer it: this and this alone is the badge of their divinity.

Finally, the psychological processes assumed towards the same tangible 'medicine' object must be supposed to vary with different persons using it. The original visionary may invest it with an air of sacredness because he has received it from a spiritual visitant. But to his fellow-tribesmen who have not shared the experience demonstration of its genuinely sacred character lies in success. If the medicine was given to insure safety in battle and the owner emerges unscathed from hostile encounters; if it was granted for the acquisition of wealth and the beneficiary secures an abundance of horses: then others will seek participation in the benefits of the vision by purchase and will ordinarily obtain copies of the medicine with instructions as to its use and relevant taboos. Now it is inconceivable that in such cases, which were exceedingly numerous, the ultimate medicine owner should retain the attitude of mind of the original visionary. To all intents and purposes the medicine becomes in his consciousness a charm or fetish devoid of *definite* spirituality. He may press his medicine to his breast and utter a prayer for long life and happiness, but even if there be a transitory personification of the object there is no individualization; the same prayer would·be mumbled to any one of a thousand other medicine objects. And as an object originally bestowed in a vision may be completely divorced in consciousness from its pristine animistic associations, so I am convinced that objects, such as rocks (p. 385), are invested with the *maxpé* quality without regard to their being the seat or transformed essence of a spirit. At all events, the burden of the proof rests upon those who in the absence of evidence insist on an animistic basis for the *maxpé* concept.

  From the variability of individual visionary experiences it follows that the number of supernatural beings is indefinite; and as pointed out above, the character of these beings is frequently ill-defined. Nevertheless, certain natural phenomena and mythological personages lend at least their names to the spirits that figure in religious belief and practice. It would be vain to attempt an hierarchical systematization of these 'deities.' The Crow have no priestly caste and there has been little attempt to standardize popular conceptions. Above all, we must beware of identifying the results of such ratiocination with the spontaneous reactions of the individual's religious consciousness. In the latter the feather granted in a vision and insuring to its possessor longevity or wealth looms larger, I am convinced, than any of ·the cosmic forces, no matter how important these may be in philosophic speculation. In other words, the Crow seem to me to be essentially individualists in ·religion. Not that a common traditional basis of religious conceptions is lacking; but the relative value assigned to specific elements of this chaotic complex varies with individual experiences.

  A partial exception may be made in favor of the Sun. I do not mean that a person who has received a revelation from the Thunder will subordinate his patron to the Sun in his own religious life. But probably a majority of the Crow looked in the first instance for a revelation from the Sun and certain important ritualistic phenomena are predominantly, if not exclusively, associated with solar worship. Thus, the oaths sworn to establish a claim to disputed war honors were addressed to the Sun; to him were offered the skins of albino buffalo; and at least preferentially the sweatlodge seems to have been conceived as a prayer to the Sun.

  The Sun, then, approaches as closely as any Crow deity to our concept of a· Supreme Being. Nevertheless, his character is singularly ill-defined, and if we have recourse to mythological evidence we merely have confusion worse confounded. For one thing, there is marked discrepancy of opinion as to the identity of the Sun and Old-Man-Coyote. There is at least a strong tendency to regard them as one and the same,

yet in his cosmogonic accounts Medicine-crow, one of my most conserva-
tive informants, constantly vacillated as to the identification.[1] On the
other hand, White-arm went so far as to say that the Sun was regularly
supplicated in prayer, while Old-Man-Coyote never was; while One-blue-
bead regarded Old-Man-Coyote as the creator of everything and the
equivalent of *Ak'-bátət-dìə* (God), but said that the Sun was distinct
(*ciərək'*).

I am inclined to take the position that we are here confronted with
the coalescence of two originally distinct conceptions. The Sun, judging
from our knowledge of other tribes, must have been an ancient constitu-
ent of aboriginal religion.   Similarly, the culture-hero and trickster
concept as exemplified in the character of Old-Man-Coyote is of great
antiquity but has rather literary and philosophical than religious significance. He is the *deus ex machina*, to whom the Crow almost automatically attribute the origin of most tribal institutions. This aspect of
his activities is at least not irreconcilable with the less definite notions the
Crow may be assumed to have had of the Sun. It may have been the
desire to give greater definiteness to their conceptions of the foremost of
their supernatural beings that led some Crow unconsciously to identify
the two characters by tacitly ignoring the less dignified phase of Old-Man-
Coyote. On the other hand, some individualities may be reluctant to
accept the mythical character as a religious being because of the part he
plays in folk-literature. It is true that the Sun does not uniformly
appear either as a benevolent or a superior being, for in the story of
"The Orphan's Contest with the Sun,"[2] he maliciously keeps away game
from the Indians because of the hero's intimacy with his mistress and is
worsted in the ensuing conflict. However, in general, the Sun is pic-
tured as both powerful and benignant and certainly never as a trickster.

The Sun is always conceived as male and is often addressed as *mḋsa'-
ka*, paternal uncle, father's clansman. Although the Sun is so frequently
prayed to, it is remarkable that he so rarely appears in visions. In-the-
mouth explained this by saying that he (as well as Cīrapé and Old-Man-
Coyote) sent the various animals that do appear, but his statement is
uncorroborated and seemed like an interpretation given at the spur of
the moment.

The manner of praying to the Sun and making offerings to him will
be considered below. As to his creative functions, however, one point
had best be made in the present connection. Though he (or Old-Man-

---

[1] Lowie, this volume, 14 f.
[2] Lowie, this volume, 99.

Coyote) is commonly identified with Ak'-$b\mathring{u}t'$$\vartheta t$-$di\vartheta$, he actually does not figure in myth as the creator of everything, but only as the creator of the Indians and the one who arranges the earth after having birds dive for it. Apart from these birds, which while figuring as the Sun's (Old-Man-Coyote's) servants are not stated to be his creatures, the Coyote, the prototype of the medicine-rocks (*bacŏritsi'tsè*), and the sacred Tobacco plant are all expressly described as beings of independent origin.[1]

Old-Man-Coyote, apart from his mythical exploits and pranks, is as indefinite a being as the Sun, with whom he is so frequently identified. Where he functions religiously, the trickster phase of his dual personality is wholly lacking. In mythology it is important to note that he is *not* represented as a coyote; indeed, a coyote is repeatedly associated with him as a distinct individual.[2] When he transforms himself into animal shape, he assumes the form of a wolf,[3] but most commonly he appears as a human character and is occasionally called by the usual Hidatsa designation of First-worker (Itsí'k'-bâric[4]), which of course has no animal suggestions.

The Moon figures far less frequently than the Sun in religious belief and practice. According to one informant, the address *mâsa'ka*, father's clansman (see above), is shared by this spirit, which would make it of male sex, but according to Gray-bull, whose opinion is borne out by the weight of other evidence, the proper address is *masa'kûare*, grandmother. It also appears as a man in one of the versions of the Grandson myth,[5] however the preponderance of evidence is to the effect that it is conceived as female. There is said to be an old woman in the moon and a pole with meat hanging from it. In a tale which is essentially the account of a vision and might in some measure reflect actual experiences of this type, the Moon appears as a woman of plain dress and wearing an elkskin robe; in another story she is an old woman dwelling near the Sun.[6] In a narrative accounting for the origin of the sacred doll employed in the sun dance, the Moon woman, dressed in an elk robe, presents the first doll-maker with this holy image, and the doll is said to represent the Moon.[7] Gray-bull's statements are entitled to special consideration on this subject, since he had a brass representation of the New-Moon for one of his medicines and occasionally made smoke offerings to the Full-Moon

---

[1]Lowie, this volume 14 f.
[2]See this volume, 15, 17 seq.
[3]*ibid.*, 31, 38.
[4]The Hidatsa equivalent is Itsi'kawâ'hiric.
[5]Lowie, this volume, 52.
[6]*ibid.*, 187, 157.
[7]Lowie, this series, vol. 16, 14.

and prayed to her.   When he obtained his medicine he was told that the
Moon was an old woman; he says that Old-Man-Coyote when visiting
the Crow[1] told them the Moon was their grandmother.   Gray-bull in a
dream once saw an old woman who gave him a song, and he identifies
her with the Moon.   Old-dog told me about an old man who had a vision
of the New-Moon, cut out a crescent-shaped hide medicine for himself
and captured four hundred Dakota horses in consequence.

Of the stars the Morningstar (*i'g'e-rɨəxe*) and the Dipper have
religious significance.   Mythologically Old-Woman's-Grandson is the
Sun's son, and after conquering various monsters infesting the earth he
returns to the sky to become the Morningstar.[2]   A fair number of Indians
stated that Grandson was regularly invoked by them.   Thus, Little-
rump said that people prayed to him in time of war and erected sweatlodges in his honor.   According to Old-dog, the Crow were still praying
to him in 1913.   Others denied that Grandson was ever addressed in
supplication.   This discrepancy is readily intelligible if we assume that
some informants simply looked upon Grandson as the hero of a folk-tale
without paying much attention to his ultimate actual transformation;
while with others the identification of the Morningstar with the ogre-
killer and his relationship to the Sun were in the foreground of consciousness.   Assuming the former attitude, they would see no more reason for
deifying Grandson than other mythic heroes; in the latter case, however,
he might actually acquire an important position in the religious domain.
On the other hand, the identification with stars of the twin heroes,
Spring-boy and Curtain-boy,[3] in one version of their myth has remained
barren of any religious consequences.

In mythology the Morningstar also appears without any suggestion
of affinity with Old-Woman's-Grandson.   It is further noteworthy that
in two of these tales he is worsted by human heroes who have received
assistance from other supernatural powers.[4]

As a characteristic sample of inconsistency may be cited the conception of one informant that Sun, Moon, and Morningstar were enemies
and that if one of them adopted an Indian, the others would attempt to
get him and eat him.   Morningstar and Sun, according to this authority,
once adopted a Crow and a Dakota, respectively.   The latter went on
the warpath but was killed by the Crow, whereupon Morningstar ate
him.   On another occasion Sun and Morningstar bet against each other,

[1]Lowie, this volume, 30 f.
[2]ibid., 57.
[3]ibid., 85.
[4]Lowie, this volume, 102 seq., 200 seq.

having various animals play shinney for them with the sunrise and sunset as their goals. Sun's players were on the east side and included the silver fox, coyote, and jackrabbit; Morningstar's players were in the west and included the elk, white-tail and black-tail deer, and another deer species called *ú"xkǎce.* During the game both Sun and Star caused storms; Star made the snow very deep so that the little animals could not run. At last the elk, being long-winded, won.

The sacred Tobacco about which center the performances of the Tobacco society, is quite generally identified with the stars,—sometimes it would seem with all of them collectively, then again more specifically with the Morningstar.

The Dipper (*i.'g̣ e-sǎ'puə* = Seven Stars) is mythologically conceived as a group of seven human brothers who had become displeased with their terrestrial experiences and decided to change their shape into something that should last forever. At the close of their discussion they decide to transform themselves into the constellation.[1] The Dipper not infrequently blessed fasters with a vision: Lone-tree was among those adopted by them.[2] The Stars often appeared painted in a particular way, holding a pipe or with wreaths of medicines, which they turned over to the visionary. As a result he would capture horses and become a chief. One Crow said that one of the Seven Stars is blind and that he has the greatest power of them all.

The Four Winds are mentioned as recipients of smoke offerings but play a minor part. On the other hand, the Thunder (*sǔə*) is important both mythologically and religiously. As usual, he is identified with the eagle (perhaps more commonly with the bald-headed eagle). In myth he is represented as the enemy of a water-monster, which destroys his young but is overcome with the aid of an expert hunter.[3] Various Indians have been adopted by the Thunder, among them Lone-tree and Big-ox, both of whom were still alive in 1911.

Another mythic personage who appeared in visions is the uniformly benevolent Dwarf, who, in spite of his diminutive stature is represented as very powerful physically.[4]

In addition to the mainly cosmic beings described above there are the host of spirits—mostly in beast or bird shape—who appear in visions and whose characteristics will appear more clearly from the account in the following section.

---

[1] *ibid.,* 126, 210, 211.
[2] This series, vol. 16, 41.
[3] This volume, 144 seq.
[4] *ibid.,* 165, 171 seq.

VISIONS AND DREAMS.

The importance of visions in the life of the Crow can hardly be overestimated. Not only the general course of sacred ceremonies but even such details as particular songs or specific methods of painting are traced to visions. Through them it was possible to rise from abject poverty to affluence and social prestige. Even war parties were, at least in theory, wholly dependent on them, for a man organized one only when prompted by a vision or when dispatched by another man who had received such a supernatural communication.[1] Since success in life was conceived as the result of these revelations, probably all men tried to secure a vision, though many of them failed. Conversely, lack of success was attributed to lack of visions. "All who had visions," said Little-rump, "were well-to-do; I was to be poor (*watsĕcik̇*), that is why I had no visions." However, through the transferability of medicine power it became possible for people not blessed with visions to participate in the benefits accruing from such experiences.

The native term for 'having a vision' is *bact̓ri*, which also means 'to dream.' One informant made a linguistic distinction to correspond to the conceptual one. A common dream, he stated, is *baré-rámmac̓re*; a vision or dream with visionary import, *baré-wac̓re*. Although I cannot analyze the second portion of the former term, it is clearly for the most part identical with the word for vision; and my impression is that in ordinary intercourse no verbal differentiation occurs, though conceptually the distinction is rigidly maintained.

There were various methods of inducing visions. Gray-bull recounted the following:—

(1) Some went to the mountains and fasted there. These men would generally dream of guns, coups, and horses.

(2) Some dreamt in their lodges. These usually became rich, acquiring plenty of horses.

(3) Others, usually poor people, would fall asleep somewhere when very tired and get a vision.

(4) Some fasted at the Tobacco garden.

(5) The Whistler got a vision at the Sun dance; so did those participants in the ceremony who suspended themselves from poles.[1]

(6) A man might drag a buffalo or bear skull fastened to the pierced skin of his back; or would lead around a horse similarly secured to his body.

---

[1] Lowie, this series, vol. 9, 232.
[2] Lowie, this series, vol. 16, 44 f.

Gray-bull's enumeration is corroborated and supplemented by the following statements secured from Scratches-face:—

Some had dreams while out lost in a storm at night or under similar circumstances. In these dreams beings would come to them while they were not asleep and showed them what kind of medicine to have. Others, having lost a sister or brother or some other close relative, would chop off a finger and go to the mountains to have dreams. All this comes from Old-Woman's-Grandson. In their dreams they would see a bird or some other animal transformed into a man who had painted his face and tied certain feathers to his head and would tell the visionary to imitate him. Those who herded horses would stay out at night with their herd and sometimes had dreams of horses. Then they went out to the enemy and brought back so many head of horses. In their vision they would see a horse turn into a man, who would talk to the dreamer. First the visionary would see a man who showed him some medicine, then the visitant would turn into an animal. Those who dreamt of a bear were not shot in battles, or even if they were shot, the arrows or bullets would fall to the ground. Badger dreams are the same. I know of two men who dreamt of a badger. One of them would not eat the young of any animal. . I saw the other deliberately shoot himself in the breast, but the bullet fell on the ground and he was not killed. Sometimes people dreamt of stones or rocks; these would be like the bear and badger dreamers. Sometimes the bear was thought to be a real bear, sometimes he would come out of the clouds. These were larger than real bears, I don't know what they were. Old-Woman's-Grandson told all the animals to help the people of the earth, and that is why they appeared in these dreams. The animals gave power to these Indians.

Scratches-face's views on Old-Woman's-Grandson were shared by some other informants, but not by all (see p. 321). It will be noted that he assigns a specific character to visions of bears, badgers, and rocks, to wit, that of bestowing immunity to missiles.

Suspension from a pole after the fashion observed at the time of the Sun dance was also practised on other occasions, but perhaps less frequently than other forms of self-torture. Bear-crane described the experience of a visionary, Red-bear, who used this method. He took a stick, went up into the mountains, planted his stick into the ground and tied a rope to it. In the morning he painted himself with white clay, cut his breast, inserted a stick, attached the rope to it, and ran round the post all day. At night he tore out the skin and slept on the mountain, dreaming that he was a chief. He returned to the Crow and announced his vision. He had dreamt of an enemy whom he had slain and scalped. He had his wife make moccasins and set out as a leader of a war party, consummating his vision.

In the various ways of gaining supernatural favor may be recognized three main types: the visionary may receive a revelation without seeking one or enduring any hardship whatsoever; he may be visited by supernatural beings in times of difficulty without a deliberate courting of them; and he may go in quest of a vision, generally subjecting himself to suffering in order to arouse their commiseration and thus obtain a revelation.

PAINLESS VISIONS.

Men who received unsought supernatural communications of importance without being placed in conditions of stress were relatively few in number and were regarded as remarkably fortunate since they escaped the necessity of torturing themselves. In such cases the Crow use the expression *bâwawá'tek'* (1st person: *bâ-wawî'tawâk'*), he gets something without working. One-blue-bead offers the best example of this type of vision, and his narrative follows:—

When I was a boy I was herding horses. I took them to the water. This was on a flat. I lay down and fell asleep. I saw something mysterious (*maxpé hawákák'*). In those days if Indians wanted anything they had to hunt for it. When I got this, I struck first coups. When I saw the camp of the enemy, I tied my feather to the back of my head, and then captured and owned horses.

When I had driven my horses to the water and they were grazing, I fell asleep. I saw a person on a white-maned buckskin horse; his face was painted red, also there were slanting lines from the eyes down. His forehead was red. He had a buckskin shirt. I saw the feather of the *tsiraxdipcîre* (a species of chicken-hawk) tied to one of his shoulders. He was like a Crow dressed for battle. I heard a voice saying, "Chief Chicken-hawk is coming from there now." He came riding a dark bay. His horse's tail was wrapped. This is the name I gave Jim Carpenter's little girl. Some time later I heard the words "Chicken-hawk woman" and gave this name to my granddaughter.

This is my principal medicine. I am telling the truth. This is a fine day. You (R. H. L.) will have good luck.

Other people have to torture themselves; I never cut myself. My only marks were those of arrows in battle. I never had to ask any one else for medicine like other men. Many people had no vision. These gave lots of property to the visionary and might get a vision through him. Some get a vision even in their own tipi. Somehow, I don't know how, they tell a vision from an ordinary dream. A common dream *baré rámmacîre*) and medicine dream or vision (*baré wacî're*) are quite different.

My medicine was good for war. I took it with me on the warpath. When I saw the enemy, I sang my song and tied it to my back. This is my song:—

mĭ rakâkam,   bôwik.
I am a bird,   I am coming.

When at home I stored my medicine; in dancing and sham battles, I took it out. I never gave it to anyone else. Just lately I made one for Andrew Wallace. He asked me for one. I saw no use for it as we have no more wars, but I gave it to him so that he might have good luck in owning horses.

My medicine forbids me to make myself bleed, for example to cut off my fingers; and if meat has blood on it, I won't eat it. At the time of my vision I was told not to eat blood, and not to make myself bleed.

When I was a boy, I was poor. I saw war parties come back with leaders in front and having a procession. I used to envy them and made up my mind to fast and become like them. When I saw the vision I got what I had longed for. I always was in something good (some good war deed). I killed eight enemies.

Young men went out to seek visions of their own accord. Before going they swam, took a sweatbath, and rubbed themselves all over with sagebrush. Before sunrise they went out, taking sage and ground-cedar for their bedding, for all the animals liked these plants. When they came back from their fast, they had a sweatlodge made and told their vision. Unless a large sudatory was seen in the vision, a small one was used. Visionaries might announce their vision to famous men either in the sweatlodge or at a feast.

I have heard some say, "I had a vision this way, but I hear I have been fooled." Some can tell beforehand when they are going to die. They say, "My father is going to take me back," then they die soon after. The only thing I prayed to specially was my feather. I might pray to the Sun any time.

On another occasion this informant gave a slightly different account, making his visitant appear as a hawk, but since he represents himself as awake at the time he was probably referring to another vision from the same source. The hawk would sing songs, fly up, and do various things. It did not give One-blue-bead any objects, but he noted the songs and actions of the bird. Afterwards he struck three coups, this is what the hawk gave him. During another interview One-blue-bead spoke of the bird as having changed itself into a young man mounted on a cream buckskin horse with a bird of its own kind at the back of his head.

One-blue-bead's account touches on a number of vital points. In conformity with other data we may harmonize the human and the bird character of his visitant by supposing that he appeared first as a man, revealing his identity, however, by the hawk feather and in vanishing assumed bird shape. That One-blue-bead adopted the feather seen as a tangible representative of his revelation, is highly characteristic, so is the tendency to confer a name on children based on one's visionary experiences. Equally significant is the contrast between his poverty and lack of prominence before the vision and his later martial success and consequent social distinction. The imposition of taboos, often of a quite fanciful character, such as that against eating blood, is extremely common in visions; in fact, practically all such regulations are traced to instructions received under such circumstances. Finally, may be noted the expression 'my father' as applied to the visitant. It is generally understood that a spirit appearing to a visionary adopts him as his child; the standard formula being, *"dī barûk' bâwik;"* "You (obj.) my child I will make." Hence the constant use of parent and child terms of relationship in the myths dealing with supernatural patrons.

Arm-round-the-neck had twice attempted to gain a vision by not drinking water, but failed. However, he was fortunate in having 'dreams' while sleeping. I cite his remarks practically verbatim but slightly re-arranged so as to bring together statements bearing on the same experience.

I had dreams while sleeping. I saw a bear and a horse two different times; also a bird. The bear I saw was singing to some people; some of them fell down while he was singing, and he jumped on them. He held his arm towards the people while singing and when he was done the trees and brush in front of him fell down. He started toward the people and some fell down. He said, "Of everything I shall have plenty." Later I achieved much in battles. I saw his face paint and used it. I also made a cap of bearskin and used it. Later I sold it to a man, who paid me four kinds of property, among them a woman, for it. The cap was from the head of a bear with the ears and was decorated with a horse tail in the rear. The buyer gave me a blanket, earrings, a Navajo breechcloth, and a girl never previously married. My mother's brother had the bear for his medicine and made me a bearclaw necklace; that may have been the reason for my dream. I like a bear when I see one, but if I wanted the hide I should kill him; I killed a bear in order to make my cap.

I saw the horses singing; they did not lie to me. I dreamt someone was kicking my foot and there were horses all round me with ropes to their necks and fastened to my body. I heard someone say, "Wherever you go, you shall have horses." Ever since then I have had horses. I think this dream was given me by dogs. I was walking, followed by several dogs. I lay down under a tree and fell asleep, with the dogs lying round me about the tent. So I thought they took pity on me and gave me horses.

I saw a bird singing. I saw a man driving a herd of horses with this bird tied to his head and singing. These were the words of his song:—

còm	barêrək,	itsíre	ítsem	bê wik´.
Wherever	I go,	horse	a good one	I shall have.

The man was riding a pinto horse. I heard someone say to me, "When he does that, he brings good horses." I don't know where this dream came from.

Another way of getting visions is to go out hunting and have dreams, but those obtained from thirsting are the strongest: the men who fasted became chiefs and were lucky at everything.

Arm-round-the-neck's narrative is interesting for several reasons. For one thing, it expresses the belief that ordinary dogs possess the power of granting a vision. Secondly, we find a definite rejection of quasi-totemic taboos inasmuch as Arm-round-the-neck did not scruple to kill bears. On this point the attitude of the natives varies somewhat, but all agreed that no man who had dreamt of buffalo would for that reason refrain from killing or eating them. Finally, the transfer, as it were, of the bear medicine from a clansman is noteworthy, since in other cases medicines are known to have descended from father to son.

Old-dog had never gone out to fast but had dreamt while sleeping in his tent. He dreamt of the Tobacco. Another dream, however, is indirectly derived from a vision. His brother had fasted and seen a little *axíaxĭpe* (kind of buzzard?), which appeared in human guise, painted his face, and sang against the enemy. He gave Old-dog his medicine power with four feathers of this bird, and Old-dog subsequently dreamt of taking a gun from the enemy and striking him. He attributes the dream to his brother's medicine. Thereafter, when he saw the enemy, my informant painted his face, tied the feathers to his head, sang towards the enemy, and would take a gun or strike a first coup.

Young-crane told of a man named He-calls-fat (*irápi'tsec*) who had been visited by the Dipper while awake and sitting down. He would send out captains of war parties and bid them bring horses and other booty. The Seven Stars told him they would take him back when he was going to die. He told his people he had to die soon and it came true.

Bull-all-the-time, who secured a martial vision through torture and fasting, was also blessed with another for doctoring while he was asleep in his tipi. He saw a horse fastened to a rope, which was lengthened up to him. He heard a person sing. The horse was a sign that my informant would get horses as fees for his cures. He was told that if anyone fell sick he was to doctor him. He saw an old man decorated with red paint and holding a pipe in his hand. This man was standing over the recumbent patient and blew through a pipestem over him. The sick man rose and then sat down. Bull-all-the-time saw all the sickness come out of the patient's blood and saw him get well. Bull-all-the-time showed me the pipestem he had dreamt of; it had a horse's track incised near one end.

Gray-bull recounted the following as an experience of his grandfather's while awake in his tent:—

A white-headed bird sat at the door, looked round and hopped inside to the side of the lodge opposite the visionary, whose wife was away at the time. My grandfather looked at the bird, which merely sat there. He looked again, and it had turned into a man with painted face and on his head was a bird of the kind seen before. He sang a song and at its close he said, "I'll come tomorrow and see you again with my wife. You have seen what I wanted you to see. I was going to let you see many things, but your wife is coming." When he had said this, he was a bird once more and went out. My grandfather went after him and saw him flying up the river. His wife got to the tent. She had seen the bird. When she had brought in the firewood, she asked her husband, "What is that bird I saw coming out of the tent? What is it?" "I don't know."

The next day he went for horses. When he returned, his wife was looking for wood. The people were going to camp there for four days. The woman cooked. He ate and told his wife to get three or four packs of wood so she might stay away longer. She went for the wood. He lay on his bed and watched the door. A bird came in and hopped where he sat and another followed. Both sat on the other side of the tipi and looked somewhere. One turned into a man, the other into a woman. The man said to the woman: "Give one song to my child." "All right." My grandfather sat up, and the woman sang. When she had finished, the man said to my grandfather, "Look at me." He did. His face was painted as before and a bird was tied to his head. "I have given you one song already, that is my only song. Whenever I want to use this bird on my head, I let a woman tie it and think at the same time that the enemy cannot shoot me." The woman said: "I have plenty of things and horses, and whenever I meet enemies they are easily captured. This is all." They changed into birds again, hopped to the door and went out. Until then my grandfather had done nothing in war and his joking relatives made fun of him. He had not even gone out with war parties.

Some time after this my grandfather saw someone kill one of these birds and asked the slayer to give him the body. He cut off its head and tail, also the wing bone for a whistle, and took them home with him. He called in all the chiefs. When all were in, his wife roasted some ribs and when they were through eating he made them smoke. One asked what this was for. He asked them to tell him how they dreamt and got medicines. All told how they had fasted and dreamt. When all had had their say, he said he was going to make his medicine, but found out that it was not good, that is, not like any they had told. The chiefs asked him to tell about it. He told them that into his very tent two birds had come and shown him something, bidding him make whatever he saw. He asked whether they knew anything like that to have been seen by a Crow before. They told him to make his medicine, to sew together the head and the tail of the bird. When he had done so, he sang the songs the bird-man had sung for him, telling his wife to sit and sing with him. After they were through, he told his visitors to see how it should turn out. He told all the chiefs he was going to take care of the entire tribe thereafter, that was why he made medicine. He gave them more to eat; they smoked and went out. The chiefs said to one another, "We'll see how it comes out, it is great medicine that he has made."

It was in the fall of the year. There were about forty enemies in a trench that fall. My grandfather came on a white horse, his face painted like that of the man in the dream, and the medicine tied to his head. He asked the Crow fighters whether anyone had struck a coup, then went to the coulée where were the enemy. He got to the bank and went to one of the enemy, who shot my grandfather, singeing his hair. He took away a gun from the enemy, laid it down, and went to the next man, who had a bow. This one broke the string of his bow. My grandfather took the bow and arrow away from him and went back. The people then knew his medicine to be true. After that he kept on striking coups and became a chief. He made one bird medicine for his son, who also became chief. The birds were real birds, and they themselves gave the medicine. The Crow believe the birds themselves have medicine powers.

It will be seen later that the medicine was subsequently transmitted to Gray-bull himself and determined one of his fasting visions (p. 336).

In the foregoing narrative the fact that supernatural powers are ascribed to the birds themselves is noteworthy. It tallies with certain statements of various informants, e.g., Arm-round-the-neck's comments on the vision granted by dogs (p. 327), but is contradicted by others, who regard the animals as mere messengers of potent spirits. Presumably we here have to reckon with individual differences of interpretation. Another feature of importance is the patrilineal transmission of the medicine (but compare p. 335). Finally, the pragmatic test of the value of a vision is highly characteristic.

It is clear that some of these painless visions were reckoned on a par with those for which suffering was undergone, but this does not apply to all cases. For example, Little-rump, who speaks of himself as having tried to get visions but failed, did, as a matter of fact, get unsought communications from the Yellow Tobacco, though obviously he does not regard them as comparable in worth to those of others, presumably because in spite of them he has remained poor. He hears the Tobacco sing songs. "Some of them I consider sacred. When I hear a song and have good luck immediately after that, then I consider the song sacred."

UNSOUGHT STRESS VISIONS.

Another category of visions, though not formally recognized as such by the natives, includes experiences not deliberately sought but undergone in times of stress or under other conditions out of the ordinary. One of Lone-tree's visions may be reckoned of this class since it was obtained during his flight from the enemy:—

We went against the Dakota; there were nine of us. I was still young and someone else was captain. I did the scouting every day. We got to the camp but the Dakota discovered us and we ran away in different directions, five one way, three besides myself another way. The Dakota caught only the former and killed them all. The rest, all young boys, got home in safety. Far this side of Bismarck, North Dakota, I thought of swimming the Missouri. Just before we got to the river, while still among the rocky hills, we saw big heavy clouds presaging a thunderstorm. I bade the others seek shelter under rocks, saying, "I'll watch for a while." As I was seated on a rock, I watched the hailstorm coming and saw the lightning quite near me. When the storm got very close, I thought I should also seek shelter. Before I got up I saw a big bird coming down from among the clouds. His color was white and he was as large as the white building at the Mission. His head faced south. In descending to the ground he made no noise. I saw him plainly. The lightning came from his eyes. He sat down on the ground. As soon as he did so, we could see smoke as though from an engine. The hailstorm did not come near but left a circle free round the bird and me. I watched the eagle going back up into the clouds. He said, "I live up in the heavens, I am going to adopt you, that is why I came down. Whatever you ask for, we shall hear you." Each hailstone was as big as a fist. That evening we crossed the Missouri. This was the first time I dreamt about him. The second night I heard the hailstones calling one another and saying, "Whatever you shall ask, we shall do it for you. I am the High Thunder (*súə*)."

Lone-tree got large white beads for a necklace to represent the hailstones.

Three-wolves in referring to Lone-tree's experience added the detail that the lightning struck the lake and something came out of it. Then Lone-tree saw a taloned bird as large as a tree flying from cloud to cloud and saying, "If you shall go to a flat rock, I will see you." Lone-tree was afraid to go; nevertheless he considered the Thunder his medicine and henceforth carried the head of a bald-headed eagle with him (see below, p. 335). When Short-bull offended him, Lone-tree said, "You will nearly die this summer." Short-bull was struck by lightning, but was not killed. Sometimes Lone-tree would take a big white bead (evidently from the necklace mentioned above), put it on a child's head and make hail. He could stop a storm and also cause rain. Big-ox had the same power.

Instances of this type of supernatural experience occur repeatedly in the myths. For example, a man and his wife reduced to extreme destitution through the husband's failing eyesight are suddenly visited by the Moon, who bids them send out young men on a horse raid; the raid is successful and the impoverished couple become wealthy. Again, a young woman who has been blinded, crippled, and abandoned by her husband is doctored by a white-tailed deer and an owl, while the compassionate brother-in-law who provided her wants till his strength is exhausted is aided by a snake-man. Similarly, a benevolent dwarf rescues from starvation a poor young man and his sweetheart, who have been driven away by the camp tyrant.[1] Sometimes the supernatural beings are explicitly represented as cognizant of the visionary's distress and attempting to relieve it either in person or through a messenger. The dwarf's wife chides him for his dilatoriness in succoring the sufferer: "'Bring my son soon,' I said, you have done it late, they almost died." The snake-man says to his protegé: "I pitied you long ago, but never reached you." In the legend of Big-iron the hero has been abandoned by his cruel stepfather and a supernatural being in the guise of an old man sends mountain-sheep to bring him to his island.[2]

[1] This volume, 186, 190, 171.
[2] *ibid.*, 291.

Sought Visions.

We may now turn to cases in which there was a deliberate quest of a revelation. These were probably the most numerous, but by no means all attempts to secure visions met with success, as has already been noted. Little-rump, e.g., often tried to get a vision but invariably failed. Sometimes the quest was abandoned from exhaustion or fear. A female informant, e.g., went out to fast for three days when mourning a deceased relative, but left after the second day because she suddenly saw a grave she had not previously noticed. Being afraid of the dead, she went off before the close of the period set by herself.

There was no limitation either as to age or sex, so far as seeking a vision was concerned. Little boys sometimes fasted, not because their parents had urged them but probably because they had listened to others talking about visions and desired to try it for themselves. On the other hand, middle-aged and even old men would go out fasting. Young girls did not seek visions, but when older they might and did. Usually this happened when a relative had been killed by the enemy or even died a natural death. Thus, Young-crane chopped off a finger joint when her first husband was killed and fasted for two days after her daughter's decease, though without receiving a revelation. It is true, however, that the number of would-be male visionaries was greater than that of the women, and that it was commonly adolescent men who were eager to get a communication that should enable them to gain martial glory and consequent prestige.

It is noteworthy that according to all informants there was no external prompting of the youth to undergo the rigors of fasting and self-torture: he went out because of the tales heard about the camp-fire and because he observed the success of those who had gone and obtained revelations.

The principal methods of inducing a vision have already been enumerated. Doubtless the most usual was to fast and thirst for several days, a procedure designated as *biricsandùa*, (not drinking water). The would-be visionary generally retired to a lonely peak, theoretically for four days, in consonance with the mystic notions clustering about that number, possibly in addition chopping off a finger-joint as an offering to conciliate the spirits invoked. That these might differ as to identity has already been set forth, though the Sun or Old-Man-Coyote w most frequently addressed. The faster was virtually naked, using buffalo skin for a blanket at night. According to Flat-head-woman, he wou! lie on his back with legs stretched out, the arms extended at the sides ar facing east all night; his bedding was framed by rocks on both sides.

Before citing accounts of individual visions it may be well to quote some generic remarks by White-arm:—

Of my contemporaries I take the lead in visionary experiences. Parents did not tell children to go out if they were well off. But if they were poor, a boy would decide not to remain so but to go out, fast, and thereby come to own property. Strips of flesh were cut off and placed on a buffalo chip, and some such prayer as the following was addressed to the Sun:—

kahé, Hallo,	isâ'kaxâria, (raising the buffalo chip), old Old Man,		bi watseck'âtem, I am poor,	mi me	arâkak', you see,
ma+ítsem something good	bakú'. give me.	mí¹ Me	xaríe, make old,	itsírem a horse	bêwi, may I have,	ûwut'baràxiə gun	burutsíwi, may I take,
dâkce a coup	marítbi. may I strike.	mi I	batsétsi, a chief,	mí k'ua I without help	mi wirəxbâki may I become a person (make a living)	makurúa plenty

wêwi.
may I have.

The Sun's name, *áx'acè*, may be used in crying for a vision; in mourning the diminutive *áxack'ât* is used. Any name pertaining to a father, father's clansman, or grandfather, may be applied to the Sun. The Sun's name may be used in cursing, e.g.:—

áx'ac bakô, To the sun I have given him, or (emphatically): áx'ac bakâce, To the Sun I have verily given him.

If a man wants a horse, he will cut out a piece of his flesh in the shape of a horse-shoe. The morning before going out he swims, takes a clean robe, and at daybreak goes to the hill selected for fasting. When the sun came up, I made my cut. Sometimes this is done on the second day. Some stayed out four days. I stayed two days or one day. A forked stick is planted the evening before the sacrifice. An old man is sought to pray for the young man. He paints the young man with white clay, prays to the sun and pierces the faster's breasts or the body near the shoulder parts and fastens him to the forked stick. The would-be visionary runs round the stick and the old man goes home. When tired, the visionary sits down, then runs round again. Some break the flesh, others do not. In the evening, the old man comes and cuts at the edge of the dried flesh, then leaves the young man. He shows the dried flesh to the Sun and prays anew, while the visionary sleeps there again during the night. Any time at night a vision might be seen. First we see a person in a vision or dream, but a few days later, perhaps while we are sleeping, the person seen is recognized as some particular animal that had changed into a person. Sometimes they found out directly through the song. In the song the visitant might say, "I am a snake" (or buffalo, or horse, etc.) If a man has a vision of a snake, all snakes will be fathers to him. Some would pick up a snake after such a vision, saying, "*dardke bîk*';" (I am your son), and the snake would not bite him.

Some were adopted by a bear. While they were asleep at home some one might strike the sole of a visionary's foot, then he would awake, make a noise like a bear, and a bear's tooth would come out of his mouth. This is one way of knowing the species of the animal giving the vision.

People who have seen a snake, do not kill snakes. I don't know how bear visionaries act in this regard. The latter put red paint from the eyes down the face in slanting lines and knot their hair to imitate bear's ears, and use a bearskin for a blanket. Bear people when in a trance (*kâxuluk*) use *isi* (Joe Cooper says, wild parsnip) incense, then they will come to. Strong men catch these entranced ones from behind, for they try to bite and act like bears. They may go into a trance whenever the sole of their feet or their face is struck.

Sometimes the Sun himself appeared to the visionary, but mostly animals came. These I do not think are related to the Sun at all. When men are praying, the Sun is first thought of, but generally other beings appear. After returning from a quest, the faster made a sweatlodge and all the famous people were called in; while they were assembled in the sweatlodge the visionary told his vision, and the audience afterwards told the other people. Snake visionaries are mostly doctors, e.g., Flat-dog; the snake tells them how to treat the sick. Some would smell the incense in a vision and thus know what weed to use for medicine.

Some are deceived by visions, go out on the warpath, and get killed, but not many are fooled about doctoring. Wraps-up-his-tail slept near Sheridan, had visions, and told everyone, yet he was killed. Sometimes everything told in a vision is false; perhaps some animal plays the part of another. It never happened that old men detected the deceit in a vision and warned the visionary when he told them. They only find out from what happens later.

It is clear that White-arm's final remarks completely corroborate Gray-bull's account as to the testing of a vision by the visionary's subsequent success. The quasi-totemic attitude ascribed to snake visionaries was certainly not shared by other Indians, as already pointed out. My informant's statement regarding the Sun is significant and agrees with data secured from some of my most trustworthy authorities. That is to say, the Sun as the most dominant single figure in the native religious consciousness is supplicated in the first instance, but rarely appears. Instead there come other beings "not related" to the Sun, which presumably means not dispatched by him but independently taking pity on the faster's distress.

From these general remarks we may now turn to some individual accounts. I will begin with Lone-tree, who had other supernatural revelations besides the one that came unsought from the Thunder.

Once I went on a high mountain and cut off a strip of my flesh with a knife. When I had fasted for three days and nights I saw the Dipper. It was towards morning. The Dipper gave me a little food, sitting down beside me as a man and saying he had brought me some food because I was hungry. "What you are eating is human flesh," said the Dipper after giving me the food. I did not know it was the Dipper, but something at the back of my head was whispering to me, "The man giving you food is the Dipper." After he had told me that the food was human I could not swallow it but vomited what I had eaten. Then the Dipper rose and walked off. I looked and saw his long braided hair hanging down in the back, and on the long queue were the Seven Stars. Then I believed that it was the Dipper. The next morning I got home.

During the winter I cut scars on my arms and went into the hills. There was a clump of trees and on one of them there was a nest. Not knowing that it belonged to the Bald-headed Eagle, I lay down. At night it stormed violently. I slept and dreamt I was in a big lodge and saw the Bald-headed Eagle sitting there. I was told that the Dakota were my only enemies and that I was to be a captain. It came true and I defeated the Dakota about ten times. People said I was the best captain.

The Bald-headed Eagle of this vision is undoubtedly connected with the Thunder (see above).

Big-ox, one of the most famous shamans of recent times (see p. 344), had become feeble-minded when I knew him and only supplied a very fragmentary account of his visions:—

I slept on a mountain and chopped off a joint of my little finger. I saw a bird, which made me a chief. The birds sat round me; they had human heads. Five balls of different color were in front of me, one of them pure white. I sat there and some of the birds vanished without my knowing it until only one sat by me. This last one told me I should be a great chief and that he would not forget me. "We shall constantly watch you." He repeated this twice. He flew away without my seeing him go.

I saw the No-drum (*birə'xdete*) dance in the daytime in the Wolf Mountains. A white woman and a white man gave me the vision and a Crow spoke to me in Crow. They gave me the stick I carry around, painted yellow and decorated with bells and feathers.

Owing to his latter experience, dating from the period of his senility, for which reason no one but himself took it seriously, Big-ox was nick-named No-drum in the last years of his life. It is not clear whether he underwent any suffering in this case or received his revelation unsought.

Flat-dog once went out to fast and get a vision. He had his back pierced and a horse tied to it, while on the other side he attached a war-bonnet to his pierced skin. Towards evening the horse got restless, being thirsty, and jerked Flat-dog's skin. Then he pulled out the stick to which the horse was tied and freed him. He fell asleep at night, tired out with his exertions and as good as dead. He saw a man come to him, who said, "Now you will remain alive a long time, you are poor now, you will be a person. I'll keep you a person for a long time (*dī wirəxbīke cíe-mā-wi-mà!sik*)." Flat-dog added: "Today people speak of me as old, then I think of this statement. My face was covered, nevertheless I saw the person."

One of Gray-bull's experiences forms an interesting sequel to his grandfather's vision (p. 329). Before dying the grandfather had given his medicine to Gray-bull's mother, bidding her turn it over to her son when he should be a young man. He still had the medicine at the time of my interview with him. His narrative follows:—

I fasted with this medicine and got a dream. I saw a bird flying over me in a circle. It descended and went down into a canyon whistling. On both sides there were rocks. The rocks began to shoot at the bird but failed to hit it, so that it came out unhurt. It had nothing tied to its head and when I heard shooting from the rocks I did not see anything either. The bird had a white head and tail. I did not know that I could not be shot till long afterwards. I was never shot. I kept my dreams secret, for I was afraid if I told them I might get shot. Once many Piegan were lying under a pine tree. One was some distance in front of us. We started out toward the Piegan. He shot at me when I was just above him but did not hit me. My horse went round as though dizzy and ran off. That night I dreamt and someone said to me, "Don't you know that you cannot be shot?"

The conceptions involved in this vision recall corresponding Hidatsa usages by which sacred objects descended from father to son and where the blessing of a vision was expected from the spirits associated with the paternal bundle. The tenor of the vision, i.e., the appearance of a person shot at but remaining unscathed is very common and should be compared with Scratches-face's as well as with some legendary experiences.[1]

The same informant had another experience, which is described below:—

I rose before sunrise, got my horse ready and went to Long-horse,[2] my father's clansman, and asked him to help me. So we went out before sunrise. I gave him four presents. He painted my body with white clay and sang a song, telling a few of his warlike exploits, then he pierced my shoulder with an arrow, inserted a stick and tied a horse to it; to the other shoulder he fastened a shield and some other medicine. They moved camp that morning. I followed, leading the horse. During the day the horse got continually more and more unruly, getting hungry and thirsty. After a while I turned to look at him and saw a stripe on one of his legs; had I seen two stripes I should have become a greater chief. I stopped there for the night and Long-horse came to free the horse and remove the medicine. I did not go back to camp, but stayed out and when I slept I dreamt. I saw a gray horse with a stripe on his leg standing in the very spot where Long-horse had removed the medicine. Someone talked behind me, saying, "This horse belongs to the Dakota." I did not see anyone. After this I went to war and captured a gray horse. I struck coups, captured guns, and achieved the other deeds of a chief, riding the gray horse. The stripe was a sign for striking coups. I named my grandson 'Chief-with-the-gray-horse' (*tsicdtaxiwatstsic*).

The most interesting detail in the foregoing narrative is the mode of self-torture employed, which exactly parallels one reported for the Hidatsa at the time of the Sun dance.

---

[1]See this volume, 184, 271.
[2]A very famous warrior.

Scratches-face, whose generic account of visions has already been cited, recounted the following personal narrative. It was not without some difficulty and considerably higher compensation than usual that he was prevailed upon to narrate this experience.

I fasted because three of my brothers (*akúpe*) had been killed, one at Pine Ridge, one on the other side of the Bighorn Mountains, one between Bighorn and Pryor. When an Indian had an *akúpe*, he could take anything they had and give it away. When all of mine were killed, I was alone, had no horses nor anything else.

I went on a mountain, chopped off a finger joint, and gave it to Old-Woman's-Grandson, saying:—

Kăricbāpìtuə,	hiné	warákuk,	îwice	îtsiə	wakú.
Old-Woman's-Grandson,	this	I give you,	pay	good	give me.

I cried out aloud a great deal. I wanted some animal or something else to help me. Before chopping my finger off, I held it toward the sky, praying and thus speaking to Grandson, "I do not steal nor do any other bad things, and you have known me. That is why I'm poor." When I had said this, I chopped off my finger. I cried, saying, "I am poor, give me a good horse. I want to strike one of the enemies and when I go on a good road I want to marry a good-natured woman. I want a tipi to live in that I shall own myself."

I fasted on the mountain near where Joliet now is. I slept one night, the next day chopped off my finger, and on the second day, about this time of day, I did not know anything then, the blood running from my hand. Far in the night I came to again and looked round; it was night and cold. I made a bed out of sagebrush and grass; on it I laid logs. When I fainted, I held my hand on my breast on the side I had cut; half of my body was all covered with blood. When I got up, I went to my bed. My arm ached and I could not sleep. On the third day I got up and sat down. I was very thirsty, but thought I should stay there till the following night. On the night of the third day I went to bed and tried to sleep but could not because it was too cold. Sometimes I heard footsteps as if of a person coming toward me, but looking up I saw no one. After a while I went to sleep. While asleep I heard a man clearing his throat; also the snort of a horse. I heard someone talking. "What are you doing? You wanted him to come. Now he has come." This is what I heard. My feet faced east and my head west. I heard someone coming toward me from the west and then standing on my right side. I saw men riding on horses, which were prancing round. I heard little bells. They got nearer to my side and I faced toward them and looked at them. They were not men or horses but shadows of these. One man was riding a bobtailed horse and had painted his horse with a lightning mark on all four legs. His horse was like fire. There were six of them, the rest were riding grays and blacks. The shadows were black. The rider of the bobtailed horse was like fire too. His rear braid reached the ground, the rest of his hair was clipped short. "I will show you what you want to see. You have been poor, so I'll give you what you want." The rider of the bobtail said, "I am going to run." All the trees and everything growing around there then turned into men and began shooting at them. They just kept on going to the east and I continued watching till they were invisible. The dust flew up to the sky. It flew up again on the east side of the horizon, where the riders had gone, and there I heard a lot of talking. After a while they got out of there and came back. They came and passed behind me. I heard them yelling and whistling.

They came and stood in front of me. The rider of the bobtail said to me: "If you want to fight all the people on the earth, do as I do and you will be able to fight for three or four days and yet not be shot." All the six horsemen started eastward. The rider of the bobtail held a spear; it was like fire. They were shooting as before. This rider knocked the people down with his spear. The dust flew up to the sky. Then followed a hailstorm. The hailstones were as big as my fist and knocked down those shooting at the horsemen. I saw them riding around in the storm. This storm was the Thunder and helped the six riders; it was caused by a man with wings. When I went out with the soldiers against an Indian tribe up north and fought in battle, I did just what I had seen in my dream. The fight started at about 8 a.m. I was not shot. They killed an enemy; I struck him first. I fasted in the spring when eighteen years old. Ever since then I have owned good and fast horses; even today I have one. I prayed for a good-natured and hard-working woman; my present wife to whom I have been married about thirty years is like that.

It is not certain whether White-arm's vision came unsought or was merely sought without tortures. It is interesting because it embodies the reminiscences of a convert to Christianity:—

I slept near Horn's place. During my sleep I saw a person riding a brown horse toward the top of a mountain and singing. He came towards me. I noticed all the feathers and other ornaments tied to his horse. The *isa'tsisé* (species of hawk) was painted on his horse's neck. I took a wing of this bird and used it for my horse's necklace. This person sang a song:—

maráká, bawaráxe dīk'uku. awé wa'kúhe k'ōk'. maráká diawátsisuk.
My child, to my song listen. The ground my ear is. My child we love you.

I joined the Church and now the one who gave me the song is teasing me at night, but I won't listen to him. I was under thirty years old when I went out for a vision for the first time. I was one of the poorest in the tribe, that's why I went. Some other times I went out, but never had a vision. I got the first one without torture, while I got no vision out of my later tortures. Before going for a vision a man took a bath, put on good clothes, and abstained from sexual intercourse. Bull-all-the-time has a bear for his medicine; he is a big shaman.

Bull-all-the-time has already been mentioned for his doctoring vision. In addition he had some fasting experiences, which unfortunately were not very fully described by him.

On the other side of the Musselshell there is a mountain called Buffalo-heart (*bicɛ̄-rasec*). There I slept and cut my left forearm. They showed me that I should become a chief. In my sleep I saw Pryor Gap and beheld a person holding out a blanket and making a sign for me to come over. The Indians began to move, and I went to the place where I had been called and fasted there. In my sleep I saw a person holding out a blanket and making a sign for me to come over. The Indians began to move, and I went to the place where I had been called and fasted there. In my sleep I saw a person coming with a war party's pipe and at the end of the stem was tied human hair in token of a killing. He sang:—

awé cóndək awúə awórək.
Country (in) any as I climb and come up.

At ——— (?) I fasted and heard a snake rattling in the distance. It came closer. It was a rattlesnake and threw something out of its mouth,—yellow paint. I made a cloth representation of the snake, painted it with yellow paint and still have it.

I told other Indians about my visions.

An interesting experience was described by Hillside:—

I was about twenty years old, and among the Many Lodges band. Over at White Mountain a big buffalo was killed. Its head was cut off and its hide skinned, leaving the tail on. I had myself cut in two places on the back and dragged the skull outside the camp. The people all saw me. My brother, the same who had made the arrow for me, pierced my back.[1] I started early in the morning and traveled all day with the skull; when the sun was low I was too weak to drag it any longer. I went to the mountain with it, my brother cut it off, and I slept on the skull for a pillow. It was raining hard. In my sleep I heard a man say: "Wait, poor fellow, you will eat now!" He had the foot of a buffalo on him. On the Pryor side I saw a large crowd of people with this person in the lead. When I was asleep, a buffalo came up to me and licked me. His hair was gray; this showed that I was to live to be an old man. His being leader showed that I was to be a leader of my people. The buffalo snorted while licking me. Leaders were supposed to carry good luck for the whole camp. I made a buffalo skin to represent my dream. While dragging the skull I was fasting. The buffalo was my real visitant; he had transformed himself into a person. On another occasion I dragged a skull. Medicine-crow's father told me that he and I were the only ones that had dragged a buffalo skull twice.

Muskrat's narrative derives interest from the fact that it represents the religious experiences of a woman:—

I was a young woman and was pregnant after my husband's death. I was out mourning the death of my husband and fell asleep. In my sleep I saw a person come up to me who said, "Take and chew that weed, and you'll give birth without suffering." I came back and it happened as I was told. The name of the weed is *batsĕkĭce.* I used the leaves, boiled them, and drank the infusion. In the same year I went out mourning for my brother (*bakúpe*). I had no dream till the fourth time. I had a vision of the *bickwarúcise* (buffalo-do-not-eat-it) weed. I was told: "This is better and more powerful than the other one." It was for the same purpose, before the birth of the child. As to the first weed, I was told never to pull out any myself, except when about to use it for medicine. Whenever anyone touches the buffalo-weed, I get into a trance (*kàxutsĕk'*). The way to get over the trance is to chew some of the weed. No one is supposed to touch my face or any part of my body with it. I have a horse inside me. Whenever the Bear Song dance is performed, I am forced over to the site. One time I was doing some beadwork while the Bear Song dance was going on in another part of the camp. I sat down, paying no attention, but it was just as if some power forced me to go there. I threw off my blanket. I heard voices, "There's one going already." Before I arrived, I was out of my senses, and the tail of a horse came out of my mouth. I was married to Bad-man's father at this time. People were astonished to see this. They took warts from a horse's leg, made incense therefrom, smoked me with it, and thus brought the horse tail back into my body again. Even

---

[1] I saw the scars—R. H. L. For the arrow referred to see p. 391.

when children bump against me, this tail will come out. So I always keep some horse wart about me. If people with a *batsiṛópe* do not get proper incense in time, they die.

I also got weasel medicine. My Weasel parents (in the Tobacco society) gavế me a weasel. There was an old man and his wife known as the Weasels; very few were in their chapter. They took the weasel away from me after giving it to me. Then I felt grieved, went out fasting, and had a vision of a weasel. I went to the mountains to fast, and could not sleep all night. A cloud came up. I went to the rocks for shelter and lay down to sleep. A weasel appeared and came on my neck, causing a queer feeling. He went into my stomach. I heard the weasel whistling with all his might. I woke up and looked round, but saw nothing. The weasel said: "This is what we want to give you." Then he gave me a whistle. He sang a song. This is the main part of the song:—

ûute ĭk·uctsíruk'.   ốpe ĭk·uctsíwa'tsềwik'.
The weasels are coming out.   The Tobacco I'll make come out.

Ever since I have had control of the Weasel chapter and through me it has become so renowned. Once an old man told me to get up and dance, and I got up and sang the song. The weasel warns me against having people strike my kidneys, lest I get into a trance thereby.

Both a horse and a weasel are inside of my body. Only lately I dreamt I owned some weasels and soon after a weasel was brought to me. People respect me and take care lest something bumps against me. Sometimes I dream of a horse and afterwards come to own it.

When I was out fasting, a gray horse came up to me and went into my stomach. He told me he should enter me. After the *batsiṛópe* once gets in, it does not go out. I doctor horses if they can't make water. I chew something and put it in their mouth. Then they can make water. I use chewing tobacco. Tobacco is one of my main medicines, I always have plenty on hand to doctor with.

I was fasting on a mountain, having heard that a man had slept there. I put down new bedding. While I lay there, I saw bald-headed hawks (?) but the eagle got ahead of them, jumped towards me, and shook one wing after the other, all in order to scare me. He came up to me and scared me. He shook his wing and one feather fell out. It was the Tobacco. I use Tobacco as one of my main medicines, as a liniment; *isé* is also used as a liniment; incense is made of it. I also dᐧctor broken bones. Some women chop off their fingers when seeking a vision; many women did it. Twice I got a vision when staying out only one day; the other times I had to fast for three days.

The Sun is the main thing I prayed to when I went out; but when I lay down to sleep I prayed to the ground-cedar and the sagebrush. The ground-cedar is owned by the Sun, I don't know who owns the sagebrush. I was fasting once and the Sun told me where to go to sleep. I went there and found many medicine-rocks (*bacớritsi'tse*). Thus I got plenty of property. Red paint was given to me at the same time. The Sun gave me power to make clouds. When a man leaves his wife, I can charm him and make him live with her a long time.

As is pointed out in my paper on the Tobacco ceremony, the *bātsiṛópe* motive was very prominent among the Crow Indians, and Muskrat's account of the weasel vision is one of the clearest expositions of what the natives imagine to happen in such cases. Crazy-head, according to Young-crane, had a frog for his *bātsirópe*, and in the winter it was heard croaking in his throat. The general conception of the *bātsirópe* is apparently found also among the Menomini.[1]

In studying the Tobacco society I obtained several descriptions of revelations, which I will merely summarize here since they have already appeared in full form.

Medicine-crow prayed to the Sun, cutting off a finger joint, and was visited by a young man and a young woman, who were identical with the Tobacco plant and gave him instructions for the foundation of the Strawberry chapter. On another occasion when mourning a comrade he saw a crane and was led to substitute a bird of this species for the otter formerly carried in the Tobacco planting procession. The crane showed him a scalp, and he subsequently killed a Dakota.

Big-shoulder-blade had a similar adventure with buffalo transformed into young men wearing buffalo caps and promising vengeance for the death of his brother. In consequence he founded the Buffalo chapter and killed an enemy about as old as his brother.

Sore-tail was very poor and went out to fast. The Sun visited him as he was lying on his blanket and said, "I'll send you my messenger." He sent the Eagle, who showed him a special kind of lodge and taught him a song. In consequence he founded the Eagle chapter and became the very richest of all the Crow. Anyone who wanted to go on the warpath would consult him and he sent them out with a blue feather on the neck. He even sent out a woman with this medicine and she came back victorious.

In 1910 Medicine-crow told me of a vision, which may be connected in his mind with the Tobacco society since a strawberry appears, but he did not explicitly state that he recognized such an association. His account follows:—

I would pray during any season of the year. Fasting makes men of Indians. At this season of the year (summer) I once fasted where there were plenty of skulls; on the other side there was a high place. I spent four days and nights without drinking anything. On the fourth morning I heard in the west a shout and a whistling sound resembling that made by a railroad train. I heard it four times, then I heard a voice say, "There is something coming to meet you from over there." I looked in that direction and saw something coming. It approached and I beheld a white man, a young man with the handsomest face, standing before me. Had he spoken to me in English, I might be able to speak English, but he addressed me in Crow. Had I been a white man and seen the vision, I think I should be wealthy today. The young

---

[1] Skinner, vol. XIII, this series, pp. 42, 45.

man said, "You are poor and I have known this for a long time. All the people around here will always know about you and hear about you; you will be a chief." Having said this, he yawned as though from sleepiness, and I saw that his teeth were all gold. He had something pinned on in front which smelled sweetly and turned out to be a strawberry. He said, pointing east, "A great many whites are in that direction; you will be taken there four times. The last time you will be an old man." Since then I have been taken East once and still expect to be taken three times.

The foregoing data will suffice to bring out the main characteristics of Crow visions. Since the vision concept enters into every aspect of Crow life, additional illustrations will be found in other parts of this paper and in publications on the whole devoted to other phases of culture.

Though I repeatedly attempted to get descriptions of ordinary dreams, I never succeeded in securing a detailed narrative. Most commonly my informants spoke of seeing ripe berries and themselves eating them; or the whole country covered with snow; or the ice floating down the river. These are quite conventional ways of designating the seasons of the year and the assumption always is that if a person has dreamt of a particular season he will live until the next summer or whatever portion of the year was suggested. It is dreams of this sort that are announced in the sudatory. For example, a man will then say, "I saw the hay crop being cut, may we all do the same."

Even in the last years of his life Gray-bull would dream of martial experiences by night and by day. He would see a big battle and himself capturing a white horse. Once he dreamt the enemy were leaving a girl behind and on coming up to her the Crow braves found that she was a woman now living in Lodge Grass. On the day Gray-bull told me about his dreams he had taken a sweatbath and had said there, "Raise the door, I have seen horses, may we all have them."

A Crow girl once dreamt that she was riding a mouse loaded with lodge poles. Dreams of flying and of falling from a height occur.

If a person dreamt that some close relative of his had fallen ill, he would cut off a lock of his hair on the following morning, take some tobacco and meat, and cast all three into the water. If the relative dreamt about is far away, the dreamer will build a sweatlodge and voice wishes on behalf of the kinsman at each opening of the sudatory.

It is believed that a bug on the head makes people dream.

Bear-gets-up told me that in the spring of 1911 he had frequently dreamt of deceased friends. At first he had not dreamt about getting anything to eat, but later he dreamt of himself being feasted by an old woman of his own clan. One day when I arrived at this informant's lodge, he greeted me with the remark that he had dreamt last night of himself engaged in conversation with me, hence I had to come:—

ṓ°tsiəc   bāwacíᶦrək   hiñé   batcírirək   bats-awáxpək   barī-wakȧ+uk.
Last night I dreamt   this   white man   mutually I with him   we talked we continued.

hᴇc   hûi-mȧtsik·,   ik·ŏt·k·.
Now   he had to come,   that is why.

Young-crane said she sometimes dreamt of the next winter, seeing ice and snow. After her husband had been killed, she dreamt of him lying down with her. This frightened her.

Dreams which definitely partake of the nature of visions have been dealt with as such.

SHAMANS.

With reference to shamans Professor Kroeber's admirable formulation of Arapaho conditions[1] applies in like measure to the Crow. There were indeed men who had received revelations of so important a character and had shown their powers in so convincing a fashion that they were designated as *batsĕ maxpé*. But they differed merely in degree, not in kind, from others who had successfully sought visions, and it is quite impossible to segregate them as a definite group from the rest of the community. As Professor Kroeber felicitously puts it, to do so would be as artificial as to recognize a distinct caste of warriors in a tribe where every one strove to achieve martial fame. Shamanism in principle has thus been sufficiently expounded in the section on Visions. It remains to discuss certain characteristic manifestations of shamanistic competence at its high-water mark.

CONTESTS.

The most dramatic exhibition of supernatural powers naturally took the form of a contest between rival shamans. This might be waged in a fairly amicable spirit, but was also carried on in grim earnest. Such conflicts are described by the term *bats-ȧn-dutùə*, seizing one another's arms;[2] it represents an opponent seizing the other's arms and rendering him helpless.

Perhaps the most serious shamanistic feud of the last half century was that between Big-ox and White-thigh. It was repeatedly referred to by various informants. Big-ox had had a revelation from the Thunder and was greatly feared as a sorcerer. White-thigh was also a great shaman, his principal charm being a medicine rock (*bacŏritsi'tse*). Big-ox lay with the wife of Shows-wings, who had got his captain's medicine from White-thigh and accordingly complained to his patron, asking that he should do something against Big-ox. When Big-ox went on the warpath, White-thigh caused him to meet a large hostile force, so that his party was obliged to flee, losing many horses. Then Big-ox waited for his rival to go out against the enemy, for both of them had the pipe (i.e., were captains). They were out several nights. Big-ox prayed to the Thunder, asking that only the captain should meet with some disaster. It rained continually and White-thigh's horse was struck by lightning, so they had to turn back. Each worked against the other four times in

[1]A. L. Kroeber, "The Arapaho" (*Bulletin, American Museum of Natural History*, vol. 18, pt. 4, 1907), 419.
[2]*bats*, reciprocal prefix; *ȧre*, arm, *dutùə*, seizing.

this fashion until neither ventured to go on the warpath.   At last Big-ox got angry.   He drew a human image on the ground, made a hole in the heart, blew smoke on it, and effaced the picture after saying, "You shall be the poorest creature on earth; finally you shall be blind and have to crawl on your hands and feet."[1]   This came true and White-thigh became so poor that he had no belt and had to use a rope in its place. The blinded man smoked against Big-ox and said, "He shall be very poor, roam from camp to camp, and end in feeble-mindedness."   This also came true, Big-ox lost all his family, and in his old age, when I knew him, he had to wander from one stranger's camp to another and on account of his dotage had lost all his former prestige.   Although both predictions were verified, Big-ox is generally regarded as the victor, for the other man died, while Big-ox in spite of his sufferings never had to go hungry.

Big-ox's practices were evidently a compound of magic and animism· On the one hand, he relied on the protection of Thunder, on the other he resorted to what savors of pure imitative magic.   It is said that he indulged in sorcery a number of times, but suffered himself each time since members of his family would die.   Once he was found trying to smite a woman with blindness, but was caught in the act and made to desist. According to one statement, such practices were indulged in clandestinely for fear of the victim's family.   However, I have satisfied myself that the notion of killing an evil shaman after the manner of some Shoshonean tribes is quite foreign to the Crow.   They would either try to pacify their powerful enemy or have him combated by another medicineman.

Evil magic is called *dúck̓ uō* (also applied to charming a person of the opposite sex), and the act of smoking against some one is literally defined by the term *kus-ŏpiu.* The methods pursued are suggested above, but accounts vary as to details.   One Crow says that the picture of the enemy is sometimes drawn near a river bank, with the head nearest the water, whereupon the sorcerer smokes towards it and burns incense. The water comes to wash the image away, and the sooner it does so, the sooner the victim will die.   Another informant says that a rock or *bắxe* weed was placed on the picture and in order to blind his enemy the shaman would put ashes or charcoal on the eye of his image.   The injury planned would, of course, vary: the shaman would paralyze his victim, strike him with dumbness; deform him, have him killed on a warparty,

---

[1]Another informant states that he saw Big-ox dig a little hole in the ground, put in charcoal and ground-moss (*awákŏtsirŭhe*), smoke and blow the smoke into the hole, whereupon he covered up the pit after saying that he was going to make his enemy poor.

or cause him to lose his property. A common motive for the use of evil magic seems to have been jealousy on account of a love affair with one's wife.

I learned of one other shamanistic contest comparable to that of White-thigh and Big-ox. The participants were Gros Ventre-horse and Dung-face (ísè-pèrec). Dung-face told his rival he would send him off to another place; Gros Ventre-horse said he could not do it: "I am not a child and will not depart." "You will not know whether you don't go away," said Dung-face. Gros Ventre-horse answered, "You shall be poor and shall have no horses or tipis." Dung-face said, "You will go off and stay in another place, it will come true." Both had their wishes fulfilled. Gros Ventre-horse went to the Gros Ventre (Hidatsa?) and died there, Dung-face came to have no horses at all. This was an instance of *batsândutùɔ*.

Dung-face had another encounter with Jackrabbit which was not quite so serious. Jackrabbit had gone out to the enemy and brought plenty of horses. He made a song in derision of Dung-face, who went into his tent and bade his brother bring an old buffalo skull. On the forehead he drew horsetracks and announced that these were the tracks of the horses stolen by Jackrabbit, as well as those formerly owned by him. He told his brother to take the head and throw it into the water, saying, "These are Jackrabbit's horses." Dung-face said, "Then Jackrabbit will not have any horses." The Crow broke camp and ascended the Little Horn. The enemy came and stole all of Jackrabbit's horses. Dung-face followed their tracks, caught the enemy, killed two of them, and recovered all the horses. Now he owned Jackrabbit's horses. Jackrabbit paid him for four of them, but Dung-face kept the rest.

More commonly the rivalry of shamans assumed milder forms. Three-wolves told of a case which was also mentioned by others. There was one medicineman who would not permit any visitors to touch the fire in the center of his lodge. Another shaman heard of this and paid his rival a visit. He found two or three men there, who were afraid to touch the fire. He said to his host, "I too am a medicineman, but I don't forbid my guests to touch the fire. Why do *you?*" The other replied, "I fear they would get hurt." Thereupon the visitor seized the fire-sticks and pulled them about, saying, "I'll see what will happen; give me your pipe and I'll smoke." The other shaman began to cough and spat out worms rapidly increasing in number and moving towards his rival. The latter struck his sides with some mud, whereupon a little bird came out and picked up the worms one after another. The host cried, "Don't let it eat up all my medicine; take your bird out and go away." "I don't like your medicine." At last the visitor covered his head with his robe and put the bird back into his stomach. Then he said, "Let us have some more fun, get out some more of your worms." The defeated shaman said, "No, you are no good. Go away with your bird, I don't want my medicine to be eaten up." One-horn added that the host, before acknowledging his defeat, spat out a big toad, but his rival again made the bird appear, which killed the toad and then reëntered the shaman's mouth.

This episode was also briefly described by Little-rump, who says it took place when he was young. The owner of the lodge, according to him, was named Cherry-necklace, of the *xúxkaraxtse* clan; he had married an Hidatsa woman and had lived among her people. His neck was tattooed all over. The other shaman was named Red-owl and belonged to the *ûsawatsiə* clan. Cherry-necklace would not permit anyone to expectorate in his lodge because if they did they would feel a worm in their neck. Once a man who had expectorated had a worm sucked out of his neck. The other taboo established by Cherry-necklace was the one described above. Red-owl's bird was a woodpecker. Both the woodpecker and the worms reëntered their respective owners' bodies.

Sometimes a number of shamans would decide to have a contest and assembled in a lodge where they ranged themselves on opposite sides, while young men came in to sing. Then, Strikes-three-men says, one might begin the performance by taking a blue bead and rubbing it, thus transforming it into a bluebird's egg. Another would rub some buffalo chips and produce chokecherry pemmican. A third would twist his blanket, thereby causing the man opposite him to drop in a faint; then by untwisting the robe he would restore his opponent. These performers were known as *ak-bākumbîre*, which my first interpreter rendered, 'the twisters,' but the more common meaning seems to be 'the transformers,' 'the jugglers.' The word without the prefix denoting the actor is applied to a white man's circus performance. One shaman said to his adversary, "I'll put a *bíwitsé* (flat rock used in pounding cherries) into your stomach." His opponent arose screaming and his abdomen was seen to protrude painfully. The other shaman smoked some medicine for incense and made the abdomen shrink to its normal dimensions. One shaman said to his opponent, "Swallow this knife." When the man had swallowed it, the shaman extracted it from his anus. Such shamans were greatly feared by other people since they could cripple their enemies through their power, 'seizing their victims' arms' (*ândutùə*, see above).

At such contests there are sometimes two or three, very rarely as many as four, shamans on each side. Sometimes a shaman is powerful enough to withstand his opponent's attack.

Three-wolves recounted a shamanistic contest attended by him in which four men took part. One side would say, "Try to prevent us from doing something to you." They sent a burr against one of their opponents, and he fainted. The singers continued singing, and the successful shamans asked for tobacco and smoked. The man who had cast the burr jumped over the 'dead' man and with his hand extracted the burr from his body; other shamans use suction. An otterskin was tied to a peg in front of a performer, who twisted it, thereby choking his opponent and making him fall down. The first shaman leapt over him and after smoking restored him to consciousness. "Now we'll go against one of your men, try to help him." They sent a red-stone pipe-stopper (?) against him. Some men cannot be choked this way. The injured man's comrades fanned him with a blanket or jumped about. Another shaman rolled up wolf hair into a ball and sent it into his adversary. One man jumped into the fire, stamped on it, then climbed a tipi pole and on getting down challenged them, saying "Now shoot at me." His opponents tried every device, but he always caught their medicine and flung it back at them. These performances take place in the evening. Only those who have dreamt of this particular power are active participants. They are usually, but not always, old men. Once a young man dreamt of a bird flying round in one direction and killing people thereby, while when it flew the opposite way they all revived.

Little-rump mentioned tricks performed on two distinct occasions. Once several old Indians had assembled in a lodge and divided into sides, each striving to outdo the other. My informant saw one man put a leaf into the palm of his hand, deposit some ashes on it, blow and rub; then he showed a shell. Another time Little-rump and his comrade were with some Indians, and there was mutual twitting about each party's having no medicine. The others challenged Little-rump and his companion to do something. His friend took a bunch of buffalo hair and some dirt, began to rub them under his blanket, and threw the product in front of the challengers, and it was a mole. Then he took buffalo hair, ashes, and dirt, rubbed them between his palms, and in a little while the onlookers saw that he had something big in his hand. When he threw it down, it was a live rat.

Arm-round-the-neck witnessed a combat between two shamans, one seated on each side of the lodge, where a big fire had been kindled.

Both had painted themselves and used all their medicine. One of them said he was going to blind his opponent. He was naked. While singing his song, he jumped into the fire and got out again. "We did not know what he did, but the other man became blind. The blinded one whistled, sang his song and did what he could but failed to regain his sight." Then the shaman who had blinded him made him see again. The second man in turn said he was going to try his medicine on the first and would make him die. His medicine was a ghost; his body was painted white and he had black paint round his eyes. He sang his song, went outside, ran up the cover of the tipi and down again. His opponent went backwards and lay down stiff. When the man who had killed him saw that he could not rise, he did not touch him, but made the motion of taking something from his victim. He had a burr in his hand. The dead man then got up. These medicinemen were named He-seeks (batsfre) and Enters-a-red-feather (bā+óc-birĕre). He-seeks jumped into the fire without getting hurt and Arm-round-the-neck thinks he had the stronger medicine. One of the two shamans went up the inside of the lodge, taking hold of the poles, went out of the smoke hole, and came down again by the smoke hole; he made a noise like an owl.[1]

The foregoing was the only real *bǎkumbírio* witnessed by Arm-round-the-neck. He was present on another occasion when four shamans tried to do something of the same sort, but without success. One of them claimed having crow medicine and said he could take out people's eyes; another tried to do something to my informant, but failed.

Another informant furnished the following account:—

It was getting dark when I heard a herald cry, "All who can make medicine shall come together! Paint yourselves according to your visions and come to where I am!" They were going to test one another's powers. They said, "We will test one another and see who will leave." Those men who had visions of ground-squirrels and ghosts always painted white. The door was opened and we all watched them. One fellow who was painted white jumped into the middle of the lodge. "I'll kill one of you," he said, and called one of the others, who immediately took his pipe to defend himself. They danced. The ghost-visionary took a rope, while the other held his pipe vertically, touching his neck. The performer tied a knot in his rope and his opponent began to choke. Another man jumped into the middle and asked the performer to try his power on him. He protected himself by crossing and convulsively twitching his arms, and the rope did not affect him at all.

All the medicinemen were singing separately. One shaman said, "You are all medicinemen; I'll knock you all down by my power." He hopped round with peculiar movements of his left hand and all fell over towards the right side. Then he made

---

[1] This is doubtless the one with the ghost-medicine. See p. 381.

movements with his right hand, and they all fell over to the other side. Another man took some bark, stuck it into the fire and blew smoke on his hands, making the sound of a ground-squirrel. When he was ready, he said, "Look what I have done." He had made a big plug of trade tobacco and gave it to them to smoke. Another shaman took ashes, burned incense, and blew on the ashes, transforming them into beads. Still another medicineman got up and said, "I'll make a handkerchief." He rolled a piece of mud into a ball, while a drum was being beaten, rolled the ball, and stuck it into the fire. When he opened his hands, a handkerchief was seen in them. He re-transformed it into mud, and threw it away. I saw this myself.

At this point all the horses ran off and all the onlookers, including myself, ran after them. After this[1] one shaman took a stone maul, lifted it and swallowed it. His stomach was inflated. He moved off and the stone dropped to the ground. Another man stuck the limb of a chokecherry into the ground. This was in the winter time. He sang, scratched the ground, and pulled out Indian turnips, which he gave to the people to eat. He told them to sing again, took the chokecherry limb, shook it over his head and looked at it three times. Nothing happened; but the fourth time he looked and though it was in the dead of winter there were ripe berries on it, which all of them ate. The same thing was done with june-berries. This magic power is derived from animals appearing in visions.

Gray-bull described the following occurrences:—

We were camping on the Plum River. I heard a crier in camp calling some men into his tipi so they might fix themselves up. I asked my mother what was the matter and she told me it was a *bākumbîrio.* I heard drums beating. I went to the big tipi, stood at the door, and looked in. The one closest to the door had all his body daubed with white clay. He sang for a while, then jumped into the fire. The singers were in the rear of the tent, singing special songs for the occasion. When the shaman got out of the fire, he said, "Make tobacco for me." Then someone on the inside said, "Give it here." He held his hand over the fire for a while, stretched out his arms, and when he brought it back he had some tobacco and kinnikinnick in his hand. He acted as if he were going to take something, then gave tobacco to those seated by him, who filled their pipes, whereupon both they and he himself smoked. The shamans were ranged on two sides, each group betting against the other. After the tobacco had been consumed, one shaman told his opponents he would knock them all over on one side with his hand. They began to sing and make medicines, telling him he could not do it and betting against him. He began to dance by the door and the fire, clad only in his breechclout and with his body painted white. He motioned with one arm as if to push them to one side, and all of them fell toward one side. The spectators cheered the shaman. After he had done this, he sat down. A man got up from the other side; his body was red. He ran round the fire four times, then hooted like an owl, jumped up, and disappeared. We did not know how he went up but heard him hooting owl-fashion from the top of the lodge. He was going to bring either a fish or a frog, but at this point all the horses in camp ran away and all the people went after them, so the performance broke up. Somehow the shaman also returned and looked for the horses. Those who performed these tricks usually had a crow, rat, or ghost for their medicine.

Gray-bull knew of no shaman of this type who gave away his medicine.

---

[1] It is not clear whether the narrator means that what follows happened on another occasion or that it merely happened after his departure and is told on the basis of hearsay.

LEGERDEMAIN.

Sleight-of-hand performances of this type were by no means con-fined to the time of formal contests between medicinemen. One of the most famous of shamans was Plenty-fingers, who is said to have been contemporary with Medicine-crow's father; One-star's wife is one of his granddaughters. He derived his power from a bear; at one time he was very poor, but when a bear was killed in camp he had his back punctured and dragged the skin about camp. He named all his seven children after the bear,—Bear-stays-in-the-wood (*naxpitsɛ́-warɛre-na'kùɔ*); Bear-holds-up-his-arms (*naxpitsɛ́-wâre-wisɑ̀c*); Bear-small-waist (*naxpitsɛ́-tsɪ̄kɪ́pic*); Bears-seek-food (*naxpitsɛ́-mārûc tsɪ̀ru*); Bear-seeks-cherries (*naxpitsɛ́-wɑ̂tsuts-ɪ̀ric*); Bear-ears (*naxpitsɛ́-a'pɑ́c*); Where-bear-stays-it-is-good (*naxpitsɛ́-anna'kɓ = ìtsic*).

One winter one of these children wanted some berries. Plenty-fingers told them to get him the limb of a cherry tree. When they had brought it, he stuck it into the ground in front of himself, covered him-self up and made medicine. When he had removed the blanket, the tree was full of cherries, which the children ate. One of the boys wanted plums and in similar fashion he produced plums. Some of the girls would long for wild turnips in the winter time. He would dig in the ground with his fingers, take some out, and give them to his children. He could also produce sarvis-berries and other berries in the winter. When people had no meat, they would go to Plenty-fingers and ask him for some. He would order them to get the bark of a tree, cover himself and the bark with a blanket, and when he was done the bark had turned into dry meat, which was given to everyone to satisfy their hunger. He could similarly transform driftwood into animal intestines.

Plenty-fingers was also able to treat illness. Once a man was on the point of death, being just able to breathe. They said, "Call Plenty-fingers." When he came, he bade the other people go outside. Then he was heard singing a bear song. He sucked something out of the patient's skull and something out of his neck and chest. While before the man had merely been able to breathe, he now began to talk and look about and was well. Then Plenty-fingers stuck one finger into the ground, sang a song and pulled out a wild turnip, which he gave the man to eat. He told the people to bring him a plum branch, planted it in front of him, covered himself and the branch with a blanket, and began to growl like a bear. When the blanket was removed, there were plums on the limb, and he fed them to the sick man. Similarly he produced cherries and plums for him. He also stuck his fingers into the ground and pulled out wild carrots (*bik'ɑ̀sa'te*) for the people he doctored.

Plenty-fingers foretold what was going to happen. He said, "There is a place where you are always going to run round in a circle." By this he meant to prophesy that they were going to have fair-grounds. He also predicted the kind of guns they were going to have, saying, "I have a gun into which I always put six shells; I have a gun that shoots far away."

For a long time he was considered invulnerable. He felt safe and accordingly acted as recklessly as a Crazy Dog. Once there was a big fight on the Bighorn and one of the enemies had a gun and plenty of arrows. The other Crow were afraid of him. Plenty-fingers asked whether any of them had struck him. When they answered negatively, he went straight toward him and was shot above the abdomen, but growled like a bear and rubbed leaves over his abdomen with his hand and got well again. Then he captured the enemy's gun. Four times he was badly wounded, but merely spat on his hands and cured himself forthwith. Once the enemy were entrenched and Plenty-fingers walked toward the trench clad in his bear blanket. They shot at him four times. Each time he fell down, but when he got back there was no hole in his blanket. Once, however, there were six Shoshoni in a trench and when Plenty-fingers started against them they shot at him and he fell down. People said, "Though he falls, he gets up again." But he did not get up; he had been shot square in the forehead. Little-rump was a big boy when this took place.

To return to tricks of legerdemain. Little-rump tells of one occasion when he saw Hunts-the-enemy give a performance at the request of those present. Taking a buffalo chip, he flattened and rounded it between his palms, then rolled it. When it first left his hand it was a round chip, but as it rolled farther it turned into a skunk. He took it back under his blanket and threw out a buffalo chip. Another tale is told of how a war party were without tobacco. One of the braves asked his companions to whittle down a piece of bark to the size of tobacco, then he put dirt on and began to rub it, blew on it, and when he showed it, it was a piece of tobacco, which he smoked. Little-rump saw another man put dirt and ashes into his palm, rub them, and produce four beads.

A similar trick was witnessed by Gray-bull. He had a comrade named Wants-to-live (*ĭm-bĭəc*). One night they were out looking for girls and wished to smoke, but had no tobacco. Wants-to-live told Gray-bull to get bark from a tree. He brought it to him. He took the bark in his hand and shook it in the air for a while, then handed it to Gray-bull, telling him to take it. It was a piece of tobacco and my informant smoked it. Another time this same man took mud, rolled it into four balls in his hands, glued them to his hand, and gave them to Gray-bull. They were four beads such as Gray-bull wore in his necklace.

Another man is mentioned who had like powers; his name was Old-man-does-what-no-one-can-do (*barê-wahirîsa-isû'ke*). When his tobacco was being consumed by himself, he managed to maintain his supply, but not if someone else smoked it.

One man had the Sun for his medicine. He had seen the Sun painting himself red all over, then taking charcoal and marking a black oval round his face, which he exhibited to the visionary. The man was able thereafter to paint his face in the same way by putting charcoal towards the sun and merely making the motion of painting an oval. The people knew about this medicine. Its owner gave the painting medicine to various men, all of whom proved successful, some even becoming chiefs.

Three-wolves narrated the following as an instance of shamanistic power he had witnessed. One winter when the snow was very deep some youths were pursuing buffalo afoot; four men went along. One man with a six-shooter said, "I'll take you where there is something to eat." He took them towards the mountains, where they saw buffalo crossing a canyon far away. "If we go there, it will take us all night." Their leader said, "We'll go to the brush and get a rabbit." He and Three-wolves went there and found a herd of buffalo lying down not far away. "I'll see whether I can kill one," said the shaman, taking off his robe. He told Three-wolves to ascend a hillock. Then he approached the buffalo, took something, and made a movement as if throwing some object. When the buffalo saw him, they rushed towards a hill, where one of them fell down, so that the medicineman could easily dispatch him with two shots. He butchered the buffalo and showed my informant a little burr he had thrown into the buffalo's back where the sinews meet. "That is what I crippled him with." He took back the burr, but Three-wolves does not know what he did with it.

INVULNERABILITY.

Relative invulnerability or marvelous powers of recuperation are credited to a number of medicinemen. Thus, within Little-rump's lifetime a man named Hole-in-his-ear was shot through the collarbone with an arrow but recovered. In another battle he was shot in the back with a gun but was restored to health. People began to think that he could not be killed, but at last the Piegan while pursuing a party of

Crow horse-raiders shot him in the head and killed him. Bull-snake is mentioned as a man bitten by a rattlesnake and apparently unable to travel back to camp. His companion left him to notify his people, but when they came to look for him he had started home by himself.[1] Another man was shot through the knee, but was well enough to walk within ten days. He was shot in the back subsequently, but not killed. At last he died from illness. After his death the Crow got to where his body was and found that his bones were all covered with iron. His name was Badger-arm. He was very strong. Once he killed a buffalo and some people said he ought to have killed it in the shade so that they could butcher in comfort; he seized it by the tail and dragged it into the shade. Another Crow named Black-elk was shot and killed by the Dakota. People saw him fall on the snow with blood issuing from his nose and mouth. The other Crow went on and stopped at the mouth of the Reno. During the night the Crow who had been killed caught up with them. They asked where he came from and he told them. It was the same man. Later he stole some Cheyenne horses and the Cheyenne killed him for good.

Miraculous powers are attributed to a legendary shaman Big-iron.[2] He is believed to have aged, died, and come back to life three times before living for the fourth and last time; thus his span of life covered four generations. He was so powerful that he ventured to challenge Thunder and succeeded in overcoming him and other supernatural beings. What seems very remarkable is that according to both the tradition and an independent statement, he told the Crow to make offerings and pray to him after he had died the fourth time and that he would then grant their requests. He also prophesied as to the coming of the Whites and his people's relations with them and what he foretold came true.

CHARMING GAME.

Calling buffalo or deer constituted a particular form of shamanistic activity based on specific visions. Thus, a brother of Bear-crane's, while watering horses, caught sight of some buffalo hair and a slice of fat some four inches long on a rosebush on the other side of the creek. He brought the hair and the fat home with him, wrapped them up, and tied them to the top of the backrest. When he slept that night, he dreamt of a man singing and shaking a rattle and a great many buffalo came to the singer. When the dreamer looked at the man, the latter said, "Make a

---

[1] See Lowie, this volume, 281.
[2] This volume, 288–298.

rattle like this, putting a buffalo hoof on it, sing and shake the rattle, and buffalo will come to you. The fat you picked up was myself; I am a buffalo. Take a buffalo hide, paint it, take this rattle, wrap it up with the hide, and hang it up." He went and carried out these directions.

At that time the Indians were starving for lack of game. The visionary went and cleaned his lodge. Beside his bed he placed dirt, in which he marked the tracks of big buffalo and of calves. He greased his lips with the fat, also took out the rattle, smudged it with incense of sweetgrass, and began to bellow like a bull. The next time he put the rattle on the same place and bellowed like a cow. The third time he imitated little calves, and the fourth time old buffalo. When the sun had gone down, he gathered together all the men in his tent and asked, "Where do you want the buffalo? "On that big level place on the other side of the hill." He sang the song he had dreamt, shook his rattle and rolled it in the mud as though it were a buffalo wallowing.

He bade all the men go home and go to bed that night. "Tomorrow morning the buffalo will be here." The next morning he heard the bulls bellowing on the other side of the hill. "Get up, the buffalo are here." They got up, saddled horses, mounted, and went. The whole plain was covered with buffalo and still more were coming. They were tired and could not run fast. The last time Bear-crane's brother worked his medicine my informant was a little boy of about five.

Big-ox is also credited with having had the power of luring game. Once the people could not find any game. Big-ox bade them get a buffalo skull and put its nose toward the camp. In the night they began to sing. In the morning they saw six head of buffalo and killed them. The following morning they again found several head. When they had had enough, Big-ox bade them turn the skull round, then they did not see any more buffalo. Another old man painted buffalo tracks around the camp, smoked incense and sang, "I want to get buffalo in." He went out and cried, "Young men, get up-hill; I think I have seen some buffalo." Early in the morning some young fellow got up and saw some buffalo going up-hill. He went home to tell the rest and they killed some buffalo. Every morning they repeated this until they had plenty of meat.

One-horn recollected several instances of buffalo-charming. Once the Indians were hungry and could not find any buffalo. They called an old man to charm the game. He told the heralds to bid a young man go to a pond nearby and they would find some. A young man rose early, went there, and discovered two big herds. He told the people, who went out to kill the buffalo. At another time the Crow were camped at the

Little Bighorn confluence. Buffalo were scared off and the people asked Big-shoulder, one of One-horn's friends, whether he could get the game nearer to them. He had a bonnet made of a buffalo head with the horns and hung it high up on a pole. Then he told the people that the buffalo were going to come close to the camp. They sent out a scout, but he could not find any. They told Big-shoulder, who bade them try again; if none were espied this time he would give up. Big-shoulder asked the same scout to go out again to Porcupine Valley, about eight or nine miles away. This time he saw buffalo, returned, and told the Indians, who went out and got plenty of meat. Another time a man told the Indians to look for buffalo near a high mountain. They sent out a scout, who espied a dozen and reported. The Indians killed them. The shaman told them that every day they would find a few head there, but they failed to find any after the first time and lost faith in his powers. Then he no longer made medicine. He had a coyote skin and an eagle wing for medicines to lure the buffalo.

One-horn also recounted one instance of buffalo charming in connection with a shamanistic conflict. Yellow-buffalo and Jackrabbit-head had quarreled about women. Jackrabbit-head got up a war party. Yellow-buffalo knew about it and made medicine so that Jackrabbit-head should fail to see any game on the warpath and starve in consequence. The party were out for two days, when a young man told Jackrabbit-head about Yellow-buffalo's attempt to starve them. Then the leader knew that he should not accomplish anything on the warpath. All were afoot. On the third day they still saw no game. The wind blew so that the deer scented the hunters. For three days they had had nothing to eat. Jackrabbit-head said to one man, "Get one nice unbroken buffalo chip." He brought it. Yellow-buffalo's medicine was the wind, while Jackrabbit-head's was the Dipper. He said, "Yellow-buffalo has been against me. I'll try to make it so we can get something to eat. I have a good medicine; I think it is stronger than his, for it is the Seven Stars." He smoothed the ground inside his tent and marked a buffalo track on the smooth surface. He put the chip on the buffalo track and took off a medicine-rock necklace he wore. This rock was covered with buckskin and shaped like a person's face. He uncovered the rock and rubbed some fat from a skin on its face; he also rubbed it with yellow paint. Someone filled a pipe and passed it round till it got to Jackrabbit-head, who did not have it passed in front of him like the others, but over his shoulder from the rear. This was a sign that he was going to stop the famine. He put the rock on the chip; then, after smoking, he picked up the rock and put it over his head where he was sleeping. He left the chip where it was. They moved the next morning. Before sunrise Jackrabbit-head sent men to Rosebud Creek to scout for buffalo. They sighted from three to four hundred head there, and the party had buffalo to eat all the way home. This showed that his medicine was better than Yellow-buffalo's.

Some shamans called buffalo by dragging buffalo skins tied to their backs and singing buffalo-bull songs on the way. Gray-bull's brother-in-law was a buffalo-shaman; he had the wolf for his medicine.

Shamanistic practices were also combined with the two methods of driving game over a cliff and into a pound. One informant says that when he was a boy the Crow were roaming over the Basin. At the end of a ridge there was a high rock pointing south and on both sides extended rocks two to three hundred feet high to the distance of about two miles. Before daybreak all the people went out. The shamans in charge sang at night and selected a man for leadership in the morning. Starting from the edge of the cliff and on each side men and women were placed with an intervening space of about fifty feet; farther back the distance between adjoining sentinels was considerably greater. Others formed an arc of a circle back of the buffalo herd, while at the edge of the rocks old people and children were stationed. The buffalo were frightened down the passageway formed by the two wings of Indians and driven down the precipice so as to be killed. The old people sang praise songs in honor of those working thus. The following day the same procedure was followed in the same place with another herd, and on the next day it was done a third time. Then the women tanned the hides. My informant knew of another place where a buffalo drive had taken place, but he happened to be on the warpath at the time, hence had only hearsay knowledge. This time another shaman directed the proceedings. The rocks in this case were only about eight feet high and the buffalo were not killed in jumping down but impounded in a corral of about the same height, which was filled with from fifty to sixty head. A space was left in the structure by which a buffalo could be dragged out to be butchered. This method of hunting was generally followed in the fall. It was in vogue long before the Crow had iron arrow-heads.

Deer were also charmed either in connection with the surround, the corral or cliff method; the procedure is known as *ûᵘx-dùtuə* (deer-catching). Bull-all-the-time recollected an occasion when Cloud lured the deer without the use of a pound. He sang his song outside the camp, and the people divided into two sides each having one man mounted on a fast horse. They went far out and formed a circle round the deer. Possibly it is the same enterprise that is more circumstantially recounted by Bear-crane as follows. When the people were camping on the Powder River, Cloud told them they were going to catch deer. He sang for four nights, and on the fourth he cried out that in the morning the Indians were to get their horses ready in order to catch the deer. All men mounted, led by two men on fast horses. One of these held a foxskin in his hand, the other wing feathers. They saw some deer about as far as from Crow Agency to Hardin. All the men were painted as though on a war party. One man led two fast horses for the two leaders so that they could mount them as soon as theirs •were exhausted. Cloud stayed behind and the other people with the children were behind him. They had all their dogs with them, leading them lest they should go ahead. The people ranged themselves in a circle surrounding the deer and were hallooing and singing. Cloud had a big pipe with a fox hide tied to it and moved it toward the deer, which kept circling around. When all got close to the deer, they turned their dogs loose. Thus they caught the deer. They got so close to them that the deer could jump over their heads and run away if not caught, but most of them were caught. The people were so glad that they sang such songs about the deer as the following: "A deer is coming running toward me; I am going to get a neck piece and the hindquarters." Cloud always wore a white cloth round his head and walked with a stoop at every step.

Another informant described the deer hunt as follows. A man while fasting would see a vision of the deer hunt. In the spring, when the grass was good, the young men and women were called with the cry: "It is time to catch deer!" Then three kinds of men were sought,—those who had medicine for speed, those having the fastest horses, and those who had earned coups. All these men were assembled and divided into two diverging semicircles, the women bringing up the rear. In this way they would enclose a tract of several miles. Two men, one on each side, rode the best-winded horses; they were carrying arrows and were called arrow-runners, (*ak-arûute-wasé*). The shaman sang four songs, wearing a buffalo robe dressed with the hair. In each hand he held a pipe and he made motions with his hands. "When I close the fourth song, you shall begin to run." Then they all began to run, the leaders taking the lead on their respective sides and meeting in front. The people all followed along semicircles so as to surround the deer and closed the circle. In those days there were very few guns; they shot the deer with arrows. It was considered unlucky to let any deer escape. The deer would circle round and round, finally gathering in a body when worn out and piling on top of one another like sheep. The young men gave their mistresses a gift of venison. The last deer hunt of this kind took place the spring after Gray-bull was born, which would make the date approximately 1848. Another method was to have two lines of rock piles leading to a cutbank, with people strung out in the intervening spaces, equipped with blankets to wave at the deer, which were driven from the rear between the two rows of sentries and ultimately down the bank.

As to the corral method, the following data were secured. One night there was singing, conducted by the headman and his four assistants, while the herald ordered everyone else to keep still except that at certain points in the song all had to knock against their lodges and express a wish to get a buck or a doe. The pound was on level ground; no posts were set up and there were no mountains there. Two men riding the best horses were chosen to lead the drive and they encircled the country from opposite directions, enclosing a much larger territory than in the buffalo chase. The people kept on closing in and the deer were kept running all the time. Sometimes some wolves would be enclosed with the deer. The last time this was done at the Yellowstone River. One man named Rawhide was a Crazy Dog; he followed the deer round acting like a dog and chasing them away till the people stopped him. Cloud, who is credited with having conducted the ceremonial side of the surround, is also described as superintending a corral drive. He selected two swift men, each holding an arrow, and told them to run as fast as possible and then cross each other's path. They scared the deer, which were impounded by the people. In another account only one of the young runners is represented as holding an arrow, while the other is made to carry a feather.

The use of sacred rocks in charming game is described under another heading (p. 389).

WAR SHAMANS.

With a people of so martial a cast of thought as the Crow many shamans naturally had special medicines for war. Their services were eagerly sought by men desirous of distinguishing themselves, who would ask to be equipped for an expedition or to be adopted by the shamans, thus gaining part ownership of their medicine, though at times the shaman himself took the initiative, offering to make the transfer. No-horse gave the following generic statement on the subject:—

If a man dreamt of a certain horse, he might say to another man, "Take my medicine and get such and such a horse." The second man would reply, "All right; if I bring the horse, you shall own it." Then the shaman would continue, "You must know something about this medicine, you may keep it." "If there is a day when I do not know something about the medicine, will you help me out?" "Yes, I will help you out, now you are my child." Possibly the warrior himself had a dream and saw a place for his party to go to. Then he would go to his adoptive father, saying, "You offered to help me; open the medicine bag and fix it as it ought to be." He did so and incensed it appropriately. "I will start out, and if I get the horses I have in mind I'll give you some." If he had good luck, he would sleep about the outskirts of the camp on his return and look for the shaman's lodge at night. He would say to him, "I have brought a herd of horses, and yours is such-and-such a horse." Then before dawn the old man would sing his song of rejoicing. When the people heard him, they knew that his son had achieved something worth while. The next morning the son brought the horse to his adoptive father.

If the warrior failed in his enterprise, he had his men form a line on a hill and sang scout songs (*tsĭtpuxùə*). Then he reported to his 'father.' "Where I went there was nothing and I have come back. See what you can do with me." "I'll send you myself now. Make a sweatlodge about four days hence, with a small one beside it. Call the older men and we'll go into the sweatlodge with them." So all would go in and sweat. Then the shaman would bid them go to a certain tipi, where they feasted, then he spoke as follows: "My son went on the warpath and came back without anything. My heart is heavy and I want to say something; I wish all of you to listen. He made this medicine, thinking it was true, but it seems not. I want to put it aside and send him out with another. Four days from now go again without hiding it. The moon is bigger now; the first time you went the moon was just dying, that was the mistake we made. When you set out, let the women ride behind you and sing. Have everything ready. As soon as the women have dismounted, go on for a short distance and sleep. I'll sleep with you there. Have another stop about the same distance, and similarly with the third. Have all your meat eaten up. On the fourth day hunt and kill game for meat. Then my soul will return[1] and you shall go right on." The medicine might be a bird. "On the fourth night when you awake a bird

---

[1] It is the shaman's soul that is supposed to have accompanied the warrior.

will come flying toward you. If it looks backwards and seems restless, turn back and run home. If it flies with ease, not shaking its wings, sing songs of joy and proceed;. in that case you may depend on success. This bird coming will be myself. When you know that you are near the enemy, see that your lodge is without a hole and put out the fire after you have eaten. When singing, look round and you'll see something. You will find out whether any of your men is to be killed or whether you are to have good luck. If the former is the case, come right back." The warrior would obey these instructions, put out the fire, and sing. He might see blankets and saddles scattered about with his men's shirts and clothes. Then he would have the fire rekindled and say, "Let us saddle up and flee." In that case he would return. Some might say, "The leader is timid" and would advance toward the enemy. Such men always met with disaster and the tribe could not hold the captain responsible for their death since they had disobeyed him.

If the brave saw a black or white or some other horse, he sang songs of joy. As soon as his companions heard these, they cried, "Thanks!" Each one would say, "I want one like this," "I want one like that," "If I get a good gelding, I shall rejoice." A bird would appear from the proper direction, possibly bearing in its beak a scalp or some hair string. Then the captain said, "I was sent out for horses, but it seems they want me to do some killing." His companions might say, "If I strike a coup, I'll give you a horse"; or, "If I get a gun, I'll give you a horse." Some possibly protested, "We have come for horses, we have not come to kill." In a war party there are generally a lieutenant (*ı̆ptse-awŭə*, inside-the-pipe), a scout, and a rear officer (*hŭkace*, the last one), who is supposed to be a long-distance runner and who pokes those in front in the back with his gun lest they slacken their pace.[1] These officers discuss the plan of action with the leader and if all three join against him he is helpless. One of them might say, "When you set out, you spoke about horses, that is why we came." Another would say, "I came to get a horse that I might display, now I want you to do as I wish." Then the leader would yield: "All right, tomorrow before daylight you will be on top of a certain hill, sight the hostile camp and come back immediately. When on top, stay till after sunrise and watch for the smoke. Look over the ground and see how we shall have to run in fleeing. Find out what place we shall

---

[1] This officer may depose any of the other scouts for sleeping too long or on account of other delinquencies. He selects additional scouts. The leading scout carries a wolfskin, the lesser ones generally do not, but may carry coyote skins. Sometimes the wolf hide is put on the scout's head when he is spying from a cliff in order to prevent discovery. In cold weather the hide is used as a covering. Some think to themselves, "If I happen to go astray, a wolf will help me out." The scout's hide is slung over his back so the head will project over his left shoulder.

reach before it gets dark. If it is near by, tell us and we'll stay where we are. Even if I have to move, we'll go slowly. If the camp is not very far, send one of your men back." If the scout sees the camp and judges it to be far off, he so reports. The leader decides to move and tells the scout, "We shall move slowly up to such and such a place. If none of your men reaches me by that time, we shall move fast." If a runner came back from the scouts, giving the coyote howl, the leader's party would sing and gather up chips into a pile. The scout who gives the signal circled round and repeated this when close to the party. At last he came directly up to the heap of chips. The leader had a pipe filled and gave it to the scout to smoke. The scout reported: "At a certain creek, as the sun came up, I saw the enemy's camp; even those boys saw the smoke." If he saw the camp at close range and distinguished horses and people clearly, he sent men back to announce it to those in the rear. A single howl indicated that the camp was seen at a great distance; two howls, that it was close. When the messenger shook his gun, the people interpreted it also as meaning that the camp was close. The messenger, whether afoot or mounted, ran over the buffalo chips, scattering them. "Our leader has given orders for you to come to yonder point. The camp is close, you had better hide in the coulée as much as possible. Throw all your heavy stuff (blankets, etc.) away, look out for your guns, cinch your saddles and have everything prepared." Then the main body advanced toward the chief scout. "Where is the camp?" asked the captain. The scout showed it to him and said, "Get out your medicines and make incense. Get ready. Some of these men had better go back to wait for the leader for four days on the way home. If I don't get there, I shall have been chased another way. When at home, make a signal fire at the outskirts; and if I am behind you I shall make a similar signal. If you see my smoke, you'll know that I have had good luck and brought horses. That is all I have to say to you." Some member of this expedition probably has a blackbird for his medicine. The captain asks for such a one, and whether he be a little boy or an older person he is put in the lead. At night the party arrives at the enemy's camp and all seat themselves at the outskirts. The captain now appoints a leading and a rear scout, and his lieutenant likewise appoints two. They go to the outside of the camp to find horses that are most easily taken. "Bring them here directly. If all the horses are tied, we'll get in and try to cut them. If any are grazing, they will capture them." Then the man getting the kind of horse promised to the captain (either in his own or his shaman's vision) gives it to the captain, who accepts it. After a while the captain says, "We have enough horses now, let us flee." They run all night and the following day. Any horses that are exhausted are made to drop behind. The party continue going for two days and two nights. On the fourth day they halt to get to the body detached from the main party, and each one of this smaller group gets a horse. They proceed till they get to the Crow camp, where they halt. The leader goes to the shaman and tells him, "My heart is good (I am glad), I have brought many." Before sunrise all his companions come to camp, circle round, and finally disperse. It does not matter how many horses are brought, all are driven before the shaman's camp. "This is what I have brought; I give them all to you." The shaman sings a song of rejoicing. "It is well. You tired yourself out getting them; take them and keep them yourself or distribute them among your relatives. I am the one that gives them to you. I rejoice. You know that I have now given you all that medicine. Go and do about it as you choose." Thus the captain gets to own the medicine and uses it as he pleases.

To the foregoing may be added a specific account by another informant.

Sore-tail was famous for sending people out on the warpath. Once a man named Hair set out on an expedition. He left his hoop medicine on a sagebrush and told his followers to take it along. They put it round a dog's neck and had him carry it. Hair said to them, "You have spoiled my luck; I was counting on victory; I'll return tomorrow." Two scouts came in and reported what they had seen. White-on-the-neck said, "Those are not elk but people." When it got dark they heard the howling of a wolf. White-on-the-neck said, "That is no wolf, you had better prepare for the enemy." They were going to send a boy for water. He said, "I'll go myself." As he dipped up some water, he heard a bush snapping. He bade the warriors hasten to their entrenchment. The enemy charged and shot one Crow in the breast. The captain reminded them that they had put his medicine on a dog. Two men were wounded, one of them took his brother on horseback and they fled riding double. They got to the Crow camp and reported that the rest of the party were surrounded in their corral. All the young men immediately set out to relieve them, but when they arrived the Dakota had made their escape with some of the Crow horses. The comrades of the slain Crow mourned publicly. They loaded several horses with presents; some stopped at Sore-tail's lodge, some at the informant's father's, some at a female warrior's, embracing them and crying. Sore-tail said, "Tomorrow make all the moccasins you intend to take along, the following day get your horses, then report to me." He said three Dakota had already been given to him in a dream. He bade all the people come out, including the women, for a ceremony before the beginning of the expedition. A big pile of buffalo chips was heaped up. Sore-tail told people to watch him at noon, to go round the camp singing, and report to him, then they would proceed towards the pile of chips. As soon as Sore-tail was ready, he took the three captains and made them sit down in front of him. He sang a song, pointing at the sun, then at the informant's father, and the latter was decorated with yellow paint there. Similarly he put red paint on him. "I'll paint him with two colors, the rest of you with only one." He put blue paint on the second captain. The fourth time he sang, pointing at the sun and the female warrior, who was painted black. The three captains cried, "Thanks!" Sore-tail, wearing a buffalo robe with a whole eagle on it, sat down on the pile of chips. "Watch me closely," he said; "I shall sing four songs, then I shall rise from this pile. Watch me when I rise." They all watched him. He rose and turned into an eagle holding the scalp of an enemy in each claw. "In seven days you shall be back here. The first one you kill will lack one hand. As soon as you kill an enemy put a new moon on your back." They sighted the enemy on the Powder River on the fifth day; there were seventy in the hostile party, so the Crow confined their attention to the three Dakota scouts. They killed two of them; the third one evaded them for a long time, but was finally also killed. It was found that his right hand lacked a thumb, hence the Crow called the year "When the thumbless man was killed."[1] On the sixth day Sore-tail told the Crow in camp to prepare black paint. On the seventh day Sore-tail met the war party, took one of the captured scalps, and went through camp exhibiting it. There was great rejoicing in the camp and Sore-tail was acclaimed for sending out the expedition.

Sore-tail on another occasion sent out the informant's father, bidding him bring two Dakota scalps. This, too, turned out true. Another time Sore-tail sent out the same person telling him to be gone for thirteen days and bring a scalp; still another time he bade him get three enemies, and he did so. Sore-tail kept a pet eagle, which would fly outdoors for a while and then return. Sometimes the eagle would whistle, then the owner looked up and saw plenty of birds, whereupon he warned the Crow to tie up their horses near camp since the enemy was near. All the Crow helped feed the eagle.

---

[1] Lowie, this series, vol. 9, 242.

Red-bear had a gun for his medicine. Once the Dakota were very near and about to charge the Crow. Bed-bear told the people to bring their guns to him. He burned sweetgrass for incense and pointed his gun towards it, asking it to break the enemies' backs, arms, and thighs. Then he pointed the butt toward the incense and asked it to break the enemies' heads. He told his followers to repeat his word. Then they all imitated his motions and words, each with his own gun. They had their gun drill. They cleaned their guns and pointed them at the Dakota. While they were going through their rhythmic movements, Red-bear sang. He ordered them not to bring arrows into his presence and told them he was about to attack seventeen lodges. One-eye came at the end of the procession with a bow and arrow, saying, "These are sharp enough, I can smoke them with incense." He did so, pointing his arrow instead of a gun at the enemy. The medicineman saw him but said nothing, thinking he had given ample warning. They made a dash against the Dakota and no one was hurt except the offender's brother, who was shot in the kneecap. When enemies approached, he would shoot off a loaded gun once, but thereafter he would shoot it without powder, by mere magic.

Some other shamans were renowned for their powers of prophecy and divination. Thus, there was an old man who knew when the enemy were approaching; he could tell in how many days and at what time they were going to come and told the Crow when to watch for them and kill them. Sometimes he prophesied that it would rain or snow on the following day. He did not dream of these things; something told him. The Sun was thought to be his medicine. He asked Indians to call him "He-sees-all-over-the-earth." His medicine consisted of a hoop to which a star was tied; the hoop was wrapped with otterskin. Another man, who was favored by the Dipper, acted in somewhat similar fashion. He would dispatch war parties, telling them precisely where to go and what to get. Though he stayed home, he knew exactly in how many days the warriors would return and what they had accomplished.

Sweet-marrow (dúp-tsik' ùəc) had the special ability of locating the enemy's camp. Once he went on the warpath with some others near the mountains. At the canyon of the Tongue River one of them said to him, "Make medicine tonight." He bade them make a shelter without any holes in it. They did so. He sang a medicine song. It was dark inside at night. He took his pipe and looked through it. He saw the hostile camp near Cold Spring. Then he sang songs of rejoicing, and his companions said, "Thanks, Sweet-marrow; when we get to the enemy.

we'll cut a mule and a horse." They stole a horse and returned. The rest of the Crow people were at the Agency. On the return of the party, Sweet-marrow acquired a great reputation. A few days later he went out again. After a while he had a dream and returned to camp while the others in the party went on. Young-coyote, the captain, was asked to make medicine one night. Then he did so and saw the camp, whereupon he sang songs of joy. The others also rejoiced. The enemy was at the site of Buffalo, Wyoming. In the evening they had a sham battle, then they moved camp toward an old fort. Young-coyote's party watched them from a high hill. Before setting out that night they made medicine. Young-coyote told the young man to go to the camp and see about the horses. They did so, but the enemy must have had dreams, for they had rounded up their horses and put them into a corral. Young-coyote sneaked into it nevertheless and captured a mule and a horse. He got out and traveled some distance, then stole two more. Grandmother's-knife said that Sweet-marrow was the only man who could find a camp by looking through a pipestem. He used an ordinary pipestem on the war-path, though he also had a special one. He would hold his medicine over incense at night, clean his pipestem and look through it. He always saw the camp in the proper place. He got his powers from his father, who got them from Thunder.

A curious method of divination is attributed to Bear-tooth. At one time the Crow were all camped on the Missouri. The Piegan and Assiniboin were in the Musselshell Valley and the Crow found out that the enemy was coming toward them. Bear-tooth told the people to bring a rifle; he would shoot it off without its being loaded. If it went off, it would be a sign that the Crow were to be victorious. He asked all the people to come and look at him. "You don't believe me, but I want all of you to see me and each bring me a little sagebrush." He called the crier to herald the performance. "If the gun goes off, we'll start against the enemy tomorrow." The Indians got out. Bear-tooth said, "Leave room for me where I can dress up in my war clothes. Some of the wise men may examine my gun to see whether there is any cartridge in it." He was wearing fur moccasins, canvas leggings smoked brown, and a similarly smoked canvas shirt. His face was painted black up to the forehead and he also blackened his chin. Around the head he wore the mane of a buffalo. He carried his gun on his arm and went to the wise men, who were smoking sweetgrass, pointed the gun at the fire, then turned the butt toward it. He got into the center of the crowd, pulled the trigger, showed that there were no cartridges there and bade the crier keep still. When ready he said, "Before I shoot I shall sing a song. If it does not go off the first time, don't worry. But if it does not go off the second time we shall be badly defeated. If I succeed, we shall beat the enemy." All were quiet and watched him. He stepped back to the sweetgrass fire, cocked his gun and sang the first song, slowly dancing towards and away from the fire. He pointed his gun at the air, but it did not go off. The people all thought they were having bad luck. He said he would try again. He sang a second song and repeated the same procedure, as before, four times. He bent his head over, patted his right ear and took something out of his left ear, putting it into the gun. Then he sang towards the fire, approached it, and shot off his gun, which went off as though loaded with a cartridge. Then he spoke thus: "At the first trial my gun did not go off, so they may kill four or five of us, but we shall get the best of them since it went off the second time." Early the next morning the Crow got ready, peeped at the enemy from over a hill, and charged them at sunrise. They took many old women, adults and children for captives. The following day they placed these in a row and counted them: there were about three or four hundred. Later the Piegan returned and recaptured some of their people. The captive girls grew up and married Crow, hence there were a good many half-Piegan among the Crow.

On another occasion there were about two hundred Crow on the warpath. They were tired out. There were about six or seven shamans in the party, including Spotted-horse, Gros-Ventre, Curses-the-whole-camp, Bear-tooth, Smooth-rump, and Crazy-bear. They were pursuing the Shoshoni, who had previously killed many of the Crow. After three or four days' journey they got to one of the Shoshoni party's recent campsites; they found fresh meat there and traces of seventeen lodges that had recently been pitched there. Trailing the enemy they got to a valley and riding at night came to camp a little above the Shoshoni. They were ready to fight but decided to wait until early next morning. Before sunrise they approached, put on their war dress and prepared for the battle. Then the leader asked Spotted-horse to use all his medicine against the enemy. They surrounded the Shoshoni camp, then Spotted-horse bade the warriors find a spring. They looked for one till they found one. Spotted-horse came up, dressed in his war regalia, and painted his face and body yellow all over. All his hair was tied in the back with black flannel. Then he pointed his finger at the Sun and drew an imaginary line round his face with it. "If I look into the spring and see a picture of the Sun there, it will be well and I shall know what is to happen, whether we shall conquer or be beaten. Otherwise I shall give up." He sang and saw nothing there. The second time he scooped up a handful of water and saw the Sun in it. First he sang a war-dance song, then two medicine songs, then looked into the spring, then went back to where his clothes were, sat down and told a follower to untie his hair. Next he asked for a pipe to smoke and asked several men to smoke with him. Then he told them what was going to happen. All kept silent to listen to him. "Our enemies are among us. We shall capture and kill many. None of us are going to be killed, but two will be wounded and one horse will be killed. We'll defeat our enemies and reach home without trouble. Don't be afraid. We are going to beat them, and while two of you will be wounded they will not die therefrom. Only one horse is to be killed. I have seen an enemy, one girl with an arrow in her shoulder, she will be a captive of ours. We are ready now and shall charge the enemy."

When they got near the Shoshoni, Red-bear stopped them to speak to the shaman and said, "They have medicinemen in the enemy's camp too, but ours are more powerful." Thin-bull wanted to work some of his own medicine and sat down before the warriors. He was carrying his medicine round his waist and opened it. He had a spear with a buffalo tail at the end of it; which he laid beside him. He called his brother Crooked-feet, who sat down beside him. Thin-bull dug a pit before his brother and filled it with red paint. Then he took a string of deer hoofs and rolled them about in the pit, whereupon he painted his brother's face and head, stuck a crow feather into the back of his head, placed the string of deer hoofs round his neck, sang a song and snorted like a buffalo. Thin-bull told him not to be afraid of any enemy in the battle.

The Crow had two men climb trees and look for the camp, which was about a quarter of a mile away. Then they all charged the enemy. The women had their children in the brush. The Crow killed and captured many Shoshoni. One Crow had a black horse killed under him, but escaped unhurt. Spotted-horse's prophecy was fulfilled. One Crow was wounded in the knee, another in the forehead, but neither was killed. They returned home without loss of a single man.

WRAPS-UP-HIS-TAIL.

Under the heading of shamanism may properly be considered the career of Wraps-up-his-tail (tsís-tsipặriəc), who is sometimes referred to by white writers as 'the Prophet.' He is connected with the one Crow uprising against the Government (1890), just before the Ghost dance began to spread among the Plains tribes. Owing to Wraps-up-his-tail's failure, some informants were inclined to regard him as a pretender, but the general consensus of opinion is to the effect that he really possessed medicine powers.

The essential points in his story seem to be these: He chafed under Governmental domination and on the basis of a vision believed that he possessed supernatural powers. His instrument was to be a sword he had somehow secured, by waving which he believed he could compass the destruction of any force of soldiers sent against him. He is said to have given a demonstration of its use by cutting down some trees. The following is Gray-bull's statement:—

I think he was medicine. He went on a war party and brought back horses. Early in the morning he went round camp, passed through the Agency and shot at the Agent's house. Rations were being distributed then and thereafter the Indians moved. Wraps-up-his-tail was living on the Little Bighorn, near Wyola. The Agent sent an (Indian) policeman to arrest him, but Wraps-up-his-tail would not come, and told the pol'ceman to bid the Agent himself come for him.

Somewhat later the war party that had shot at the Agent's house were brought to the Agency, then Wraps-up-his-tail went along. He said he wanted to die and the Agent should hang him. The white soldiers were camped at the foot of the hills, just below the Agency. The Agent sent for Wraps-up-his-tail and asked whether he preferred being imprisoned or killed. He answered, "I want to be killed." The soldiers were all lined up. The followers of Wraps-up-his-tail began to make medicine, painted their bodies, faces and horses, and rode round camp. Wraps-up-his-tail sat on a gray horse. He painted black stripes on his horse's legs; he was wearing a red shirt and leggings, with fringes at the sleeves, leggings, and at the bottom of the shirt. His foretop was very short. He used red paint and white clay on his face, decorating it with a lightning line, and tied a whistle to his head. After painting up he went round camp, carrying a sword. There were no clouds at the time but raindrops were falling. The Agent sent for Wraps-up-his-tail and had him brought to the office. He offered to make him chief and give him cattle and other property, but Wraps-up-his-tail refused, saying he wished to die. There was no fighting that day.

Spotted-rabbit arrived and asked Wraps-up-his-tail whether he might fight with him. He said, "Yes." Wraps-up-his-tail made a shirt for Spotted-rabbit and the following day he painted up and acted as before. The soldiers were also lined up again. Spotted-rabbit was carrying both a pistol and a sword, Wraps-up-his-tail only a sword. When the soldiers had formed their line, Wraps-up-his-tail approached them and said that if they did not kill him by the time he reached the end of the line he would kill them. The soldiers were waiting for him. The Crow Indians tried to dissuade him; Crazy-head and Deaf-bull were the only chiefs siding with him, the rest of the Crow merely looked on. Spotted-rabbit and Wraps-up-his-tail were like the Sun that day. They ran in front of the line and the soldiers began to shoot at them. They could not hit him. When he got to the end of the line, they shot him in the arm. Then he and Spotted-rabbit went to the river. The soldiers sounded the bugle and went in pursuit, but could not hit them. About ten Indians fought the soldiers then, killing one of them. The soldiers surrounded Knows-his-coups and from time to time he shot at them. They shot Two-whistles through the arm and killed an old woman. Wraps-up-his-tail got to the spot where the old woman had been killed and laying down his sword asked the Crow to kill him; but they refused. After a while Fire-bear (Crow policeman) came up and asked where Wraps-up-his-tail wanted to be shot. He said he wanted to be shot in the forehead. So Fire-bear shot and killed him. Crazy-bear and some others were seized and imprisoned. There were only about ten Crow who took part in the fight; the old men all advised against it, saying there was no reason for fighting. Had all the Crow participated, they would have killed all the soldiers. I have never heard why Wraps-up-his-tail wanted to fight.

I have heard that Wraps-up-his-tail had cut down pine trees with his sword. An Indian said that he similarly tried to cut down the soldiers and that a noise was heard overhead when he made the motion. Had he made it a little lower down, he would have cut the soldiers down.

Wraps-up-his-tail received his name from his guardian, who had dreamt of a dog calling another by that appellation.

Another informant presented the occurrence as follows:—

There was a complete circle of enemies round the Crow. Wraps-up-his-tail of the Kicked-in-their-bellies clan, went out with a pipe,[1] brought back a great many horses, and paraded through camp. He went through the Agency, where they were issuing beef. He shot at the Agent's house, telling him he was not afraid of him. The Agent, whose name was Armstrong, sent the (Indian) police after Wraps-up-his-tail, but he refused to go with them. The police were afraid and would not touch him. He said to them, "You are poor ones; I may kill all of you." He put on red leggings with long fringes and wore a red fringed shirt. He put a whistle crosswise at the back of his queue, together with a flying-squirrel (?). His hair was done up in a short pompadour and decorated with white paint. He painted his face yellow and put a white oval round it. He painted his horse's face with charcoal; from the shoulderblade and hip joints to the hoofs he painted him black. His only weapon was a sword.

The whole Crow tribe was camped at the Agency. The Agent wanted Wraps-up-his-tail killed and sent for the soldiers. Wraps-up-his-tail burned incense and placed his sword over it. He said, "When all the soldiers are lined up, I shall wave my sword and they will all die." The Agent came with all the soldiers and said, "Since you are chief of all the Crow, make known your request and we'll agree to it." The Indian policeman asked Wraps-up-his-tail to make a request on behalf of the Crow, but he refused. He said, "You are Crow Indians, I don't call myself a chief. You have treated your own people as prisoners. I want to die, that is why I shot at the Agent's house." To the whites he said, "I want to destroy you all." They were camped by the fair-grounds. The soldiers were ready to fight. The young Crow all supported Wraps-up-his-tail, who said he would point his sword in the four cardinal directions and kill the whites. He and his followers mounted horses. The Indian police took their kin to the Agency, where they would be safe. The soldiers practised shooting at effigies. We got tired. We heard they were trying to shoot Wraps-up-his-tail's effigy.

In the morning a herald told all the Crow to mount their horses and get ready. "They have your power, Wraps-up-his-tail." "No, I don't like you any more, I want to die." There were about ten young men with him. Then others got tired of it and left him. The soldiers extended from the hill back of the school to the Agency;

---

[1] The captain's emblem of office.

they were all armed. Wraps-up-his-tail rode a few feet in front of their line. They all shot at him. We were standing farther back looking on and thought he would fall but he was never touched. Spotted-rabbit was accompanying him. Wraps-up-his-tail waved his sword and all the soldiers seemed to fall, but straightened up again. One soldier said they heard something whizzing by when the sword was moved past them. When the horses got to the end of the line, all the soldiers formed a ring round him and shot at him. One man tried to stop him, but he hit him across the head with a sabre, knocking him down. Then ten Crow Indians went right among the soldiers. At last Wraps-up-his-tail fled across the river and the soldiers gave up trying to kill him. He talked across the stream, bidding them come and kill him, since they had shot him in the arm. He advanced towards the soldiers and threw down his sword, but they did not go toward him. The police ordered the Crow to go to the Agency. Wraps-up-his-tail said to Spotted-rabbit, "Go alone and hide, I want to die." He crossed the stream below the slaughter-house. On the other side Knows-his-coups was lying in a little hole, popping up and down; the soldiers shot at him, then gave up the pursuit.

Wraps-up-his-tail had surrendered to the soldiers, who would not seize him. The Indian police arrived. He sat down, pointing at his breast. Then he said, "Point at my forehead." Then Fire-bear shot and killed him. The soldiers killed an old woman hiding in the woods. They shot Two-whistles in the arm, breaking his bones, and after having the arm amputated they sent him home. Three-foretops was also in the fray. All the Crow hated Fire-bear. Wraps-up-his-tail's brother tried to catch him alone and kill him, but never succeeded. Crazy-head and Deaf-bull, both Kicked-in-their-bellies chiefs, were blamed for the uprising by the Government and imprisoned in the East.

Before this time Wraps-up-his-tail had never been recognized as a medicineman. After his burial it was reported that there was a red flame above his grave. The Crow still consider him medicine because the soldiers' volley did not kill him; also because on his return from the war party he moved his sword before some pine trees and made them fall down.

Still another informant said that Wraps-up-his-tail had gone to the mountains three times in quest of a vision, staying from two to four days. Gros-Ventre says he has seen him paint his face by pointing his finger at the sun, and though he used no paint he would produce a red stripe. There was usually a storm when he went through camp. It was said that he chose the wrong season for fighting, hence his failure. He was powerless in the winter time, but would have succeeded in the summer.

One-blue-bead also said that in his opinion the outcome was Wraps-up-his-tail's own fault. His vision was to come true in the spring when it thundered, but he waited until the fall. Half of his vision was true (*tsûsa k'ŏt'ûk'*). In part he was fooled. "He claimed that he could not be shot, that part was false. Our hearts tell us that part of what he said was true. He had a sword, went up to the mountains, made a motion of cutting the pines, and the trees fell down. But with the soldiers it did not work. Muskrat saw the trees fall."

MISCELLANEOUS.

When Fire-weasel was a boy he accompanied the Crow to the Hidatsa; there was a shaman in the party. An Hidatsa stole one of the shaman's horses. The shaman made medicine, calling for a good rain. Then it rained every day and night. The Hidatsa gardens and their earth-lodges were soaked, and the horses sank down in the mud. The Hidatsa chiefs asked the thief to return the horse lest they be destroyed. Accordingly, the horse was brought back at night and tied to the shaman's tent, but the horse's mouth had been tied with corduroy and was badly cut, so the owner was very angry. The chiefs made the thief give the shaman another horse and some property, then the rain ceased. That winter the Hidatsa were starving.

One informant told about a man named Hunts-the-spring, who generally traveled afoot and would sometimes walk up to the top of big tipi poles, then down again. The same informant knew of a woman, said to get out of her head (*dúciuk*), who could tell who it was whenever anyone peeped in through a little hole. She was a good runner.

THE PRACTICE OF MEDICINE.

A person who administered roots and other medicines in our sense of the term is known as *ak' bārɔ*, a word extended to include white physicians. As a special class of practitioners the Crow segregate the wound-doctors, *akûwɔcdiu*. Those, on the other hand, who are shamans, i.e., derive their powers, whether relating to medical treatment or not, from a supernatural source, are in a literal sense 'medicine (= holy) men,' (*batsɛ́ maxpé*). But this classification cannot be rigidly maintained in practice since many forms of treatment are traced to a vision, and the method of healing wounds is probably uniformly so derived.

Apart from special medical assistance there are of course certain remedies which are extensively used. Of these the *isɛ́* root, which is dug up in the mountains, is used in a variety of ways, but especially as a liniment. This is the same substance that serves so largely as incense on ceremonial occasions. It may be applied with various other ingredients; for example, a mixture of *isɛ́* and buffalo chips is rubbed over a swelling. Once I observed Muskrat treating an interpreter's little daughter for a swelling. Sitting at a distance I could see her chew some root, very likely *isɛ́*, which she rubbed on the girl's leg. This root is said to be eaten by bears; the stem of the plant closely resembles that of a carrot. Among other things, *isɛ́* is also boiled with tallow for a cough medicine. In Pryor I bought some 'sweet-sticks' from Sharp-horn's wife; they are chewed, soaked in water, and drunk as a remedy for diarrhœa. Henry Russel, oddly enough, said this medicine also contained a cathartic principle and was used accordingly. Elsewhere I heard of a plant called *átsirûxe*, which the Indians pull out in order to chew the juice, which is good for the teeth and the health generally. Certain river weeds are boiled into a tea (*cúcuɔ*).

The sweatlodge was not used primarily for medicinal purposes and even in recent times seems to have had rather a ritualistic function or to have assumed the character of a sport. It is true that in a myth Old-Man-Coyote cures his companion Cirɔpɛ́ through a sweatlodge,[1] but the circumstances admit of a different interpretation. Cirɔpɛ́'s sickness resulted from his having been offered to the Sun; hence danger is naturally averted by substituting the sweatlodge as a Sun offering *par excellence*.

---

[1]Lowie, this volume, 20.

In cases of stomach trouble the Crow even today employ an implement called *i⁺'tsipâtsiruə*, stomach-kneader. It is a stick about 18 inches long widening out at the bottom after the fashion of a darning-last. The lower part is pushed against the stomach and upward. This device is mythologically derived from the Dipper, who instructed a woman in its application, telling her she should gain property thereby in the way of fees.[1] However, its use nowadays is quite devoid of any religious implications. I saw Gray-bull knead a young man's stomach; he explained that the Crow were careful not to press hard on the navel.

Muskrat, as shown elsewhere (p. 340), derived some of her methods of treatment from her own supernatural experiences, and Bull-all-the-time made a corresponding claim (p. 328). Since visions differ and are of specific character, it follows that most practitioners are specialists conversant only with the mode of treatment to be followed for particular kinds of disease. Thus, a man bitten by a snake, but surviving the effects, would regard the snake as his medicine and would treat people who suffered from snake bites. Wounded men, on the other hand, were treated by men having a buffalo vision. Again, Gray-bull's wife was an obstetrician, having obtained instructions from a man who had dreamt of a certain mode of treatment in confinement cases.

Crow theory of disease is not affected by the belief in sorcery to nearly the same extent as that of many other primitive peoples. Of course evil magic is practised (p. 345) but it does not pervade the entire intellectual atmosphere. On the whole, far greater significance must be attached to the taboo concept. Illness is often ascribed to the transgression of a rule laid down in a vision or associated with some sacred object. For example, a person may be forbidden to eat chokecherries or a special part of the buffalo, and disobedience will lead to dire consequences. Others are afraid to come into close contact with menstruating women lest they bleed from the nose or contract a headache; if such men went into battle after contact with a woman in this condition, they would probably be killed. Tangible pathogenic agents are also reckoned with. Sometimes the soul of a deceased individual puts a tooth or lock of hair belonging to the corpse into a person's body, producing insanity. Persons afraid of corpses seen in battle are said to be liable to this affliction. Gray-bull ascribes his temporary deafness at one time to a stone put into his ear by the hand of a slain enemy (see below).

---

[1] *Ibid.*, 126, 128.

Turning now to the medical treatment given, it is natural that doctors contending with real or putative material agents of destruction sought to extract them. Some blew upon the affected part, others used suction. A favorite method was applying a pipestem and sucking out the fatal substance; this, e.g., was done in extracting the hair or tooth of the ghost causing madness.

Gray-bull called this procedure *bǎkōriuk'*. Once his son White-hip was ill; he had eaten some food and something stuck in his throat, and though he drank water he could not get rid of it. Bull-all-the-time was summoned and ordered everyone out of the lodge except the patient and Gray-bull, whom he asked to look at him. The doctor rubbed some substance on White-hip's breast, abdomen, and neck. He sang some songs, sucked at the patient's throat with his mouth, making a popping sound, and produced a morsel of meat which had lodged in White-hip's throat. Bull-all-the-time himself referred to this episode, as well as to several other cures he had effected. Thus, he once extracted a black beetle from Flat-dog's nose in the presence of many onlookers. On another occasion a big crowd were ready to mourn over a man who had swallowed a fish bone that stuck in his neck. They offered Bull-all-the-time a gun and other presents, and he drew forth the bone, curing the patient. Still another time a woman had a swollen leg and my informant sucked at it with his pipe and made the swelling go down. He also knew how to doctor spider bites, but did not treat snake bites or wounds. I saw the pipe used by him, which was that revealed in a dream; it had horse tracks incised near one end.

The mother of Bull-does-not-fall-down fasted when one of her sons died and became a doctor for both wounds and illness. Once Gray-bull was returning with a war party after an enemy had been killed. The men cut off the enemy's hand and tied it to a long stick. As they were walking along at night, Gray-bull came to walk beside the staff-bearer and the hand struck him on the ear. He immediately became deaf. When he got home, Bull-does-not-fall-down's mother treated him. She took him into a sweatlodge, stuck a pipestem into his ear, and sucked a little red stone out of it. Then Gray-bull recovered his hearing. He believes the hand, that is, the enemy's ghost, put it into his ear. The stone was of the kind usually found on ant-hills.

Goes-ahead had a pipestem that was painted red, and used it to draw some blood out of a man afflicted with pneumonia. He drew it into his own mouth and then spat it out. The patient recovered.

Other practitioners blow or rub chewed medicinal substances, _bắwîtăre_, on the patient, the rubbing process being designated by the word _báptsisùo_. Any therapeutic potion is called _îwa+ict wa'tse_ (by means of it they make them drink). How largely such draughts were administered by the recognized doctors, I do not know for certain. They were surely prescribed to some extent and also employed as a domestic remedy by the laity in general. The 'sweet-sticks' have already been referred to; Bull-all-the-time showed me a bunch of pine needles, which he said were boiled into a tea and drunk for medicine.

Gray-bull described certain modes of treatment for specific affections. For _èrapùo_ (literally, rotten stomach) the stomach was kneaded towards the heart and bleeding was resorted to. Rheumatism (_irîts-arè_) was treated by snake or mole visionaries, who would burn incense and rub on some tallow, or use the pipe to suck out blood, which they would expectorate. They left no mark where the blood had been extracted. Bull-all-the-time extracts blood in this manner to cure a colic. For a venereal affection called _icìse bāku'pâk_ (literally, loins sick) the doctor placed hot rocks under the patient's genitalia, made him drink some powder (ammunition) put in warm water, and threw some of this mixture on him. Another disease, apparently also of venereal nature, involves a swelling of the groins and is known as _arùɘpùsuɘ_. The doctor heats _isè_, places it on the groins to relieve the pain, and blows on them. If this does not prove effective, he will lance the swollen parts, for if these were to break of themselves an inflammation of the face would result. Gray-bull lanced a swelling of this sort himself when on the warpath. Heated stones are continually used in treating this disease, the body is kneaded, and there is an attempt to keep the bowels open. There is another disease characterized by a mass of sores and aching joints. In this case the best physicians are called, who wash the sores and use a poultice with a special mixture.

Of all the wound doctors (_ak-ûwɘc-dìu_) remembered by the Crow one named Dap'îc takes precedence, for he was the only one who could make his patients well forthwith and hardly ever failed. Gray-bull had never seen him, but an old woman, Young-crane, recollected him. Graybull said he had heard that once a man was so weak that he could neither walk nor stand, so that Dap'îc had to make medicine to make him rise. In going towards the creek, he acted like a buffalo cow with a calf. The patient followed him. At the creek a fish came and ate up the matter about the wound. Dap'îc took his patient out and showed the spectators the hole in his body, then took him back to the river, dived with him for a while, got out, and repeated this procedure. Then the patient was as well as before.

Dap'íc acquired his power by fasting at the hot springs of what is now Thermopolis, Wyoming. One informant says he swam out to a little island in a pond, sat there for three days and observed the underground spirits treating wounded men. Others narrated that some being took him into the spring, sang medicine songs for him, and gave him his own name, the one by which he has been known since, and the springs are called *Dap'íc irúpxe* (father of Dap'íc). After his return to camp, Dap'íc went on the warpath and was shot. He told his comrade that he was a medicineman. His friend answered, "You are a medicineman and you have forgotten that you are half dead." "I am going to doctor myself." "If the people see you cure yourself, they will wait to have you cure them and will give you plenty of property." Many people looked on as he treated himself. The bullet had not gone through him, but was in his body. He held an otter in his hands, showing its teeth. He was going to dive into the river and have the otter remove the bullet. He sang before entering the water, then dived into it. After four breaths he came out again and the otter had the bullet in its mouth. Then all the people knew about it. There was another battle and a man was shot with an arrow; the shaft was pulled out, but the head remained sticking in the wound. People asked the doctor to cure him. He told his patient he would dive with him and have the arrow point extracted by the otter. He sang and painted himself, as well as the patient, then dived with him, and when he came out the otter had the arrow-head in its mouth. The man was cured. On another occasion an old man was shot in the forehead and the doctor took out the bullet. Once in the Wolf Mountains a Crow was shot below the navel in a fight with the Dakota. There was a watercourse nearby and after damming it up to make it deep enough they laid the patient in there. Dap'íc used the water-bull (*bímuin tsírupe*) and the long-otter for his special guardian spirits. He sang over the patient, hopped over him, and rode to camp with him, singing on the way. In the morning the people formed two lines of spectators. They made the patient rest on a high pillow and several men sang for him. No person or dog was permitted to pass in front of him. The doctor had his wife and daughter wear a robe and with them he approached the door of the lodge, where the singing was going on continually. Dap'íc transformed himself into a bull and made a snorting noise over the patient, who rolled over. Then he bade the wounded man seize his tail and forthwith he was able to stand up as though well. Dap'íc led him to the water, re-assuming human shape on the way. He took him where the water reached up to his chest and then dived down alone. Before so doing, he whistled upstream, then downstream. The patient's blood flowed downstream, and he stood there for a long time awaiting the leech's return. His wound healed. Only the wounded man saw the doctor in buffalo shape. Later in life Dap'íc became blind because he had transgressed one of his spiritual patron's rules.

According to one informant the legendary shaman who recovered a drowned Crow's necklace[1] became a wound-doctor when he had returned from his diving expedition.

Gray-bull remembered two famous wound-doctors; one was Bull-does-not-fall-down's mother, who also treated other afflictions (see p. 375), the other was named One-eye. Neither permitted dogs about while administering his treatment; it was said that if a dog crossed their path at that time the patient would die. My informant saw One-eye at work on three occasions. When he treated Crazy-head, who had been shot from side to side, he painted white rings round the patient's eyes and touched all his body with the tip of his hand, which had white clay on it. He painted his own forehead with white clay, wore a buffalo robe, and tied a plume to the back of the patient's head. He stood at the door of the lodge, singing his song. The singers, including Gray-bull, were indoors. The relatives of a wounded man always got as many young men as possible to act as singers during the performance, and they would sing the physician's song. One-eye danced at the door, first with one foot, and rubbed a buffalo tail, which had a plume tied to it, against the ground so that the dust flew. Everyone cheered him. He went to the patient, blew on his abdominal wound, stood back, extended his arms and bent his body. Crazy-head imitated these movements. Pus and blood came pouring out of his wound. When all had come out, the people in camp were told to stand in two rows extending from the lodge to the river. Gray-bull did not see the procedure in the river since he was one of the singers and thus obliged to remain in the lodge and continue singing. Young-crane, Crazy-head's one-time wife, said that according to her husband he was not cured by the doctor. Some time after that, however, he went out to ease himself and in the morning there were masses of blood there; from that time on his health improved.

Another informant mentions seeing four or five women take part in the singing in company with the male drummers. He says the doctor

---

[1] This volume, 231.

pawed the ground like a bull and licked the patient's wounds, drawing out blood and pus from both sides. He made the sick man walk toward the creek in the usual fashion, making four stops and each time causing water and blood to run out. He waded into the river to the depth of the patient's wound and made the blood and water flow out of it. Then the man got well.

Arm-round-the-neck added only a few details on the basis of one performance he had witnessed. In this case the physician blew into the wound and ran back to the lodge, followed by the wounded man. This informant said that some doctors had seen buffalo treating one another's wounds in a vision and imitated what they had been shown. Others might see other animals (otters?) and would then use an otterskin and whistle instead of the buffalo tail. The wound doctors might purchase their medicines.

The association of wound doctoring with the buffalo is of comparative interest since it occurs elsewhere, e.g., among the Omaha, where a whole fraternity of buffalo visionaries treat cases of this type.[1]

The treatment of a woman in labor has already been sketched elsewhere.[2] Sometimes no physician was called because there was no time. In ancient times, according to Gray-bull, only women were obstetricians (*bīə-ĕnde ak-dīə*) but now there are also some men who act in this capacity. A man was certainly not normally permitted to attend during his wife's travail, and it seems no other males, not even boys, were allowed in the lodge since their presence was believed to protract the period of delivery. Otherwise the husband was not subject to any taboo.

Gray-bull's wife had obtained her obstetrical knowledge from a visionary, to whom she paid a horse. She regarded the information as a secret. The medicine was a combination of a horned toad and a root; she would rub it down the patient's back. The woman in labor clung to a post planted by her bed and assumed a kneeling posture. Not the doctor, but anyone present, cut the navel cord (*ictĕ'pe*). After the delivery the mother received a portion of *iəxciwe*, a kind of fatty food (probably pemmican) which she ate just once. For several days she abstained from cooked meat and was not allowed to stoop.

There were no special beliefs as to twins (*dătsg'e*) and Gray-bull did not know of any case of triplets.

---

[1]Alice C. Fletcher and Francis La Flesche, "The Omaha Tribe" (*Twenty-seventh Annual Report, Bureau of American Ethnology*, Washington, 1911), 487.
[2]This series, vol. 9, 218.

SOULS; GHOSTS; HEREAFTER.

The metaphysical tendency is very moderately developed among the Crow. There are no profound theories as to the soul and such reflections as may occasionally be garnered on this and related topics are not infrequently mutually contradictory.

The word for soul is *irâᵃxe* (my soul, *barâᵃxe*; souls, *irâaxùə*). It is used in speaking of a person's will power and is clearly connected with the word for 'shadow,' *irâxaxe.* Gray-bull said that all animals (*bâxuambicè*) have souls, that is why the Crow do not kill dogs. The sacred stones taken along on war expeditions also had souls. Another informant, however, denied that animals were believed to have souls. Sometimes the soul of a dead person will put a tooth or a lock of hair of its own into a person's body and cause him to go insane. The soul is believed to stay by the burial and sometimes an owl-like cry is heard there. In this last statement there is probably a confusion between 'soul' and 'ghost,' for below we shall find that the deceased live in camps of their own, while hooting like an owl is generally described as an attribute of ghosts.

The word for ghost is *a'parâaxe*, which is also sometimes used to render 'devil.' It seems to be etymologically connected with that for soul, but I am unable to explain the first part of the word. Another word recorded for 'ghost' is *maxuěretè* which denotes lack of body. Ghosts are feared and to compare a person to a ghost is to offer a grave insult. In a myth a woman at once leaves her husband when he likens her to a ghost.[1] The whirlwind is taken for a ghost and an approaching one will be thus addressed:—

an-daré	k·awîk·,	dí-t'at'	dā!
Where you are going	it is bad,	you alone	go (imperative)!

Ghosts are not regarded as uniformly malevolent, however. I heard of a woman named Gun, who had had a vision of a ghost. She would invite a crowd of people, darken her room, and make everyone sing and listen. Then something came and the people could not make out what the being had said. Gun would interpret its words and prophesy what was going to happen. The gift of detecting lost property and of determining the fate of lost individuals seems to be preëminently derived from ghosts. In the most recent times an old couple had lost money and asked an Indian policeman for assistance. The latter, being a great wag, pretended to recover the money by means of his medicine,—a whirlwind ghost. He smoked incense, made the sign of a whirlwind in front of his face, and after chanting a song hooted like a ghost.

---

[1] This volume, 118.

Once the Crow were on the Musselshell, while the Dakota were near Sheridan. A Crow party went out and captured some Dakota horses. Two of the braves did not come back; even after ten days they had not returned. Their brother went to an old man who had ghost medicine, gave him horses and property, and asked him to find out where the two men were and whether dead or alive. That night the old man told everyone in his lodge to go outside. All the relatives of the two missing men came and stayed outside the tipi. The old man put out his fire and began to sing, shaking his rattle. He made a noise like an owl, went out of the smoke hole, and returned to the tent. The whole lodge shook when he came back. The spectators heard people talking but could not understand them. Then the medicineman called the outsiders and lit up his fire. He told them the two young men had not been killed, but were in camp at that very moment and bade them look for them. That very night one of the two missing men came back to his tipi. The old man had seen the two in camp and told the other people. They were there looking on while their tribesmen were looking for them.

A sister of Horn's wife once went to St. Xavier for a visit. On the same day Gray-bull and others went there too. The following day they got to the Bighorn, where a Fourth of July celebration was being held. The Lodge Grass people stayed for the festivities, but the woman did not appear. They looked for her all over the district, but failed to find her. Her horse returned to Gray-bull's herd without a saddle. Then a ghost medicine woman, Stops's mother, was called. They gave her two horses and other property and asked her to find the lost woman. That night she did not tell the people to leave, but put out the fire and closed up the smoke hole. She began to sing and hooted like an owl and the whole tent began to shake as though from a whirlwind. The audience heard talking but could not understand what was being said. They also heard the medicine woman, but could not understand her either. When a child who was with Gray-bull began to cry, all the noise ceased. The medicine woman kindled the fire and told the people that if the child had not cried she should have learned about the woman's whereabouts; she had been told that she was close but the exact place was not revealed. More presents were offered to the shaman to make her try once more, but she refused and the woman was never found. The Indians thought she might have been killed by some white man or turned insane, for she had gone crazy several times before.

The following curious tale was recounted by Gray-bull as a personal adventure.

I went on the warpath toward the Missouri River. Right above the mouth of Plum River I came to a square-tent camp of about a thousand tents. There was a little house there, and a tall white man, who talked Crow, took us all to this house, and told us to look inside. In this house there were bunks covered with gray blankets. The white man told us to take off the covers and then we saw under all of them the skeletons of men, about thirty of them. The joints were fastened together with wire. When we got out, we stopped there for the night. The Indians began to sing. The white man told us to keep quiet for they were going to make the skeletons alive again and if we wanted to see it we might. We told him we had never known of any one dead coming to life. He said they were going to raise the skeletons to live in four nights. That night we heard a band-drum and cheers from the whites all night. We stayed there for two nights, consumed our food, and told the white man we were going to leave. He told us to stay and killed a beef for us. For four nights we always heard the band. After the fourth night the white man came and told us the skeletons had risen to life. He took all of us to the house, opened the door and told our captain to look, but he was afraid. One man was very brave and said, "I'll go and see," for he doubted it. His comrade said he would go in also and a third likewise said he would do so. Wolf-head was the first man who wanted to go in. Wolf-head asked me what I was going to do and I said I would do it. Wolf-head told the captain to keep quiet. When all four of us were inside, the white man closed the door. It was early in the morning. The white man took the cover off one, and then we saw a white man lying there very thin. He looked at all four of us. Wolf-head shook hands with him and said: "Ho!" The other just shook his hand and while he was holding his hand Wolf-head asked, "Are there people yet over there in the ghost land?" The white man answered, "Ho!" The Indian said: "Whenever I become a chief and people honor me, I'll see your people." The next Crow shook hands and said, "When I've given horses to all my relatives and captured picketed horses, I'll see your people." The third one shook hands and said: "Are there people on the other side?" "Ho!" "I want to see your people soon." I shook hands with him myself and told him I did not want to be afraid, but wanted to be an old man and a big chief. The white man said, "Ho!" We shook hands with the other whites in the bunks and repeated our conversation, then we went outside. The rest of our party asked, "How is it?" "They are living."

Then the white man who spoke Crow told our captain if he doubted he should stay till the next day and see the people come out of the house. We stayed till the next morning, when we dressed and painted up and came to the place. We saw all the white men seated outside on a bench. One white man had a hole in his cheek where he had been shot and matter was running out of it. This man asked us whether any of us could speak Dakota. Our captain said he could talk Assiniboin. The white man with the hole said he was also an Assiniboin. He said he was going to talk and wished the Indian to listen. He talked in Assiniboin and asked the captain where he was going. The captain answered that he was on the warpath. The white man said, "When you get to camp, don't be afraid; go to the camp, take a picketed horse and kill some of the enemy; don't be afraid, for you are to be people twice. Don't be afraid of anything. The Crow who died are living in a camp. I myself can't help myself and have to stay with the whites." The other Indians told the captain to ask what was the matter with the man's face. He asked him. "The Piegan killed an Assiniboin on top of a hill, where there were rocks and trenches. While the Piegan were in the trenches, I went up and struck at them, shouting that I was the first to strike a coup. The women and men said I did not strike a coup, but only rocks. I tried again, sang a song and made medicine. I went to the trench. One man was pointing a gun at me. As I was going to stab him, he shot me in the face. From that day I knew nothing until the day I saw you Crow." The Indian asked the white whether he was going to die again, but he answered he did not know.

We got back to the Crow camp. The one who said he wanted to see the other side soon died about two seasons later. What he wanted came true: he died soon after. Wolf-head, who had said he was going to see the other people when the Crow all liked him, was killed some years later. What he had said came true. The Crow honored him very much. The third man who said he would give horses to all his relatives did what he said; he was killed on the Bighorn. What I said is coming true: I am a chief and pretty old. I believe those men were ghosts. At first I did not believe in it but after seeing that it came true for the others I believed in it. Since then I have never seen any ghosts.

This last narrative, whatever experiences it may be based on, connects beliefs as to ghosts with the conceptions entertained of the hereafter. This subject seems to have exercised the Crow imagination to a very limited extent. So far as there is any standard belief it is to the effect that the dead live in camps like those of the Crow and have a superior way of living. This might be used as an encouragement to the warriors, as in Gray-bull's mysterious story. Sometimes before a battle the heralds would cry out: *kuké asûk'*! "Over there there are (also) lodges!" A number of informants declared they knew nothing about life after death and none seemed to exhibit any particular interest in the matter. Those who had any conceptions based them on the reports of tribesmen who are believed to have died and returned to consciousness. These accounts, such as they are, follow.

The dead go to an Indian camp. Once a Crow died. He got to two rivers and beyond there was a large camp of buffalo skin tipis. He was invited into one lodge. Indoors everything was furnished after the old style, with buffalo robes on the ground to sit on. The owner looked at the visitor and said, "I see something about you I don't like. I don't like otters. Your people are down below." The visitor said, "Then I'll go back home." He came to and told what had happened to him. He was eager to go back to the dead again and died once more soon after.

There was a Crow who was shot and was brought back to camp. He died of his wound. The next morning he got up again, went round, and told the people that all the dead were camped together and had a better way of living than the Crow; hence he said, "Don't be afraid to die." When I was seriously sick, I was eager to see my parents, who were already dead. I remembered what the old man had told me. If it was so, I thought, I might be happy with my relatives since all the dead camped together.

Two men went west to the coast, where there were no more white men. The Crow believe the dead are living over there. The two travelers met a man without moccasins who knew their names without their telling him, and he sent them back. They set out in the summer.and came back in the fall.

There was a man who died and came to life again. He said that all who had died were still living and that they were better people than the Crow. The Crow believed it.

One of my (Old-dog's) own brothers got sick and weak and ready to die. He took a knife and tried to stab himself but was too feeble. Then he lay on the ground with his body on the knife and thus killed himself. He lay there for a while, then woke up and told his story. His younger brother, who had owned a fine gray horse, had died before him. This younger brother took him on his horse riding towards the camp of the dead. "I could hear the singing of praise songs over there; also loud talking. They were singing, 'Is that person coming already?' As we proceeded, he said, 'My horse is fast, but we have brought him.' Then my brother angrily struck me in the chest, saying, 'You are stingy and think too much of your horse. If so, go back.' He jumped off and I came back to life." This man told us he had found that the dead had a camp like ours and a good way of living. After this experience he did not die again until relatively recently (since the Crow have been on their present reservation).

SPECIAL MEDICINE OBJECTS.

Since most objects derive their sacred character from a vision, the number of medicines is theoretically unlimited. However, they can usually be classified in certain categories. The relative paucity of medicine bundles is remarkable considering their prominent place among the Hidatsa and the Blackfoot. Similarly the notion of painted tipis plays a very subordinate part. Altogether it seems fair to say that while probably no important class of sacred objects characteristic of the Plains is wholly unrepresented, the Crow differ in a decided shifting of emphasis.

MEDICINE ROCKS.

The medicine rocks (bacŏritsi'tse) occupy an important position in Crow religious thought. In some respects they correspond to the Blackfoot iniskim, but the notion that their prototype is the oldest part of the earth and a being independent of all others, the Sun (Old-Man-Coyote) included,[1] rather suggests Dakota metaphysics.

A bacŏritsi'tse is primarily characterized by its appearance, which suggests that of some part of an animal's body, perhaps most frequently of the head (Figs. 1, 2). These stones were not as a rule bestowed in visions, but were found accidentally by anyone and then adopted as the finder's medicine. They were wrapped up with numerous offerings, such as beads or decorative strips of skin, greased with castoreum, and supplicated for long life and wealth. More particularly were they taken to a performance of the Singing the Cooked Meat festival, at which each guest owning such a rock pressed it to his breast, kissed it, and addressed prayers to it. According to In-the-mouth, the bacŏritsi'tse are found by the odor they emit, which also indicates what kind of incense they demand, e.g., whether isé or sweetgrass. All Indians agree that bacŏritsi'-tse have a tendency to multiply like living beings. According to one informant it was customary to unwrap them when the first thunder was heard in the spring.

In 1910 I purchased several of these medicine rocks, generally from young Indians who had inherited them and no longer used them. I recollect paying as much as ten dollars for one; another was offered to me at the price of thirty dollars.

Gray-bull owned several bacŏritsi'tse. He showed me one resembling a mule hoof. Soon after finding it, he had obtained three mules and had come to own a hundred and twenty head of horses. This stone he never

---

[1] This volume, 15.

Fig. 1 (50.1-4008a). Medicine Rock with Offerings.

Fig. 2 (50.1-4010).   Medicine Rock with Offerings.

took to a Singing the Cooked Meat feast, though a subsequent statement indicates that he used it with his others when he himself arranged this ceremony. One of the other stones resembled a buffalo head, still another had horns and the semblance of eyes but Gray-bull did not know what it was. His principal *bacóritsi'tse* he kept enclosed in several cloth wrappers, the whole being stored in a rawhide container of envelope shape. The body of the stone was completely covered with buckskin, which was decorated with rows of beads. The rock itself was said to have natural horsetrack markings on one side and to suggest a human head on the other; a deer was also marked on it. With the rock there were the usual trimmings of weasel-skin, elk teeth, and the like; also some sweetgrass. The stone always faced upward (*tse wákus-ä+uk*). In the same wrapping, but considered a distinct medicine, there was a very small bundle containing a little stone on which might be seen or imagined a face. This had been found by a little child and according to my authority had since then grown to twice its original size. Gray-bull would pray to it as follows: "May I have horses and property, live till the next year, and fare well (*itsik ä́ta baká 'kuwi*)!" While wearing it suspended from his neck, he had captured a rifle, two horses, and an eagle feasting on a buffalo, besides experiencing other forms of good luck.

Normally *bacóritsi'tse* were not sold but inherited. Gray-bull inherited his principal stone from his stepfather.

In-the-mouth told of a remarkable *bacóritsi'tse* shaped on one side like a buffalo with a bird on top, on the other like a horse mounted by a little being in human form. In going on an expedition the owner would ask the buffalo for success, e.g., for a horse. This stone gave birth to two stones ("had two children"), which multiplied in turn. The 'children' were given to some men as captain's medicines. Some people offered as much as ten horses for the medicine, but the owner would not sell it. The owners would open up the bundle and show the contents to close relatives, but would not permit any handling. Sweetgrass was used for incense with this stone. It was discovered by the wife of Sees-the-bull's-member, a reckless young man who had squandered all his property at gambling and deserted his wife. She went out crying and scented sweetgrass, whereupon she saw the *bacóritsi'tse* shining and picked it up. That night her husband returned and through the stone he secured a captain's vision. By means of it he was able to cause buffalo to come when they were scarce.

Two points are noteworthy in connection with the last-named stone. The circumstances of its discovery, for one thing, align it with medicines secured in visions. Secondly, its use for charming buffalo constitutes a specific point of resemblance with the Blackfoot *iniskim*.

Gray-bull told me that Medicine-crow owned one *bacĉritsi'tse* that he esteemed above the rest. It had been found by Medicine-Crow's mother and had reproduced itself since then. When people unwrapped it, they saw horsetracks, would go on a raid and bring back horses; also an enemy was killed. It is marked with a man's head and indications of a bird, horses, and buffalo. Medicine-crow did not use this stone at the Singing the Cooked Meat ceremony, for he is under a taboo against eating tongues and at the feast other people who did eat tongues might touch the rock with their faces. Medicine-crow's parents had owned the stone and abstained from tongue, so he does likewise.

Another informant gave more details concerning this stone. It had been seen in a vision by Looks-at-a-bull's penis (tsĭrup-ĭr-ik˙ac) and later found by his wife, Medicine-crow's mother, whom he married in accordance with the levirate. The woman always kept it under her dress. Her husband wanted to see it. One day she said, "We'll go out and I'll show it to you." They went to a coulée, and there she took it out and showed him the medicine. One stone looked like a bird, another like a buffalo, the third like a horse, the fourth like a person resembling Two-leggings. There was some hair hanging down from a willow and the man tried to take it, but his wife asked him not to do so. Then they went home and on the way they found a bunch of hair and a piece of fat; with the latter they greased the *bacĉritsi'tse* and wrapped it up in the hair. They got to a hill. The woman bade her husband remain there in order to get another vision of the stone and went home alone. In the night the man dreamt about all sorts of things the stone told him to do; they showed him how to lead a war party and how to make medicine.

Medicine-crow was growing up as a boy. One day he told his (step-) father that he was hungry. All the people were starving, for there were no buffalo. Looks-at-a-bull's penis made medicine. He made buffalo tracks and that night he sang his medicine song, shaking his rattle. The next morning they saw buffalo wherever they looked. His medicine was genuine. Now Medicine-crow had plenty to eat.

Looks-at-a-bull's-penis made medicine for Medicine-crow and two other men, who would go out and bring horses for him. Thus he came to own a great many, all of them black. Early in the spring his stones were light in weight, later in the summer they would get heavier. In the coldest winter there would be frost on them, for they breathed. The owner made hoop medicine[1] for Medicine-crow and bade him go on the warpath and bring a pinto from camps on the Rosebud. His son went there and brought a herd including a buckskin pinto. Looks-at-a-bull's-penis made medicine for Two-leggings, asking him to choose between killing a person and capturing horses. Two-leggings chose the latter and brought two horses, one of them a buckskin. The owner dreamt about Takes-it-back-twice and gave him the *bacóritsi'tse* to take on the warpath, but on the way one of the horns of the stone broke off and he was not successful. The next time, however, he captured a white horse and gave him to Looks-at-a-bull's-penis.

The *bacóritsi'tse* always told this man where the Crow should go so as to avoid a bad winter and have plenty to eat. Whenever he received such instructions, he had a crier proclaim them. Thus they avoided hard times. According to my informant, this medicine stone descended to Little-nest, Looks-at-a-bull's-penis' own son, who unwrapped it last spring (1915).

Charges-camp told me about an old woman named Otter-woman, who discovered a *bacóritsi'tse* that brought her good luck. The owner was always fortunate in getting property. When the camp was moved, this rock was always taken to lead the people to the right hunting-grounds. War leaders would go to Otter-woman, pay her a fee, and get her medicine with whatever dreams she had had about it.

---

[1] This refers to another medicine seen by him in a vision.

BUNDLES.

In a certain sense it seems artificial to segregate one class of Crow medicines as 'bundles.' Literally, almost all medicines are bundles, i.e., wrapped-up aggregations of sacred objects. This, e.g., would fully apply to the medicine rocks. On the other hand, even where this might not hold it remains true that for the native the material characteristics of a medicine are quite subordinate to its spiritual significance, which from the nature of the case must be at least generically uniform. Nevertheless, from a comparative point of view it seems proper to separate those medicines which are not only physically more complex but have greater dignity and even tribal significance. Such bundles are not numerous among the Crow and unlike those of the Hidatsa and Blackfoot they do not conform to a single pattern. The Medicine Pipe and the Horse Dance medicine, both of which are described elsewhere, are known to be of alien origin, the former being derived from the Hidatsa, the latter from the Assiniboin. Among the Crow medicines derived from indigenous visions, the Sun dance doll,[1] the Tobacco medicines, and the Medicine Arrow probably approximate most closely to the bundles of other tribes. Owing to the importance of the sacred arrows among the Cheyenne, it is quite possible that even in the last-mentioned instance we are dealing with at least the adaptation of a foreign idea. Both the Medicine Arrow and the Doll were evidently passed on from one close relative to another, differing in this respect from the Tobacco medicine, which was acquired by a selection of sacred objects from the adopting chapter of the society at the time of initiation.

Since the other bundles have been described elsewhere, I will here confine myself to the Medicine Arrow (*arúut maxpé*) concerning which I interviewed Hillside and Flat-head-woman in 1914. I will begin with Hillside's narrative.

Hillside's Account of the Arrow Bundle. Cut-ear's father was my brother. He was young and very poor. Near Forsyth there is a peak called Búatárɛc. There he went up; in order to get up he had to make a kind of ladder. He chopped off a finger and fasted there. Then he had a vision of the Seven Stars; they appeared as seven persons and sang songs to him. One of them had a medicine arrow in his possession. This one sang a song. The arrow was covered; it was notched and was held with the notch pointing the other way. He sang a song and threw the arrow,

---

[1]This series, vol. 16, 12 seq.

which alighted by the Crow camp. Then the visionary heard the Indians crying for joy and saw a big herd of horses. This was the song:—

awɛ́ cṓndət hiríacɛ.
Land in any say this.

He threw the arrow as in the arrow-game. The one who sang had a red arrow, which I have now. Four of the seven visitants had arrows. The second took a black arrow. He sang a song with the same words, then threw the arrow, which went toward the Dakota and struck their land. Then the Crow were heard shouting and praying for first-coups, and people were seen entangled in a fight. The Crow were heard saying: *ahṓ*! (Thank you!) The third arrow was green, this now belongs to Flat-head-woman. Another star held it and sang:—

hutsé   húwa· tsēwik·; hutsé hú wĭk·.
The wind to come I'll make; the wind is coming.

He threw the arrow. It struck the Dakota country. The visionary heard horses making a noise and the Crow shouting 'thanks,' and saw many dead enemies. The fourth arrow was white. The fourth star picked it up. The first star said to him, "That arrow is no good, don't throw it." Nevertheless, he sang and threw it, but it wiggled and came back. The first three stars must have made it come back.

I was about ten years old when among the River Crow. At about eighteen I came to the Ac'arahó band to visit my brother. I had heard about his going out on war parties as captain and being successful. I joined his party. He gave me a black wolf and sent me out as scout. I was not sleepy, but a good runner, an early riser, and a good marksman. Whenever I caught horses on my trips I always gave one or two to my brother. I had a reason for so doing. The wolf was the first thing he gave me. When I had proved a good shot, my brother said, "You are all right now, you may be a war captain."

I made several trips to the Dakota, but came back empty-handed three or four times. Then I went out with a magpie my brother gave me. On one trip in the Wolf mountains the Dakota tracked me. I got scared, but made my escape, though they followed me. I was tired out and fell asleep. I had felt badly before falling asleep, saying, "That medicine of mine is bad, I have no medicine." In my sleep the owner of the arrow visited me. My brother had never told me about his vision, but in my sleep I saw an arrow thrown toward where he had fasted. It alighted on an island there. There were plenty of horses, the best of them a bay with feathers on his forehead, and I heard the Crow shouting for joy. I woke up and bade my followers be ready when the snow should melt and make their way to me wherever they might be. It was the beginning of winter then. "I'll go out and bring a big herd of horses. In all my troubles so far I have done no leading at all, but now I'll take you out in a different way, I'll take the medicine arrow with me." I did not know yet whether the owner would give it to me or not.

When it was time for me to start, I said to my brother, "I shall go out on the warpath." Then he asked of his own accord, "Do you wish to take the arrow?" "Yes." "Very well." When men made their first expedition as captains, their following was composed of poor young fellows. Of the men whom I had offered to lead with the arrow, the majority did not trust me and said they would not go with me. Only Spotted-horse had confidence and accompanied me, otherwise I had new followers. Where I had seen the arrow, there I came upon the enemy. Flat-head-woman was with me. We saw the smoke from the enemy's camp. The snow was ankle-deep. We packed ropes. In my dream I had seen horses on an island feeding on cottonwood bark, and we captured fifty head of horses. Flat-head-woman got the bay. We got away that night. We got near the site of Billings, where the Nez Percé were camped. The Crow had left. I got to the Nez Percé camp next morning. Flat-head-woman captured a bay and a gray horse. I gave him the gray.

I took pity on Flat-head-woman and thought I'd make him a war captain. So when I returned I asked my brother, "Is this the only medicine arrow?" He asked in return, "Have you seen any?" "Yes, a blue and a black one; I want to make one for Flat-head-woman." "He is no relative of ours." "That does not matter. He was my younger brother's comrade, and I want to give it to him."

The next time I went to the same place as before with a larger following. The people began to believe in me. This time the camp was below the first place. I had dogs and children with me. I took my party to the edge of the camp, brought back horses, and gave them to the young boys. Then I sent the rest to get all the unpicketed horses, and came home with a hundred head.

The next time I went with a large party. Long-horse had been killed and I went to avenge him. At Tallick's (?) Fork there were seven Dakota in a camp. I was on a good horse, killed one, took his gun, struck a first-coup, and scalped him. We killed all the Dakota but one.

The Crow were camped on a creek above Billings. The Dakota were there and stole some of our horses. I trailed them, stole thirty of theirs and got home with them.

When Long-horse was killed, the Dakota had stolen some of our horses. The Crow were on Trout Creek. The Dakota came to kill the

Whites, instead they had to flee, and the Whites told the Crow about it. The enemy got to the Musselshell, into a clump of pines. No one followed them except me, who killed one, scalped and struck him.

I thought I was using my medicine all alone and decided to give part of it to Flat-head-woman. So I gave him all my power and ceased using it myself, not going on the warpath thereafter.

The medicine arrow was taken out only on the warpath when the enemy was seen, and early in the spring. Now it is taken out only once a year. When we saw the enemy, we took it out and prayed to it. Now we pray for horses and property. This spring, when Flat-head-woman seemed to be dying, they opened it for him and prayed on his behalf.

In a tipi where the arrow is kept no one is supposed to throw anything; further, no menstruating women are allowed there.

My arrow is red; Flat-head-woman's, made by me, is blue; Firebear had the black one. Old-tail has a red one patterned on mine, and Bushy-tail had a black one in imitation of Four-bear's.

When my brother gave me the arrow, he gave up his right to the medicine. When I thought I had enough, I passed it on to Flat-headwoman. Nú' pa-kurutc (Takes-back-a-woman-twice) was the nickname of my elder brother, given on account of one father's clansman[1]; his real name was Bear-in-the-water. My brother gave me the name Woman-with-plenty-of-horses (mí isắcg'e ahốc).

The stone arrow-head (about 2½ inches long) worn round my neck is the head of my medicine arrow.

* * *

Flat-head-woman's Arrow Bundle. For the opportunity to see an arrow bundle, I am indebted to Jim Carpenter, my interpreter, who prevailed upon his father-in-law, Flat-head-woman, to unwrap it for me on June 20, 1914. Flat-head-woman began with this preliminary statement:—

"The Cheyenne also had a medicine arrow, but when the Crow got theirs, they no longer had an advantage over the latter. In the old days of war parties men had to pay a good price to see the medicine, but now I am willing to show it for $5."

The medicine bundle was about five feet long, with feathers extending at each end beyond the outermost cloth wrapping. Flat-head-woman had a little girl bring some live embers from the iron stove, and divided them into two heaps, about three feet from each other, one much

---

[1] This series, vol. 21, 41.

smaller than the other. Then he strewed some material for incense
(ground cedar?) on each heap, and alternately lowered each end toward
the heap nearer to it. The bundle, after being taken down, had been
resting on a blanket spread on the ground of the tent. With some mut-
tered words of prayer Flat-head-woman opened the bundle. The cloth
wrappings were folded back on the sides without disturbing their relative positions. There were two outer cloth wrappings, then a sack made
of a complete buffalo calfskin with the head on, out of which was pulled
a rawhide cylinder open at both ends and of more uniform width, as
well as rather longer, than the common cylindrical medicine bags.
Turning the tail end of the calfskin sack inside out, Flat-head-
woman exposed paintings of horsetracks and human figures, the latter
representing Dakota. "This picture was drawn before I started; then
I went out and killed some Dakota. The horsetracks represent a horse
named to me by a visionary adviser to be stolen from the Dakota. The
calfskin is the main cover of the bundle, but I keep it wrapped up in
cloth for fear it might be struck by lightning." In the rawhide cover,
there are two sticks about three feet in length; originally there was
a third, but it was lost. "We hunted for it in the mountains. It was
foggy. At last I found it, but then I was afraid to touch it and left it
there." Inside the rawhide cylinder was another sack of canvas.
Though it is of poor quality, Flat-head-woman explained, it is the one
prescribed in a vision. Inside of it was a colored wrapper; then followed
a blue wrapper; a reddish (?) wrapper; another cloth wrapper; a green
wrapper; and when the last-mentioned cover was thrown back there was
nothing to be seen but a large bunch of feathers. Now Flat-head-woman
combined the two incense heaps and strewed incense on the top. Then he
carefully arranged the feathers and took out from among them the arrow.
It had a stone head about one inch long, a shaft of birchwood (?), with
a standing feather at the end, and four tails of horses Flat-head-woman
brought home from war. Every time he captured horses a tail was
added, each representing a different war party on which good horses
were cut loose. My informant's narrative follows.

Flat-head-woman's Tale. In the old times when there was disease
people would offer fine calico cloths to the arrow. In time of war people
would say to it, "If I am not killed, I'll give you new cloth" (or some
other gift).

In order to own this I had to go through a good many hardships.
(Here he took smoke out of a redstone pipe and pointed the stem at the
arrow.) "Why," the owner asked me, "do you want this so badly? You

are not related to us, you are a different person altogether." Then Hill-side, his brother, said, "He was the comrade of my younger brother who is dead. They loved each other, that's why I wish to give it to him. Don't say any more about it (*dirisa!*)." So the owner said: "Tell him to fetch four birch (?) sticks." I went to look for four good ones, found them and brought them to him. The owner peeled them, trimmed them, and put them up to dry. There were about seven lodges of the owner's relatives who camped together. I took buffalo meat and put some in front of every one of these lodges, thus the owner became well-disposed toward me and willing to give me the medicine. After the sticks were dried, they were turned over to me. Nothing was said about the feathering of the arrow till spring, when word was sent that they were ready to feather the stick for me. The snow was melting. The owner called all his brothers and me to his lodge. A buffalo hide with its tanned white side up was used to put the stick on. Then they tried to find out who was a good arrow-maker. One man was named, but the others did not consider him suited for the purpose. Finally I was sent to an old man, who happened to be related to me. I said to him, "Brother, they want to give me the arrow." So the old man came, smoothed the arrow between two rocks and notched it. Then the owner told me the red plume on the shaft represented the fire. "If you are in battle, carrying this bundle, don't be afraid of the enemy, they can't hit you with their arrows. Since we have made this one, we'll take the Dakota by their bangs and have their foreheads to the ground." The owner said that he had seen his arrow crossing that of the Cheyenne, i.e., the Crow arrow was superior. (At this point Flat-head-woman offered smoke to his arrow.)

The owner said, "The day before yesterday, as I came out of my tent, there were seven cranes flying in the air. Go and bring one of those seven. Get one of your friends who is a good shot to go with you." I thought it was impossible: the cranes must be far off and were possibly already in some foreign land by that time. I felt badly, still I went out, and told my comrade what was to be done. He laughed. "How can we see them? We can't see them; it is impossible." Still he went along to please me. We pretended then to go out hunting, went up-stream, and looked about in the marshes. We kept going. There was a sleety snow-storm. Suddenly the clouds were gone, and my comrade, pointing at the prairie, said: "Look at the white-tail deer there." When I looked, it was the seven cranes making their pr—— pr—— pr—— sounds. There happened to be a coulée leading up to them, so we got about as close as Jack's tent from here (about fifty feet). Then I told my comrade,

"You are a good marksman, kill the biggest one." So he aimed, shot, and missed. The cranes went straight up. I was down-hearted. Only black spots could be seen where the cranes were flying on high. "You pretend to be a good shot, you have caused my downfall," I said to my comrade. As I looked up, the birds began to come down and alighted again in the spot where they had been shot at. When they alighted, my comrade again wanted to shoot, but I took the gun away from him, aimed at the big one, fired, and missed him. The birds went up. I was down-hearted, but looked up and thought the birds would come down again. They came back to their old place. Then my comrade took the gun, shot, and missed again. They went up straight in the air. We lay on our backs and watched. They came down again. My comrade took the gun, made medicine, and fired. We heard a dull sound as if the shot had struck something. The birds all flew straight up into the air,—small specks hardly to be seen, but we could hear the noise they made. I scolded my companion, but he said, "Only six of them are gone, there's one coming now." The seventh alighted in the same place whence they had flown up before. I was going to shoot it, but my comrade would not let me, ran after the crane, threw his blanket over it, and caught it. (Here smoke was again offered).

The owner, in sending me out, had told me he should wait for me in a certain place. I took the bird, and we ran back to camp. The bird had a long neck, and I had its neck hanging out. When I approached the lodge I was laughing and full of joy; those inside were all astonished. The owner called for the bird, and had it sitting in front of him. I expected that he would pull out the long feathers, but he only took two long ones, one from each side of the wing, and one from the middle. These three he put down. The two long ones are on the arrow now. The old arrow-maker was to do the fixing up.

Now the owner said to Hillside: "You, too, claim to have had a vision of it. Do you make half of it, and I'll make half of it. You'll give him some of your power, and I'll give him some of mine." Hillside said, "Very well, we'll make it all green. We'll make the plumes green that are to go on. We'll have the enemies' horses for its plumes, and I'll make a covering from the skin of a young buffalo calf. That is all for me; now do you start yours." The owner said: "I will make a red plume to represent fire. We'll shape an arrow-head of rawhide. If (to Flat-head-woman) in your vision you see the rawhide paint gone, open the bundle, and if it *is* gone, then make a stone head." That is what happened, and so I have a stone point. "If either you or Hillside, or I, should see the arrow point of rawhide gone in our visions," said the owner, "we'll replace it with stone. Get the hide of a four-year-old buffalo, we'll use that for a cover." I went, killed a buffalo, and brought the hide. When it was not yet dry, the owner painted the rawhide. "This represents the painting on your blanket when you return from an expedition on which an enemy has been killed. Such and such a cloth shall be used for a wrapping. Put a plug of tobacco at the bottom for the arrow to smoke." I was about thirty years old when this bundle was made, and the tobacco is still there.

The arrow-maker was told how to put the different paints and other decorations on the arrow. He covered it with green paint. He was instructed by the owner and Hillside. When it was completed, they laid it down and told me to get all kinds of feathers for the arrow to rest on. Then the bird was given back to me, and they told me to send it home. I went out some distance and set it down. It began to run and disappeared. It was not dead.

Everything looked common to me till the sacks were made, then it began to look like real medicine to me. It was wrapped and tied. I took it up. After a while the owner came to tell me to tie two eagle wing-feathers to each end of the bundle. After several years he came to me and said, "Open your medicine, I had a vision last night that it (the arrow-head) was gone; let us see whether it is true." I do not know how it happened, but the arrow point was gone. The owner put on a stone head then, and ever since it has been there.

Everyone heard that I owned one of the medicine arrows and talked about it. I would be at home when Hillside or the owner would visit me and tell me to go to the Dakota in some region they had seen the night before and to fetch such and such a horse. They would tell me they had seen an arrow thrown and alighting in a certain place, and had heard a rumbling noise and the whinnying of a herd of horses. Thus they sent me out. That is how they started. After a while they no longer sent me out. Then after a while they said, "We see you are well posted, now go out of your own accord." I was now to have visions of my own. I did not see an arrow as they did, but a long species of grass. I would see the stalk flying like an arrow and follow it with my eyes till it alighted somewhere, then I would go thither. From now on everything depended on myself. I had visions of different things. I made a little notched stick about four inches long myself, because I had a vision to that effect. If the enemy had stolen our horses and I put this on their tracks, they would sleep too long or be otherwise delayed, so we would catch up if I led the party.

At the Old Agency one time the Piegan stole some of our horses. All the young men were out, and I came late with the arrow. They were glad to see me and wished me to take the lead. I got to the tracks, planted my stick there, and we did not have to go far. They had over- slept. We got all our horses back, killed some, brought back the hair, and none of us got hurt. When I got home I put this medicine back into the bundle again. I did this two or three times.

When Dakota were sighted, young men would come to me with calicoes, pray to the arrow and say, "I wish not to be hit and to come back alive (*bámbi*)." There came to be a big bundle of these cloth offerings.

Once I went out in the dead of winter. When a considerable distance out, I had a vision. I heard a voice say: "Keep going, when you get to a certain land you will see a snake. This will be a sign that you are to get horses and will rejoice on your way back." The other men laughed at me because there are no snakes in the winter. About noon we came to a little creek, and there was a snake there. Then they believed that what I had said was true. My old comrade stayed with me, we changed direction and brought back some horses.

The arrow in a vision forbids me to do certain things. It told me not to throw anything and not to let anyone else throw anything where the arrow is. It told me: "If that is done in your lodge, it will be the same as throwing away some of your property." It forbade me to strike the tipi harboring the arrow in order to knock off the snow. It said, "If you want to remove the snow, take a long willow and gently scrape off the snow without hitting it." It forbade me to cook the fat above the paunch or to throw ashes out of a tipi. "If you don't keep the rule, the owner of the arrow will be blind."

Once I went on the warpath. The buffalo scared our horses away. I took my little arrow and planted it in the horses' track. They heard a horse whinnying and found a gray with a rope on it, wrapped round a bush. It was my horse; the others could not be found.

The owner came to me once and said: "You must have visions of your own. If a young man should ask you for it, it is your place now to make a bundle for him." I spoke to Hillside about this, but he would not allow it. He said, "If it were not for me, you would not own it; I gave it to you because you were my brother's comrade, otherwise I should not have done so. Do not make it for anyone else. When you have children, give it to them." My eldest daughter (Jim Carpenter's wife) owns it now.

The owner of the medicine originally got it (in a vision) from a woman with black hair and white face, wearing a buckskin suit and a string of beads round the breast.[1]

On a war party I found red plumes, and I put them into the bundle with the feathers.

Before Hillside and I started on the warpath the owner would call us in and brush us with one of the feathers from his arrow bundle. We would not have to pay for this, but other young men who desired to be brushed by him would have to pay a fee. When I got close to the enemy's camp I would sing my song and open the bundle. Then it got dark and cloudy so that we could hardly see one another. In most cases the arrow would protect us, so the enemy could not see our tracks.

In the original vision there were four arrows: red, blue, green, black (dark blue). Of these four the white one was the most effective and its owner would become a great chief. However, he was soon to be killed, and for that reason people were afraid of owning it, and it was left out. In singing the owners must not point the arrow toward themselves lest they be hurt, but toward the enemy. Through the arrow the Crow became people again (i.e., after suffering reverses from other tribes). When we opened the bundle formerly it got windy and cloudy, but it is not so now. Something must have changed. When there was a battle, a virtuous young woman (virgin) would open it. More recently the owner said, "Now you can have your wife and children open it. It does not look well to have strangers do it."

One time when on a war party along the Yellowstone I had a vision near Forsyth. "Go up where the arrow originated, and in one of the cracks there you will see an eagle feather of the kind next to the foremost. Take it out." I searched for it, found it, and took it on the warpath. The people never saw it except when I returned from a successful party, when I would expose it on a pole. But even then they could not see it near enough to see just what it was like.

In battle young men tried to be the first ones to carry the bundle and would give presents for being permitted to do so. These arrow-bearers were not afraid of anything, for they knew they could not be hurt. They had to pay for this privilege. Sometimes the owners themselves carried their bundle; then they felt as if no battle were going on at all. The owner would point the arrow at his associate-owners and sing, and then a wind would come up.

---

[1]This is of course at variance with Hillside's account (p. 391).

In giving me the arrow the owner said, "When you go out on the warpath, you'll see a white buffalo and kill it." It came true, and this proved to me the truth of the medicine.

Before the Custer massacre another general (Terry?), named Three-stars (I' ge ráwic), was helped by the Crow. Two young men both wished to carry my arrow and had a dispute over it. I and Medicine-crow took the lead in this fight on account of our medicines. When Three-stars went away, Custer came. The Dakota tried to kill off all the Crow, but on account of the arrow they could not do it. They lost plenty of property and horses. Custer was unlucky; he was destroyed. The Three-stars fight belongs to the arrow. It always protected me. Custer heard of it.

PAINTED TIPIS.

Painted tipis did not play the important part they did among other Plains tribes. In 1907 on a short visit to the Northern Blackfoot of Gleichen, Alberta, I saw a fair number of painted tipis pitched at the time of their annual festivities; but though I have repeatedly visited the Crow on like occasions I recall but a single painted tipi, which was decorated with the figure of the Thunderbird. Nevertheless, there were a number of painted tipis in the old days and their owners were esteemed as medicinemen and took precedence in moving the camp. Enemies' scalps were always taken to such tents and subsequently given to women who had lost brothers in battle; sometimes they kept the lock for a while and would then throw it away.

Painted tipis were of course revealed in visions. Returning from his experience, the visionary would have some men gather, had the buffalo-skin cover spread out and the paint lying about ready for use. Then he would say, "I saw this when fasting on a mountain," and would give a full description of his vision. He would close with some such words as, "I am painting this tent on behalf of the Crow. You will fare well, horses and scalps will come into our camp from everywhere."

The most noted owner of a painted tipi recalled by Gray-bull was White-lip. He chopped off a joint of one of his fingers and burnt it up with a buffalo chip. He had a trance. When he regained consciousness, he was in a tipi with two black stripes by the door and another stripe in the center of the rear. Someone said, "Walk round, look, this is your tent." They gave him a pipe. When he got home, he went on the war-path and the Crow met five Dakota. White-lip asked his companions, "Why did you let the Dakota escape?" He pursued them on horseback, jumped off in front of one of them, shot him and took his gun. He shot and killed a second man. The third fled but was also killed by him. He did this very soon after his vision. No one ever achieved what he did,—killing three enemies single-handed.

White-lip wore a necklace with plumes, hanging down; in the center there was a red clam shell, which Gray-bull thinks symbolized the morningstar, possibly the sun or moon. He also wore a shell above the point of attachment of his switch in the back. He had weasel-skin trimmings in the back.

White-lip was leading the camp as chief. The people were on a buffalo hunt and there was a strong wind blowing so as to throw the scent to the game. White-lip pointed his pipe in all directions, drawing a circle. The wind forthwith blew from the opposite direction. Plenty of buffalo were killed. White-lip was never shot in battle. He lived to be about 110 years of age; his skin would tear when he moved.

The manner of decorating the sacred tipis varied. Some had the picture of a moon on them, sometimes the whole lodge was painted red or with some other color according to the revelation.

No Crow, according to one informant, put up a lodge of twenty or more buffalo hides unless he had dreamt to that effect. Otherwise, the Indians believed, he or one of his close relatives would die.

SHIELDS.

Shields (*mínnatse*) were sacred objects inasmuch as their decoration was revealed in visions; plain shields for ordinary use were not considered medicine. The protective quality of the former type was naturally attributed to the supernatural experience and men going into an important battle desired to carry one of them. Consequently they would approach the owner and ask for his shield, saying, "If I achieve such and such a deed, I will give you a horse" (or some other property). If successful, they would then fulfil their promise.

Shields were made from the hide of a buffalo and White-arm says that the ventral-thoracic part was utilized. According to this informant most shields were decorated on the rawhide itself, but my impression is that in the majority of cases the painting appeared on the buckskin cover.

In moving camp the owners would entrust their shields to their wives, who fastened them on one side of the pommel while to the other side was secured a stick about four feet long and wrapped with otter-skin; the cantle had a cylindrical bag attached on the left side and the spear-holder with erect spear or sabre on the right. If a man had two wives and only one shield, they would sometimes quarrel as to who should carry it, for the one doing so was regarded as the husband's favorite. Usually the owner took no part in the dispute, letting the women settle the matter between them, but sometimes he assigned it to the one he loved more.

In going on the warpath the owner of a shield had it carried by a young man, who took the lead. Whenever the party halted for smoking or resting, the bearer would put the shield on some sagebrush, for it must not touch the ground; further he was not allowed to carry any weapons. When in sight of the enemy's camp, the captain owning a shield took it himself, as was the custom with other medicines too. Sometimes shields were taken from and by the enemy; such capture was mentioned at dances in the recital of coups, though it was not reckoned on a par with that of a gun. White-arm recollected the case of Long-piegan, a Crow, taking a Dakota shield, but said the Piegan Indians excelled all other tribes in getting into a hostile camp and stealing shields or other medicines.

When a man was about to die, he would will his shield to his son or otherwise to a younger brother. It was never inherited by a woman. If the owner had made no disposition of it, a man he had adopted as his son in selling him some medicine might mourn in conspicuous fashion and subsequently announce, "I have done this for that shield." Then the family of the deceased felt that he deserved to own it and gave it to him. White-arm knew of no case where a man had been buried with his shield, but my interpreter thought Ten-bear had been and Medicine-crow told me he would under no conditions sell his shield at any price since he wanted to be buried with it.

As already noted, no shield was supposed to touch the ground. A shield-bearer carried his shield on the left arm and horsemen charging the enemy did not pass on his left side, otherwise their horses would fall down. In other respects the notions associated with shields varied. When in my presence uncovering his shield, which had two covers, Medicine-crow followed a procedure which may or may not have been typical. He took a few live coals and burned *isé* for incense, then held his shield above the fire and raised it a little distance, lowered it and raised it a little higher than before, and repeated this performance till the fourth time, when he raised the shield high above his head. Then he removed the buckskin covers.

A magnificent collection of Crow shields was made by Dr. G. A. Dorsey and Mr. S. C. Simms on behalf of the Field Museum in Chicago and is housed in that institution. I do not know what notes were secured in connection with these specimens. Owing to these previous purchases the number remaining on the Reservation was very small and since their owners either declined to sell at all or demanded extravagant prices I was able to acquire only two complete shields (Fig. 3 and 4) and two shield covers, (Fig. 5) but was permitted to view one or two others. Fortunately my informants were able to give some data about other shields they had seen or heard about, and below I give all the information secured.

Medicine-crow's shield was decorated on the cover with a series of parallel vertical lines resting on a horizontal line; these were said to symbolize clouds. Below the horizontal line there were two triangles with long zigzag appendages; the triangles represent Buffalo-above's eyes, the zigzags his breath. According to another note, the buffalo is represented as urinating, and the black lines symbolized the glancing off of bullets. On the shield there were also some buffalo tracks. Zigzag ornamentation is rather common on the shields exhibited in Chicago; for example, in two cases I noted that the decorative surface was tripartite, the central third being occupied by a number of parallel zigzags, while above and below were symmetrical series of parallel lines. To the middle of Medicine-crow's cover there was attached some horse-hair representing a scalp. At the top of the cover there was a bunch of mountain-grouse feathers, below an eagle feather was hanging.

White-arm and Grandmother's-knife spoke of a type of shield painted yellow, decorated with a buffalo representation in the middle and with weasel tracks; to the upper edge was tied a yellow weasel. There were several of these shields owned by men of the *xúxkaraxtse* clan.

Another shield, also painted yellow all over, was decorated with rabbit tracks. The owner's wife had to take care of it. As soon as the sun rose, she placed it toward the east and as the sun moved she changed its position westward, wrapping it up at sunset. Owners of this type of shield were not allowed to eat any kind of kidney and did not permit others to bring kidneys into their lodge. Shows-a-fish inherited one of these shields.

Another type, greatly admired by White-arm, was covered with a light layer of red paint and streaked in spots by a heavier application of the same paint. Two-bear's ears were represented, and attached to each was a six-inch cord tipped with a plume. The streaks represented

Fig. 4.

Fig. 3.

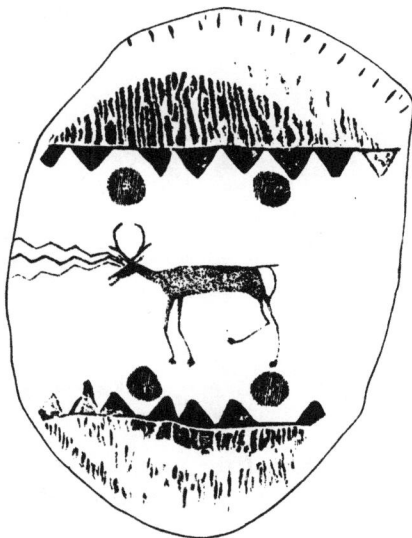

Fig. 5.

Fig. 3 (50.1-3894a). Magpie's Shield.
Fig. 4 (50.1-3895a). Wolf-lies-down's Shield.
Fig. 5 a(50-6932), b (50.1-3896). Shield Covers.

clouds. This shield was owned by Búətac (Coyote). In the rear of the lodge where it was kept people were prohibited to put any moccasins for fear of some stroke of misfortune.

Another shield said in 1916 to be kept in Sheridan, Wyoming, had a buckskin cover painted with the figure of a buffalo, over which was tied a buffalo tail. The painted cover was in turn enclosed in a second cover. A shield in the possession of the Museum before my purchase seems to belong to the same category (Fig. 6).

Fig. 6 (50-5710b).   Buffalo-hide Shield.

One of the most noted shields because of the fame it brought its owners was called *minnatse c'pewac-bicè*, shield having a short intestine. It was painted white all over, except for a red spiral, which represented the intestine.

A shield so highly prized that it was never exposed in sham battles and accordingly never seen by White-arm is or was owned by Two-white-birds of Pryor. It was abundantly ornamented with feathers and other decoration. Unlike other shields, it was not tied to a woman's saddle in traveling but carried on her back.

One shield was known as *mínnats i'tsíne hawátec*, shield supported on only one pole. White-arm thought it had a bear painted on it and might be identical with Flat-head-woman's shield.

Bull-weasel's mother was said to own a shield covered with white paint and having real bear's ears tied to the middle; between the ears was the tail of a sage-hen and at the bottom there was some beadwork. This shield is called *mínnats tsí'tsġ iséwicè*, shield having a big sage-hen.

A shield known as *mínnats i'ġ é sá'puɘwicè*, shield with the Dipper, was painted all over with a light yellow. The seven stars were put on at distances of from five to six inches from one another.

White-arm himself made a shield, though a small one, which he had seen before becoming Christianized. He cut four horsetracks on one leg and three on the other, also cutting his arms and dragging horses' heads. He placed the cut flesh on buffalo chips as an offering to the Sun. The cuts on his arm represented coups he was paying for, the dragging of the skulls any gift that might be made. My informant did not describe what decoration was on his shield.

Each shield had distinctive taboos. In some instances no person was permitted to borrow coals from the owner's fire; in others, visitors to his lodge were obliged to sit down immediately on entering; still other shield-owners insisted that no one must strike their tipi with any object.

Charges-camp was said to have owned a shield decorated with the figure of a man in black; this man was shown with open mouth, exhibiting teeth resembling a dog's. Once the Flathead stole Charges-camp's horses and also his shield. Another Crow then dreamt of it and made it, my informant's brother paid the visionary for it and my informant inherited it from his brother.

I saw a shield with several buckskin covers, of which the outermost was decorated with parallel vertical lines in red. Across the center of the shield from top to bottom and beyond it there was an otterskin; on each side there was a bunch of feathers, which was tucked under the skin in wrapping up the shield.

Tattooed-face was said to own a shield painted all over with a light red color and with a decoration resembling a buffalo's guts. The owner's horse was never shot in battle.

Grandmother's-knife told me of a shield owned by a chief named Rotten-belly (*ɛra-púɘc*). A man named Hanging-foot had separated from the main camp and he and all his male followers were killed by the Cheyenne, who captured the women and children.[1] Some of the captives

---

[1] Cf. this volume, 185.

escaped to the main camp and offered the pipe to the two chiefs, Red-plume-on-the-forehead and Rotten-belly, in order to have them undertake an expedition to revenge the death of their kinsfolk. Rotten-belly smoked the pipe and bade the young men get ready. The military societies got together and danced in the afternoon. Rotten-belly asked the warriors to get ready early in the morning and saddle their horses. They did so and proceeded to the top of a hill. There he ordered them to dismount and gather buffalo chips, which were then piled up. The sun had just risen. Rotten-belly said, "I'll sing and walk upon this pile of chips and it will stay exactly as it is. When I get up on top of the chips, I'll sing again. Then I'll roll my shield, and if the painted side falls next to the ground, we'll turn back. If the other side falls to the ground, you must all cheer." The picture on the shield was that of a man in black with his ears disproportionately large. Rotten-belly sang and walked up the pile of chips with his shield in his hands. He made the painted side face toward the sun and began to sing. When done, he threw the shield, which rolled away and fell with the painted side up. All the men cheered. He descended from the pile, picked up the shield and sang a praise song. He said, "Don't kill any birds on this trip." They set out. Young birds began to fly and one flew over a woman. She struck it with her hand and it fell to the ground; she picked it up, but it died. They reached the enemy's camp and attacked them, killing many of the enemy. Only one Crow was killed,—a brother of the woman who struck the bird. The shield was noted for its medicine power and was in constant use until reservation times. It ought to be at Pryor.

In 1910 I was approached by Yellow-brow, who offered to drive me to his house and sell some valuable specimens. I accompanied him and found that he and his father Magpie really had a veritable treasure-trove of ethnographically interesting material. I noticed a shield and wanted to see it, but Yellow-brow at first refused to unwrap it, saying that he had no desire to sell it. After I had bought a number of medicine objects, he relented in response to my importunity so far as to uncover it, still insisting that he would not sell it. When I saw the shield, I made him an offer and after considerable parleying he agreed to sell it for $75. In driving me back with my acquisitions, Yellow-brow handed the shield to his father, who clasped it in his arms and with great display of emotion recited a prayer to it. My interpreter, Jim Carpenter, told me that if any accident should befall the seller, the Indians would ascribe it to his selling the shield. The shield (Fig. 3) has a buckskin cover decorated with two vertical zigzag lines, one on each side; to the center

is attached a whistle and on each side of it a yellow bird. Several years
after the purchase a favorable opportunity presented itself for inter-
viewing Yellow-brow as to the history of the shield and his narrative
follows; unfortunately it does not explain the ornamentation.

The Tale of Magpie's Shield. Dries-his-fur was leader of a war
party. Humped-wolf, then about eighteen years of age, accompanied
them. When they had gone a great distance, they were attacked by the
enemy, who drove them out of their trenches and killed many of the
Crow in the night. Humped-wolf was shot through the legs above his
knees, but still went along with the survivors. That night he ran off.
He had no clothes and it was snowing; he thought he was going to die.
Then he came to a big black object,—a dead buffalo. When he touched
it, it was not dry. He went inside, where it was warm. He stayed there for
a while and was just about to go to sleep, when the buffalo snorted. He
did not know what it was and was afraid. He heard something coming.
Someone called him, "Full-mouth-buffalo (*tsípkarìcti-ŏric*), come."
He did not know who it was but there was daylight and he rose and went
towards the sound. "What are you worrying about?" "I was shot by the
Dakota, that is why I am worrying." The visitant opened his mouth.
"You shall be the same as myself." He had no teeth. "You cannot die
until then (when you have no more teeth). That is the first thing I will
give you. Face towards the east and look!" It was a buffalo bull with
another behind him; the first changed into a man, the second into a bay
horse. Humped-wolf noticed what the buffalo-man was wearing.
He wore a horned bonnet with a short streamer decorated with eagle
feathers, a calfskin shirt with the hair on it, sleeve-holders of buffalo
tail, a necklace of buffalo horns between dewclaws. In his hand he held
a buffalo tail mounted on a pointed stick and he was carrying the shield
I gave you (R. H. L.) He was painted white from his nose downward
and all over his body. His horse was also painted white below the eyes,
from the knees down, and about the middle of his tail; a plume was tied
to the horse's forehead. This man came up to Humped-wolf and said,
"I have made you go on the warpath and come where you were and go
inside the buffalo. Look towards the place where you came from."
When he looked, he saw men lined up behind him and all dressed like the
buffalo-man. There were also dead people lying all about with guns,
bows, and tomahawks. "Look to the west." There, too, he saw dead
people with guns and bows. The buffalo-man spoke to Full-mouth-
buffalo (this being thenceforth Humped-wolf's name) as follows: "Other
medicines do not last. Give this to your children and grandchildren and

so on till there shall be no more fighting. I have given you this medicine. That plume is the body of your horse (meaning that it could not be shot). When a person is shot, he is considered a man. I have placed you among the Crow. Henceforth you shall not be driven back by the enemy. I have given you everything that makes a man. This is all. Give the medicine only to your brothers (*dakúpe*) and your children (*darûke*)."

After his vision Humped-wolf went homeward. It was still snowing but he no longer suffered from the cold. About daylight he saw a person coming up in front of him. He[1] told Humped-wolf that he had forgotten something and began to sing. Humped-wolf saw another person coming, whom he recognized as a Dakota. The first man sang against the Dakota, who was armed with bow and arrow, a knife, and a tomahawk at his belt. When he had done singing, he went towards the Dakota and held his shield in front of him. The Dakota was ready to shoot his arrows and let one fly. It struck the shield, broke, and fell to the ground. He dropped his bow and arrows, took his tomahawk, came up to the Crow, and struck at the edge of the shield. His tomahawk broke. He took out his knife. The shield-bearer stepped back, then started towards him again. When the Dakota made a motion as if to stab him, he threw the shield in front of him, and the knife touching the shield was broken. Then the Crow jumped aside, stabbed the enemy's breast with a lance, and killed him. Then Humped-wolf looked and saw that it was a coyote. "You shall be the same," said the visitant.

Humped-wolf went toward his camp. The rest of the survivors of his war party had returned to camp and told the Crow that Humped-wolf had been shot in the leg and left behind. The people mourned for him. When he arrived, he summoned all the older men to his tipi and told them his vision. He described it and told them he liked it. "Make it," they said. One of them asked, "Have you any songs (*dicû-wici*)?" "Yes." "Sing." He sang the following:—

bāp'	hirí at bicìt,	bik·	baráwarawik·.	arûut
Whenever	there is any trouble,	I	shall not die but get through.	Arrows
ahú'ta,		bówik·.	barasé	batsék·:
many though there be,		I shall arrive.	My heart	is manly.

The man who asked for the songs had no faith in Humped-wolf's vision and said, "You had better look for safety."

Humped-wolf made what he had seen. Riding a dark bay horse, he accompanied a war party. On the day they set out from camp the enemy attacked them. Making the rest of the company lie in a coulée,

---

[1] This is the visitant.

he alone fought the enemy and killed several of them. He was shot by
the enemy, so were some of those who hid. The Dakota ceased fighting
and thus spoke to Humped-wolf: "Go home, you are no good, have your
will of the women and rejoice." They meant that he was a man. They
did not pursue the Crow, who came back with none of them slain. Some
of the enemy had been killed and scalped. Then the Crow liked this
man and the whole camp knew about him. Whenever he went with a
war party, the enemy always attacked them. He always fought alone
and was always shot, but sometimes some of the party were killed in-
cidentally. When the Crow discovered that parties he accompanied
were attacked by the enemy, captains did not like him to go along. They
recollected his song and said, "He was to fight, he is always giving
trouble."

A man was setting out as captain for the first time. He had many
brothers; they were not good people but were always looking for a fight.
When Humped-wolf tried to accompany them as before, they turned back,
saying he was no good. When they had been out four days, he overtook
them, thinking they would not turn back after having traveled for four
days. They said, "What are you coming for? You are no good. We
are not very good captains, we are just going to try. Turn back, or we
shall beat you. We give you only this choice: turn back, or if you don't
we shall beat you." They went on. He asked them to beat him once
and he would go with them. All surrounded him and beat him till one
of the party who was not a brother of the captain asked them to desist.
Humped-wolf was covered with blood. He rose to a sitting posture and
said, "If you achieve something good, I'll be in it; if you are all killed,
I too shall be killed." They bade him turn back lest they kill him and
went on.

Humped-wolf sat there, thinking of the man who had adopted him,
though his medicine was worthless, and cried, "If it had not been for
my medicine, I should have gone with the party." After they were all
out of sight, he considered whether to turn back or follow the party, not
knowing what to do. While he was sitting there crying, he heard hooting
and whooping and someone was saying, "Humped-wolf is nearby."
The party ran towards him and said, "The enemy came and drove us
back." He said, "You did not like me. I could have joined the enemy,
but because I am a Crow I did not do it." He put up his blanket in a
heap and ran around. He bade the war party get behind him. The
enemy surrounded him. They fought from early in the morning till
sunset. He made gestures to the Dakota. "Bring me some water; I

am very thirsty. If you don't do it, I'll go for water myself and follow you to your main camp, fighting you all summer until winter." The Dakota brought some water and left it at a distance for him to take it. They told him to go home, that he was no good and should have his will of women. "Quam maxime penem insere," aiunt. They returned to the rest of the party, who had hidden in a coulée. They now liked him and treated him well. He was shot all over and was not feeling very well; some of his teeth had been knocked out. They got to a river on the way home. His wounds smarted. The captain asked, "Why did you turn back?" "My leg smarts, that is why." The captain told the warriors to carry him across the water. He refused to be carried. "We'll do it nevertheless." He remembered the time they had beaten him and asked the captain, "How many times did you strike me?" "I did not count, but it was many times." "About how many?" "About ten times." There were large stones in the creek and the water was flowing very swiftly. He asked the captain to carry him across, and the captain alone lifted him on his back. When he got to the middle of the creek, the water was almost up to his waist. He slipped on a stone, fell, and both floated downstream. There was a whirlpool just below and they could not get out, but the captain was pulled out by his brothers; they left Humped-wolf in there and proceeded homeward. He had been shot in the arms, so he could not swim but climbed a log and floated on it till night, crying continually. About dawn he saw a black object approaching. He wished it were an enemy coming to kill him. It was singing medicine songs. It said, "Child, I am coming to see you, we'll do it again." It was the man he had seen coming from the east in his vision. "I made a mistake," said the visitant. "I asked you before why you were grieving; you answered that you had been chased and shot by the enemy. That is what I have given you, that they should never chase you. The Dakota have bidden you go home and have your will of the women, they always bade you go to camp. Henceforth give no help to war parties, help the camp. The Dakota and Cheyenne have driven you away and captured your people." He was still floating on the log. "Get up, come." He thought to himself, "How can I rise and walk?" "Get up and come." He made an effort to rise and the water was hard, so he stood up. He walked on it and got to this man. He told him to go home. "Make this medicine for your children and brothers, your having it alone is bad." Humped-wolf proceeded without pains of any sort. The rest of the party had returned and reported him drowned. The people had been mourning for him. Henceforth he stayed in camp. He must have been about forty years of age then and had owned the medicine for a long time and achieved great deeds. This was about 173 or 174 years ago (*sic!*) The people were staying between Powder River and the site of Columbus, Montana.

Humped-wolf had three sons, and his two sisters had two sons each. Early one morning he told his wife to take everything out of his tipi. He sent for his four nephews (*itsûke,* younger brothers or a man's sister's sons[1]), who sat down beside him, while his three sons were on the opposite side. To the one next to him Humped-wolf said, "I'll give you a name,— White-young-buffalo (*tsîpkarìcta-tsìəc*)." To the next one he said, "I'll name you Full-mouth-buffalo." To the third he said, "I'll call you Bull-always-living (*tsîrup-dāwîc*)." To the fourth he said, "I'll call you "Buffalo-walks-to-the-river." Of his sons he named the first Colored-fur, referring to the yellowish or reddish color some calves are born with; the second, Buffalo-with-high-withers; the third, Small-backed-bull. He asked them all whether they were satisfied with their names and they said, "Yes." "Don't go out on war parties. The rest of the Crow are men; they can go out and look out for themselves. Look after the children and women in camp. The camp has been attacked, and women and children have been captured by the enemy. When you are there, this will happen no more." Then he told them all about his medicine and told them to go out and seek some medicine of their own.

They went out. The first nephew was looking for something on a hill at the junction of the Rotten Grass and the Bighorn. He did not get what his uncle had wanted. He reported as follows: "A jack-rabbit came to me and told me not to take the medicine because you have always been shot. He said to me, "You shall be a chief without trouble; old people are poor; you shall grow up and die without trouble or sorrow." Humped-wolf replied, "You have erred. A person wants to get enough of life. I will not make this medicine for you." The second nephew reported: "I did not get anything. While I was seeking medicine, a bob-cat and two different kinds of hawk came to me. They said, 'The animal that gave him the medicine is heavy, we are more powerful, don't take its medicine. You will be liked by all the Crow and shall die without trouble or sorrow. Old age is bad, old people have no teeth or eyes.' I do not want your medicine." Humped-wolf answered, "Not all the people on this earth desire to die forthwith." The third nephew reported as follows: "While I was seeking a vision, a hawk came to me on a cliff and

---

[1]Lowie, this series, vol. 21, 60.

said, 'I'll make you help your people.   The owner of the medicine you are about to take has always been shot.   Old age is not good.   He has had to suffer a great deal of trouble.   When you are shot, your body shall not be penetrated.   You shall do whatever you please in battle.'"   Humped-wolf spoke to his three nephews thus: "I wanted to live with you a long time, but you will not."

The fourth nephew, Full-mouth-buffalo, said that he had brought the medicine: "I am like (?) the rest of these, but have a different way. I don't know what it is, but I saw a vision and was told to fight.   It was the sacred Tobacco (*i'tsi'tsìə*).   On the return trip I was caught by a bear. He lifted me up so that I could see all the earth.   He made me touch his teeth; he had none at all.   'You may jump among high cliffs or do what you please,' said he, 'you cannot die.   When you have no more teeth and all your hair is white, you shall fall asleep without awaking.   You'll have a good death, so don't be afraid of anything.   When we are in trouble, that is what makes men of us.'"   Humped-wolf replied: "You have done well.   Those three are like the plants.   They will grow up a while and then wither.   Had I been in their place, I should have taken the medicine you obtained and also the one I am about to give you." His three sons all brought what he had asked them to bring.   He made the medicine for them.   The first three nephews did not get either Full-mouth's or Humped-wolf's medicine, but only what they had themselves seen.

When Humped-wolf had made the medicine for his three sons and the last of his nephews, he bade them sit down.   The camp had separated into distinct bands in the wintertime.   He said, "When the whole camp is engaged in a fight, help the tribe and keep the enemy from taking captives."   "Yes, we'll do this." ' "I am slow (*ahôkātək*), I am heavy; no matter what happens, I have no place to run to.   When you wish to flee, remember this and you'll remain strong and brave."   "Yes," they answered.   "When all the people are hungry and you bring buffalo, give meat to the poor.   Look out and scout for the camp, look for buffalo, move the camp to where there are buffalo.   Treat your people well, die for them.   Be men for your people, don't fight with them.   If they dispute with you, don't mind it, treat them well.   If they strike you, do not hit them back.   Have you heard what I said?"   "Yes."

One of the bands that had separated was almost completely destroyed by the enemy.   All the Crow got together in a camp circle. Full-mouth's father had two wives, and each of them had a son with a month's difference in their ages.   These boys had grown up and loved each other. Thus there was an eighth man to go out. This brother of Full-mouth was called Wants-to-die (*cĕce*), though his real name was Owl-head. Full-mouth had a horse nicknamed Face-on-both-sides, which name was subsequently transferred to himself. Bull-always-living frequently changed the painting on his face, for which reason he was called Plays-with-his-face. Buffalo-walks-to-the-river, while looking for some woman, passed a bevy and looked for a woman where there were none; hence he was called Passes-the-woman.

The enemy had killed a man and his child; the mother was alive. Wants-to-die and Face-on-both-sides were camping in the middle of the circle. The Crow liked these two, knowing that they could get help from them; that is why they were camped in the center. The mourning woman went round the camp crying and saying, "The Dakota have killed my husband and child, who is going to kill one of them for me?" After a while she got to the two central lodges and walked round them. "Who is going to kill a Dakota for me? If no one will kill one, I'll be miserable." She went to Face-on-both-sides' lodge, saying, "You have a body and you are still here. I wish you would kill a Dakota for me, no one else can kill one, you are the only one who can do it." She went and pressed his head, as was the custom then. His father said, "You have done wrong, you are going to make my son die. You ought to have stayed outside wailing." She went outside. Face-on-both-sides said to his father, "Don't worry. I shall not die during your lifetime. I'll die as a very old man, don't worry about me." He called Wants-to-die, who was in the next tent. "At this very moment we have a good thing. There are plenty of men but she has come to us, and it is well. Bring six others, bring the old man (Humped-wolf) also." The old woman prepared good food for the visitors. "Why have you sent for us?" asked the old man. "You told us not to go on war parties, but a woman has asked us to kill one of the Dakota. Will you let us go?" "How are you going to kill Dakota without going anywhere? I told you to help the children and women. A child has been killed, a woman has asked you for help, that is why I want to help." The Dakota camp was close, and it was large. Of the other tribes they were not afraid. Face-on-both-sides said to Humped-wolf, "We'll start this evening, I'll go with you." It was in the morning. "Go home now and get your horses, we'll go with any-one who wants to join. Go out and herald that we are going to sing (*actä-wawaráxbōk'*)."[1] The old man heralded. Face-on-both-sides

---

[1] A special kind of singing is referred to.

was very anxious, he did not eat. He sent for the old man, who entered his tipi. "What is the matter, Face-on-both-sides?" "I feel like crying, yet I also feel like singing Big Dog and medicine songs." "Your medicine is anxious too, that is why." "Paint me up." He did so, also painting his horse. Face-on-both-sides used all the medicine he had as he was riding his horse. He cried, "A woman and children, who are timid, have been killed by the Dakota, who have captured some. They alone want to be men; they do not consider us, the Crow, men. Sun, if I die today, it will be well. Whenever they have killed children and women, I always grieve. If I die for my people, it will be well." He went round the circle and returned to his own tipi. Everyone cried as he went round crying. He went round again, singing the Big Dog songs. The women cheered him. He got back to his own tipi, then went round again, singing the medicine songs. "There is only one man, Face-on-both-sides; I am he. I am among the Crow. There is none among the Dakota. I am your helper. Remember me when you have a hard time. Tomorrow I'll kill an enemy, from now on I'll keep on killing them." When he got back to his tipi, all his brothers and the old man were there. The old man said, "This is what I have brought you up for, for the time when the Crow tribe would come to you for aid."

That night they sang and then set out. A great many went along, there must have been about a thousand. They traveled on till they saw the Dakota camp. They stayed there all night. A Dakota captive escaped from the Crow to the Dakota camp and warned them, so no Dakota ventured out. The following day the old man spoke as follows: "This is a fine day. Your mother must have been waiting for you, thinking you were going to bring a Dakota scalp. When a woman gives birth, it takes her a long time and she does not know whether she will live or not. You have it easy, the camp is right there. Mount your horses and go, there is nothing to hold you back. When you get there, you will either be killed or will kill an enemy. Let me know how your heart is (what you think)." Face-on-both-sides rose and said: "My people, I am going to speak. Listen to me. Now you are miserable, you are weak. Go home and wait for me on a high hill this side of the Crow camp. When you have been gone a long time, then I'll kill an enemy; otherwise the enemy might overtake you too." They did what he told them to do. Then he spoke to the old man: "Where are your nephews and your sons today? To all of us you spoke, where are the rest? Have they heard or not? You ought to have spoken to me alone that time, there was no use speaking to the others. This is all." Wants-to-die said, "I am going to speak; listen. I heard what this old man said when he spoke to his nephews and sons. He wanted to make men of his nephews and sons. I am going to excel them. Let us all mount our horses. When I am old, I shall die. I will die at any time; I want to find out how it is. It is like going up over a divide." He sang this song:—

bak·ótsi·te	awáxe	awérək;	bāxaríə	kawá+uk·.	bātsiríreta.
Eternal (are)	the heavens	and the earth;	old people	are bad.	Do not be afraid.

All mounted their horses. One man named Tears-the-tipi said, "They are not the only men, I am a man too, I'll be the one to kill an enemy." The old man answered, "Thanks, you are doing well. I was wishing that some of the other men might help my nephews and sons. You have done it and I want you to keep it up." All, including this man, stood in line and Humped-wolf behind. The bulk of the people had departed long ago. The old man said, "Full-mouth,[1] what you have shown me I will do today. Wherever you are, you will know. Give your power to Face-on-both-sides, I want him to get through in safety. I will go, I am old and shall be tired." Then he left them. They bade him go faster; they were going to kill the enemy when he had gone far away.

When he had departed, Young-white-buffalo proposed a plan. "When we kill, do not take a scalp. They won't believe us, they'll think we did not kill anyone if they see no scalp. The one who scalps shall be the first to strike. If we only strike the Dakota, we shall not have it."[2] "All right," they said, "you have a good plan." They mounted and set out towards the camp. There were nine of them. A coulée extended to the camp. They proceeded without halting till Tears-the-tipi bade them stop. "I thought you were going to kill. If you act as now, they will chase you and kill you all. I don't want to be in it." "We'll go right into the camp." Tears-the-tipi said he would turn back. "You may go." He turned and went. Near the camp he halted and sang his medicine song. The coulée ran through the camp. They went right up to the edge of the camp. There on top of the bank a woman was dressing a hide. Face-on-both-sides said, "No one has left the camp, so we'll kill that one." Plays-with-his-face said, "You are no persons, I'll be the one to scalp." Passes-the-woman answered, "You are not of much account, I'll be the one to scalp." Face-on-both-sides said, "Thank you. I thought I should be the one to scalp, I did not know you two were." When 300 yards within camp, they saw a man coming

---

[1] This refers to his visitant.
[2] This paragraph is obscurely worded.

out wearing a blanket. They said, "There is a man coming, we'll kill him." He went some distance to ease himself. The eight men ran towards him. He rose and started back to camp without cleaning himself. At the door of his tipi they were upon him, but instead of entering he went toward the center of the circle. They shot and killed him and fell upon him. The Dakota had been expecting the Crow and were already shooting at them. Plays-with-his-face scalped the man, his companions ran away, and his horse with them. Thus he was left all alone in the camp circle. Everything looked high to him, and it seemed to him as though he were standing in a hollow. He did not know whether he was walking or running, but followed in the direction of his friends. The fugitives saw his horse and looking back saw him alone in the center of the hostile camp with the enemy surrounding him and shooting at him.

Wants-to-die caught Plays-with-his-face's horse and took it to him. He passed him and threw him the reins so that they hung over his shoulder. All this time the enemy were shooting at him. He seized the reins and jumped on the horse. They ran through the camp. The Dakota were in pursuit. When they got out of the camp they turned and drove the enemy back, then they ran back. There were two parallel coulées. They ran along one, then turned off to the other and went in the reverse direction, so that the enemy were going the opposite way. The Crow said, "They have killed a child, so we'll kill one of their children." "All right." They ran into camp. A boy was running from one lodge to another. Wants-to-die struck him in the temple with an ax and Plays-with-his-face dismounted and scalped him; then they fled. They galloped till night. When they returned to the rest of their party, these said, "We thought you had been killed by this time and were going to mourn." The old man rejoiced and sang praise songs. The next morning they returned to the Crow camp.

Thereafter the Crow were never driven back by the Dakota, since that medicine was with them, but they repelled the Dakota. These men each had one shield of the same kind, but those who had visions of their own dressed a little differently.

VARIOUS MEDICINE OBJECTS.

Though sacred objects were almost uniformly derived from revelations ultimately, many individuals owned medicines which they had merely bought from the original visionary or even second-hand from another purchaser. When a person saw another man prospering on the acquisition of some medicine, he would be tempted to acquire the medicine also in order to share the owner's success. In such cases the visionary made copies for the buyers to the number of four; with the fourth replica he lost his property rights. Below I enumerate a miscellany of medicines concerning some of which no detailed information was obtained, but which serve to suggest the total range of relevant ideas.

In 1910 I bought a 'big weasel' ($\hat{n}^u te$ *isáte*) medicine from a Pryor Indian. It consisted of a weaselskin stuffed with buffalo hair (Fig. 7). The seller told me that it had once been owned by a famous warrior, who would unwrap it when on an expedition, smoke it with incense, and hold it toward the hostile camp.

Some men tied both ears and the tail of a jack-rabbit to the back of their head when going to fight and also put green paint on their face from the lower lip down to the chin. Charges-camp had nothing to tie to his body in battle, but regarded the dog as his medicine and would sing dog songs when fighting. Lone-pine had a stuffed white-headed eagle for his war medicine; attached to it and worn round the neck was a whistle without a hole but which the owner was able to blow in making medicine. Where-the-sun-sits (áx'ace-arawátsic) used a stuffed magpie with iron eyes and horse-

Fig. 7 (50.1-3995). War Medicine.

hair in the beak to take the lead in war. Another man, who had had a vision of a gun, would smoke incense at the end of the gun, point it and say, "I should like you to hit the enemy and break his backbone or head." When he struck an enemy, he would break his spine. Dung-face used a common stick for his war medicine and was a successful warrior; the stick was called *t̄'pace* (marrow-pumper?). Another captain used a *matsápuəte* (birch?) stick with five or six prongs at the top, each tipped with magpie tails and decorated with red plumes at the bottom. Unlike other medicines, this one was never wrapped up but kept exposed.

Bull-all-the-time received various medicines from an old shaman including a stuffed chicken-hawk (*ba+ǐ'pūctsìǝ*) and a hoop (*mâxe*) wrapped with otterskin and decorated with eagle feathers. My informant used the hoop in war with great success. He accompanied General Miles and destroyed a whole Shoshoni camp, killed two Dakota on his next venture, stole horses from the Flathead on another occasion, and later recovered horses and saddles from thieving Dakota,—all through the medicines received. When he destroyed the enemy's camp, Bull-all-the-time presented the shaman with two horses; when he came home empty-handed, he did not give him anything.

Bull-tongue showed me his war medicine consisting of one male and one female hawk (*isâ'tsisé*). He tied the male to his own head, and the female to some other person's in battle; the wearer would take a gun and·strike a coup. This medicine was made for my informant by his father-in-law. Bull-tongue regards the female as more sacred because he sees it in dreams showing him the next winter or some other season. He does not really *see* the bird in his dreams, yet he feels that it is the female, not the male, that shows him the next season.

A visionary once made a coyote medicine for Gray-bull and prophesied what he would do against the enemy, e.g., "You will meet an enemy in such and such a place and kill him," or he might describe the kind of horse my informant would capture. All his predictions came true. Another medicine secured by my informant consisted of a tooth from the skull of White-cub, the greatest of Crow shamans, who had been killed. One of his teeth was kept for medicine and Gray-bull got it. Whenever he went out with it, White-cub would always speak to him so that he was afraid of it. He always advised Gray-bull what to do. Soon after getting the tooth, my informant went on an expedition and put it over his bed. It made a noise, saying several times, "They are coming!" The other members of the party were terrified and ran into a little shelter. They asked, "What is the matter? We heard your medicine speaking." Gray-bull was the only one who understood about it and said that about dawn a man would come close to their resting-place, he did not know whether a Crow or an enemy. At dawn a Dakota was seen near by and driven off, Gray-bull capturing his horse and all his belongings. A number of Crow horses had been stolen by Dakota, and these were recovered. Gray-bull used his medicine on four expeditions.

A maternal uncle of Gray-bull's gave him a bird tail to be tied to his head when fighting; attached to the tail was the head of a bird and a piece of beaded buckskin was sewed to it. Gray-bull paid a horse and other property for it. The same kinsman gave him a necklace consisting of beads and bird claws. This was supposed to be connected with the Moon, and subsequently Gray-bull had a dream in which the Moon appeared and gave him a song (p. 321). His uncle had not given him a song with the necklace because he himself had not had a vision of the Moon. Gray-bull was a young man and a scout at the time of this experience. It happened sometimes that a man would dream about a medicine after receiving it; sometimes men would take a medicine after acquiring it and fast with it, so as to get a revelation. For this medicine Gray-bull did not pay anything.

A crescent-shaped brass breast ornament, though apparently also connected with the Moon and received from the same uncle, is regarded as a distinct medicine. Gray-bull lost the original and made three copies. It did not matter since the Moon knew him. He was the third man to own this medicine. Old-crow had a brass full-moon for his medicine; when he went out as captain, he would dream the position of the enemy but did not see the Moon herself.

Several informants mentioned a war medicine carried on the back that was called *íriə*, after the dart used in the hoop game (*batsík̄isuə*). It was wrapped in black cloth, had feathers at the end, and lacked the white clay painted at intervals on the *íriə* used in playing the game. White-arm described it as a stick of some wood resembling the *masûpuəte* and about three feet long. At the center was a sea-shell (*maxûxe*) ornament; between it and either tip there was this succession of decorative appendages: red plumes (*ma+ôce*), magpie tail feathers, red plumes, and at the end a weaselskin fringe.

According to White-arm this *íriə* was discovered by Long-otter when he was mourning the death of a daughter on a peak on the other side of Bozeman. Some being had seen him before he fell asleep; it was seated under a pine tree with this medicine over it. The man rose, took the *íriə*, laid it on the ground, unwrapped it, sang a song, and threw the stick, naming some country. It fell there, and Long-otter heard praise-songs and words of thanks. Then the visitant sang a praise-song and walked to the mountain top. Long-otter returned to camp, not knowing whether he had been sleeping or not. Everything he saw came true. His visitant was an eagle. Long-otter made three or four copies after his vision.

Looks-at-a-bull's-penis is also credited with a vision of the *íriə*. He once went out fasting, but could not endure the hardships for more than three days, when he returned. Then Cunning-man[1] gave him instructions. He told him to put on new clothes, also to make a sweatlodge before sunrise and to leave camp as soon as possible when he wanted to go for a vision. Whenever he returned from a quest thereafter, Cunning-man went to him and asked whether he had seen anything, but he had nothing to tell. Once he went again, going up the same hill as before, and stayed three days and nights. Then at sunset he saw an *tria*, and returned on the fourth evening. Cunning-man again visited him and asked, "Has anything happened yet?" He told what he had seen. At that time he was so poor that he was obliged to walk. Cunning-man said, "What you have seen is a great thing."

The people moved to the site of Yellow-crane's present dwelling place and camped there. Several men went up the mountains. Looks-at-a-bull's-penis went lower down, fasting two days. In a dream he was told to come this way. When the would-be visionaries returned, all built sudatories, sweated themselves, and told what they had experienced. Looks-at-a-bull's-penis said that nothing had happened to him except that he had been told to go in a certain direction. He went and stayed there for three days. He was shown a place where there was light. He came home and saw another vision. He saw a spot up the creek near Lodge Grass canyon and a child-woman there. Returning after a few days he came near Black Canyon. His first vision had been an *tria* but he had not understood it. Now he stayed for three days, dreamt, and understood the *tria*. He saw the child-woman again. He returned and after a few days set out with five men for another revelation. He said to himself, "Now I will try to stay four days." He stayed four days and was always on the point of starvation. A hawk (*ma+tpxdxe*) adopted him, then he returned home. He walked slowly from weakness. A bear jumped up and caught him. He thought he was being killed, but the bear held him up and asked whether he could see all the world. "Yes." Then the bear said, "Put your fingers into my mouth." The bear had no teeth.

The woman he had seen in a vision was married by one of Looks-at-a-bull's-penis's brothers, who was killed the following year. His widow was with child and gave birth to Medicine-crow. Looks-at-a-bull's-penis married the widow. The light he had seen in his vision was a *bacôritsi'tse* (see p. 385).

---

[1]This volume, 256 seq.

Looks-at-a-bull's-penis made an *íriə* and called all the children to make them touch it and pray to it.   He built a sweatlodge, bade the children bring firewood, and made them sweat.   Then none of them died young and they grew up increasing the population.   When he saw big birds up in the air, he would make medicine and they would come down to him forthwith.   He had frogs for his *bātsirśpe*.   He had medicine to make horses run fast.   People with race horses would give him four presents so that he might make their horses swift.   He made hawk-medicine for Medicine-crow, who was subsequently also adopted by a hawk in a vision.   Looks-at-a-bull's-penis was a member of the Tobacco society and would make the Tobacco grow by making medicine with *isé*.

A war medicine of some consequence, part of which was secured by Mr. Simms of the Field Museum in Chicago, is called *batsípe*, Digging-stick.   It is derived from the witch Hícictawìə[1] and consists of a number of sticks, of which the largest is decorated with a lightning line;   the smaller sticks were kept out of sight.   This medicine was carried by the captain of war parties.   According to Flat-head-woman, it was made by the owner of the Sacred Arrow (p. 391).   Another informant says that Takes-twice first saw the *batsípe* in a vision granted by Hícictawìə, that Dúritɛc (Humpback) made the specimen owned by Whinnies, and that Robert Raise-up must have sold the medicine to Mr. Simms.

Dr. J. A. Mason of the Field Museum has kindly sent me the following detailed description of the bundle —

The principal stick is 1 m. long and 3 cm. wide at the head, 2½ cm. wide in the middle.   It is entirely covered with red ocher.   The lower end comes to a rather blunt point, while the upper end consists of three rings.   At this end there are tied with thongs of buckskin seven pendent eagle feathers also covered with red ocher.   The length of the stick is incised with a zigzag line consisting of just about a hundred angles.   On the opposite side there is a crude representation of two arms and hands incised, as you will see in the enclosed rubbing.   Then there are three plain sticks about 1 cm. in width and covered with red ocher.   They range from 103 to 107 cms. in length.   There are four sticks about 88 cm. long and 1 cm. wide, well-rounded and covered with ocher.   The lower end is pointed, while the upper end is left in two bands which still retain the natural bark, evidently a cherry, to which stick are tied with buckskin thongs two pendent eagle feathers which have been dyed purple and then covered with red ocher.   On each stick one feather is complete, while the other feather has been stripped for half its length.   In each case there are smaller red feathers attached to the base of the large feather.   The last stick is like these latter, except that it is shorter, 69 cm. long, and apparently made from a manufactured turned and varnished rod.

---

[1] This volume, 128, 204.

When leading war parties Gray-bull took with him the skin of a bur-
rowing animal, decorated with numerous woodpecker feathers.   A piece
of wood was attached to the back, and on the ventral side there was a ring
of beads representing a hoop.   Two strings served to tie the medicine
round the neck.   Hawk-bells and an elk tooth below formed additional
decorative features.   During horse raids Gray-bull used another medicine, which he showed me.   It consisted of a buffalo-skin representation
of a horse, supplied with strings so it could be tied round the neck.

MAGIC.

With a people who stress to so great an extent as the Crow the importance of visions and the aid supplied by the supernatural guardians
appearing on such occasions it is difficult to divorce magical from animistic practices.   That is to say, a certain procedure resembling the
magical performance of other peoples may ultimately derive its efficacy
from the revelations of a spirit.   Nevertheless, there is little doubt that
to some extent imitative magic is used without a clear-cut spiritual association.   Thus, at the close of the Tobacco adoption ceremony all spectators raise aloft whatever they are holding in their hands and this sym-
bolizes the growth of the Tobacco.   So, in the account of sorcery under
the head of shamanism (p. 345) the employment of imitative magic in
conjunction with reliance on animistic aid has already been pointed out.
Altogether, however, it may safely be stated that pure magic occupies a
very subordinate position in Crow life as contrasted with activities
based on visionary experiences.   Such performances of weather magic as
are attributed to Lone-tree and Big-ox (p. 344) are explicitly or implicitly
derived from their guardian spirits.   Perhaps the *bacóritsi'tse* form the
most important case of a group of objects not ordinarily revealed in
visions and possessing powers independently of spirits.

Bull-tongue showed me a stick used to attract women.   It was over
a foot long and was decorated with buffalo hair twice that length; near
the bottom of the stick there was a dewclaw on each side.   The owner
carried this implement in dances, using it as a fan.   Unfortunately I did
not ascertain whence the stick derived its power, but from all I have
learned concerning Crow notions I feel convinced that it must have been
revealed in a vision.

This was certainly true of the majority of love-charming methods.
The term *dúck'ûo*, also used for casting an evil spell in other connections
(p. 345), is specifically employed for love-charming.   Charming a woman
is called *bīə-rúck'ûo* and a woman who charms a man is designated as

ak-batsɛ́-rúckʼuɘ. Both in legend and in every-day life the elk is credited with taking pity on a man spurned by a woman and endowing him with irresistible powers of fascination.[1] Sometimes a tangible substance is given to the visionary to attract his mistress, e.g., different kinds of perfume or moss and an eagle plume, or elk dewclaws strung together and attached to a little sweetgrass. In revenge for his mistress's cruelty the legendary lover is represented as repudiating her after having gained his ends. At Pryor I saw a robe of elk hide on which was depicted a female elk in front of a male. This blanket, I was told, had been dreamt by a man eager to possess a woman who had spurned him. After going to the mountains and praying, he saw the robe in a vision and subsequently captivated the girl with it.

A woman deserted by her husband might go in quest of a vision and receive instructions. She might be told to burn incense and smoke her clothing with it; also to use certain songs and then walk toward her husband. These words were given as typical of such songs:—

frɘk		batsɛ́c		húrθm,		awáka		húreke.
That		man		is coming,	I see him	coming.

According to one informant the woman receives a special weed-medicine to be incensed and it is its odor that compels the husband to come to her. Then other women will come to her when in similar difficulties and ask for doses of the same medicine.

---

[1] This volume, 191, 196.

OFFERINGS AND PRAYERS.

The Sun is preëminently the recipient of offerings and the object of supplication. In the old days a man setting out on a war party would say to the Sun: "If I bring something back, I will give you eagle feathers." Sometimes fox hides and later red cloths were substituted. The latter were always decorated with a black circle and usually a bunch of broad-leafed sagebrush was tied to the cloth together with a horse's tail. There was first a gathering of about ten persons in a tipi, and about sunrise they would begin to sing, singing four songs. When they had done, they took the cloth out, brought little children over to where they were holding it and made them touch it, the children themselves voicing the wish that they might live till the next winter.

The sweatlodge is generally conceived as a Sun offering, and all albino buffalo skins were ceremonially given to this supernatural being.

The presentation of a white buffalo to the Sun is already mentioned by Maximilian.[1] It was described by a number of informants. Three-wolves said that the Crow sometimes encountered a yearling buffalo calf, white either on the back or heart or tail. The man who killed such a calf went home without touching it, gave a present to one of his father's clansmen, and told him he had slain a white calf. The father's clansman would go out, locate the calf, which invariably fell with its face towards the east,[2] and skin it carefully so as not to cut the hide, which was then turned over very slowly. The meat was not touched at all, for it was said, "If you eat of the meat, your hair will turn gray prematurely." The father's clansman took the hide to camp, singing a song in praise of his clansman's son and praying that this man might have good luck. Then he would take the hide to one of *his* father's clansmen, saying, "I have brought you this hide for you to offer it to the Sun." The old man would take the skin, tie it to a long pole, carry it through camp with a laudatory chant, and say, "I shall offer this to the Sun; I want everybody in camp to touch this hide." He went from the camp towards sunrise, planted the stick into the ground, and said, "Sun, I have given you a blanket." Then he prayed for coups or horses, or that his relatives should live to the next season without illness. He might say, "The people have done a great thing in giving you this, they wish for . . ." Usually only old people asked for gifts. Four offering songs without words were sung. This offering was made just before sunrise.

---

[1]Maximilian, Prinz zu Wied, *Reise in das innere Nord-America in den Jahren* 1832 *bis* 1834 (Coblenz, 1841), vol. 1, 401.
[2]This is confirmed by all other informants.

Gray-bull recollected an albino buffalo that was killed near Hardin, Montana; it was the fastest buffalo in the herd and when a hunter crossed its tracks, his horse would be exhausted. On this occasion the man who usually made Sun offerings was not of the party, hence the leader himself made the offering. The hunters counted coup on the white buffalo and the four coup-strikers ate the kidney, no other part of the flesh being touched. Gray-bull struck the second coup and got a piece of the kidney; holding both hind legs he wished that he might capture a gun, get an enemy's body, and strike a second coup. That autumn the Crow killed some Piegan, and Gray-bull struck a coup, got an enemy's body and gun, and also captured a medicine pipe; the last-mentioned he got without having prayed for it.

Gray-bull distinguishes an albino buffalo, *bicê+ictsè*, and a yellow buffalo with a black spot on the back, *nîkawate*; instead of having the black circle, the latter sometimes was black from the sides down. The *nîkawate* were usually calves. The ceremonies for white and yellow buffaloes were alike. The songs used with them differed from those sung in offering red cloth.

One informant said that the killer of an albino buffalo rode home with the skin in front of him, singing praise songs, and presented the hide to the chief, who painted pictures of the sun and the rainbow on the back and tied a plume to the tail. At daybreak he sang a song, telling the Sun of the offering, attached it to a high pole, and placed it on a hill, where it was left to fall; no one would touch it thereafter.

Sitting-elk said that only a medicineman was permitted to skin an albino buffalo. The skin was suspended from an ash or cottonwood pole.

I secured two versions of the prayer uttered at the formal presentation of an albino skin to the Sun:—

1.

áx'acè, disâace díəwak'. baré-ambirəxbâk'e ítsi. bak'âte,
Sun, your robe, I make. Our way of living good (may it be). The children,

birəxbâk'e ítsik'âte á'tsipâre ahúi-mâtsik'.
the people peacefully (may they) multiply and be plentiful.

2.

kahé, mâsa'ka, kan-disâace díəwâhik. kam-barí'k'u,
Greeting, father's clansman, now your robe I have just made. Now I give it to you,

k'ôk'. ambìbirəxbâke ítsiə mak'ú. bac-birəx bâk'e ítse awírupe
this is it. My way of living good give me. My people (object) safely the next year

awâwi. bac-bak'âte á'tsipâri, barâk' dúxirek'âte
I shall reach with them. My children may they increase, my sons when on the warpath

itsírik'âte arûo, barâk' dúxire íse cipítə
horses (may they) bring, my son when on the warpath (with) face black[1]

---

[1]Indicating victory.

k‘úi.   amarîre   hutsé   biíc-k·oi,   bicé
may he return.   When I am on the move,   the wind   to my face may come,   the buffalo

bís   əxiə.   hinné bīəwəkce bac-bāpāre ítsi,   bátsurək
towards me   (may) gather.   This   summer   my plants   (may they be) good,   the cherries

ahúi.   báre   ítsi,   bá+isánde bɪ   hí-sai.   bīəwəkce
plenty.   The winter   (may it be) good,   illness   me   shall not reach.   Summer

bik·é - raraclə awákawi,   á²pe   arakúxke hɪ′irək   awákawi.   á²pe
grass   new   may I see,   leaves   full-sized   when they come   may I see.   Leaves

d ɛəxe   awákawi.   bíi′pe   basákāce   awákawi.   ambíawakusè awákawi,
leaves yellow   may I see.   Snowfall   the very first   may I see.   Spring   may I see,

bacbirəxbák‘e   xaxúə   ítsik·áte   awáwi.
my people   all   in safety   may I reach it (the season) with them.

From various statements it appears that making a ritualistic offering to the Sun, whether in the form of an albino buffalo skin or of red cloth, was viewed like other ceremonial privileges, i.e., was vested in individuals who directly or indirectly derived their authority from a vision. The Hardin offering ·was made by someone else avowedly as a makeshift; Medicine-crow's father and grandfather are mentioned as preëminently persons who presented the Sun with red cloth; and so forth.

Offerings are not restricted to the Sun, but may be made to any supernatural agency. Pryor Creek derives its name, *arû*ᵘ*t-â²ce*, i.e.,, Arrow-stream, from the injunction of a mythic dwarf who decreed that all the Indians passing a certain spot should shoot arrows into a cleft as an offering to him. The legendary incident reacted on actual practice for within the lifetime of my informants the rule was followed by the Crow.[1] Offerings were sometimes made to the fire, to water, or some curiously shaped rock, accompanied with some such utterance as, "Eat this, Water, so that I may live long." Beads were presented to the medicine rocks (*bacóritsi'tse*). Of course, the cutting of one's flesh in the quest of a vision is also regarded as a form of offering.

Offerings tended to ensure longevity. An old woman volunteered the information that she had made many offerings in her day; hence she had lived until her hair had turned gray. ·

The sweatlodge (*awúsuə*) is a form of offering that plays an important part in the life of the Crow Indians and has already been described in connection with the Tobacco ceremony. It is clear from the best accounts that primarily it was a distinctly ritualistic institution and was not indulged in without some definite religious purpose. Nowadays anyone may put up a sudatory and sweat, and there are men who have a passion for frequent indulgence in sweat-bathing which an interpreter compared to that of white people addicted to the cigarette-smoking

[1] This volume, 169 f.

habit. Anciently a sweatlodge was held sacred and might not be erected except by one who had acquired the title thereto either by personal vision or by purchase. Even those who had the privilege would only sweat, according to Bull-all-the-time, when prompted by a dream. Gray-bull and Bull-all-the-time agree that formerly only or mostly old people went into sudatories. Gray-bull stated that their use for medicinal purposes is relatively recent; they were formerly built when going on a war party, when returning from a successful raid with a horse or after striking a coup, and in connection with the Tobacco society. Bull-all-the-time says people would make conditional pledges to put up a sudatory. "If I get well, I'll erect a sweatlodge." "If I live till the fall, I shall make a sweatlodge." According to him the original use of the lodge was for old people, later the Crow came to use it for medicines (the Tobacco?) and in going on war parties, and finally anyone came to use it without particular reason.

Bull-all-the-time declared that the Moon originated the sweatlodge, that formerly sweatlodges were put up in Moon's honor in the evening and in Sun's in the morning. Only lately this informant has taken to putting up sudatories at noon. The sweatlodge had been his adopted father's medicine. According to Gray-bull, the sweatlodge was put up in honor of the Sun, who was regarded as the owner. This he remarked, appeared from the formula used in making the vow of erection, viz.:—

mäsa·ka,	bä+ítsem	acέ	āwä́-rək,	awúsuə	díəwä̂wik'.
My father's clansman,	something good	camp	if I bring to,	sweatlodge	I shall make.

The point of this argument is that the stem for father's clansman is used in vocative form only when praying to the Sun. Little-rump says that in going to war the sweatlodge was erected in honor of Old-woman's-Grandson.

Today the same sweathouse frame may be used repeatedly, but in the old days when the people were constantly on the move and sweatlodges were much more rarely employed there was little chance to use a frame a second time. The number of willows used for the frame varies from twelve to one hundred. Medicine-crow, in describing the Tobacco ritual, said the number might be one hundred or any number with four in the units' place, from fourteen to ninety-four. Three-wolves asserted that twelve-willow frames were reckoned less sacred than others and had the fireplace on the side instead of in the center. Others did not associate the latter detail with the number of sticks but declared that the fashion of shifting the fireplace to the side was a recent innovation borrowed from the Nez Percé.

Three-wolves furnished the following account of the procedure:—

The first four stones are put into the fireplace, one by one, by means of a forked stick. When the fourth has been deposited, the stone-bearer voices some wish, whereupon he may throw in as many rocks as he pleases, two by two. Water is set down by the stones. The bathers enter, one by one, never walking in front of the stone-tender. The lodge is covered, then one man dips his hand into the water and sprinkles four handfuls on the rocks, whereupon four wishes are expressed. The man nearest the entrance tells of a dream, such as, "I have seen snow on the ground," or, "I have seen horsetracks." The rest cry, "Thanks!" and pray aloud: "May I get there!" (if a season has been mentioned.) The door is flung open and the inmates cool off. The dreamer recounts a second dream, then the cover is put on again. Now seven handfuls are poured on the rocks to symbolize the Dipper. After the period of sweating the second man from the door tells his dreams, and the lodge is uncovered for a while. Next ten cupfuls are poured on the rocks and the third man tells his dreams. The fourth time they throw on an uncounted (*tsimúsuə*)[1] number of handfuls. The fourth man tells only one dream, then cries, "Throw the door wide open!" All now jump up and run into the river. While inside the bathers scourge themselves with horsetail[2] or sagebrush whips in order to perspire still more. In the smaller lodges five or six sweat themselves at a time; in the larger ones from ten to twelve.

Other informants add some interesting details. Bull-all-the-time says that in the winter some men would roll in the snow after a sweat-bath. According to him, the lodge is carpeted with sagebrush. Four times they pretend to put *isé* incense on the fireplace, and the fifth time they actually do so. This, if I understand my informant correctly, takes place before the deposition of the rocks. Gray-bull explained that the dirt removed from the fireplace is piled up outside the frame between the door and the fire in which the rocks are heated and that no one is permitted to pass between. The man to pour water entered first and sat down on the left side from one entering; the rest passed in behind him, all going on the left side. While the first four rocks were deposited, all in the lodge kept quiet. After the fourth stone they all expressed their wishes (Three-wolves only mentions the stone-carrier in this connection). When the water-pourer has told of the season he has dreamt of, the people both inside and outside cry, "Thanks!" Then the door is opened. After a while the pourer says, "Close the door! All of us shall get there[3] together." While the door is open, water is put in and all the bathers drink of it. One of them will say, "I am drinking the long rain" (*xar-átsgʿe kʿō icbĭkʿ*). This refers to the long rain in the fall and is equivalent to a prayer that the speaker and his companions may live to see the next fall. When all have drunk, the dreamer says, "Close the door. I want

---

[1] From *tsimé*, to count; *su*, not (plural form).
[2] Buffalo tails mounted on short sticks are perhaps more common.
[3] That is, to the season mentioned.

to drink in peace" (*itsik ăta biricbiwik*). Gray-bull describes this drinking feature as if it belonged to the second intermission; it is not clear whether it is restricted to that period or not. As an offering the sweatbathers would tie red cloth to a stick and lean it against the sweatlodge. Little-rump says that the stick with the red cloth, for which an eagle wing might be substituted, was put on top of the lodge and the owner would say, addressing Old-woman's-grandson, "I have made this sweatlodge because you told me to make it. (*Kăricbāpituəc, bā-wi-diə-ra'tsic hinném kan-diəwak'*.) I give you this red cloth (or eagle wing)." On the red cloth were marked stars or moons and sometimes a circle to represent the sun. The owner sat on the left side for one entering and would sing songs; all who came in were expected to sing. The floor of the lodge was nicely prepared, being covered with ground-cedar, and charcoal was sprinkled on it. Little-rump bought the privilege of making a sweatlodge and puts one up twice a year, in the spring and in the fall, in obedience to the instructions received at the time of the purchase. Sometimes he has made a hundred-willow lodge.

Women are not excluded from the sweatlodge but they enter it more particularly in connection with Tobacco adoptions, when they normally sit by their husbands.

My personal experience with Crow sweatlodges is the following. I omit matters of routine described above. In the summer of 1910 Medicine-crow was telling me about the sweatlodge and offered to take me into one since he had intended going in that afternoon anyway. For several hours the rocks were heated in a big fire. Medicine-crow, One-star, and Plenty-hawk entered the open frame stripped to their geestrings, while I retained my drawers. Into the uncovered lodge were passed the rocks, which even then created a terrific heat. When all had been passed in, the blankets were thrown on the frame, covering it completely and making the lodge pitch dark. When water was thrown on the rocks, producing steam, the heat became almost unbearable and I availed myself of the utter darkness slightly to raise a flap of one of the blankets and thrust my nose into the air. When the blanket was raised I saw that my companions were like myself bathed in perspiration. I had had enough and withdrew. The Indians assured me I would catch cold unless I immediately bathed in the nearby creek, but I declined and of course suffered no disagreeable consequences. The Indians continued their sweat-bathing in the prescribed fashion and after the final lifting of the cover they proceeded to plunge into the cold water of the stream.

Prayers have been cited in different connections, notably under the heading of Visions; also in the earlier part of this chapter. The concept of praying is an old one, and a modern church is designated as *aratsiwaká+u,* the place where they pray. Women as well as men offered prayers. Young-crane said she only prayed when there was a specific reason for it. For example, when her kin went out to fight she would thus address Old-Man-Coyote or the Sun:—

Isá'kawùətəkāt,   bI wakúte   napforetì.
Dear Old-Man-Coyote,   those around me   may they not be killed.

When one of her relatives went away somewhere, she offered a corresponding prayer:—

Isá'kawùətəkāt,   ìtsik'àta   k'ûi.
Dear Old-Man-Coyote,   in safety   may he come back.

When her husband was killed, she mourned his loss and cut off a finger joint, but did not pray then.

In smoking it was proper to point the pipe first up, then down, next offering it to the four cardinal directions. In so doing, Gray-bull would pray to the four winds; he had learned the prayer from Bell-rocks, to whom he was indebted for other religious instruction. Occasionally he also offered smoke to the full-moon. Men owning medicine-pipes also pointed them in the manner explained above.

TABOOS.

Tribal taboos are by no means prominent, and individual ones are naturally based on specific visionary instructions. Maximilian mentions the superstition against smoking a pipe in a lodge where footgear is suspended; he also states that when men smoke in a group each one takes not more than three puffs, whereupon he hands the pipe with a special sort of movement to his left-hand neighbor.[1] I am inclined to regard the former custom as a purely personal regulation. Since the connection between moccasins and smoking is not obvious, it is worth recalling that according to Lewis and Clark the Shoshoni as a sign of friendship removed their moccasins before smoking. Personally, I failed to get this corroborated, but an old Lemhi told me that medicinemen formerly took off their moccasins when smoking during the treatment of a patient.[2] Mr. Spier learned of a similar rule in the case of certain Kiowa Sun dance participants.

Taboos were common in connection with a *bàtsirópe*. In this case the usual consequence of a transgression was the appearance of the *bàtsirópe*. For example, there is an old woman whose *bàtsirópe* does not like to hear crying. Once her grandchild was crying, and a cedar (spray?) began to come out of her mouth.

In this as in some other instances the observance of the rule is not necessarily dependent on a person's volition. One informant said that he was told never to allow the young of any animal to be taken to his lodge. Some one must have taken some young animal there unknown to the owner, which would account for the rheumatism that has afflicted him for eleven years.

Food taboos were sometimes imposed at the time of a vision or when medicines were bought. Thus, when Gray-bull slept in the Tobacco garden, he was ordered not to eat the manifolds of a buffalo or cow; and when he secured some bird medicine he was told not to eat birds' eggs. He was still obeying these prohibitions at the time of my interview.

---

[1] Maximilian, *ibid.*, 400.
[2] Lowie, this series, vol. 2, 213.

MISCELLANEOUS DATA.

Jim Carpenter tells me that children must not lie on their stomachs, facing the fire, and are scolded if they do so, because it is a sign that their mother will die soon.

If a cocoon (*ak'iréwe*) is tied round a baby's neck, it will not readily wake up; hence this device is resorted to in the case of infants who cry too much.

Horned-toads were not regarded as persons, but they were believed to understand the Crow language. Girls would take a horned-toad, lay it on its ventral (?) side, gently rub it, and then say, "May I become a good bead-worker! May my children be born without difficulty!" Then they slipped the animal down inside the neck part of their dress and allowed it to fall down. A boy would say, "May I be able to make a good bow and arrows!" Gray-bull consulted horned-toads with regard to the location of buffalo, judging by the direction in which the animals faced.

Before going on the warpath a man would sometimes kill a buffalo, take some of the blood from its shoulderblade, and spill some badger blood over it. In this mixture he could see a reflection of himself. If he saw himself with a wrinkled face, it meant that he would live to be an old man; if his image showed the scalp cut off, it meant that this fate would befall him. In the latter case he would be afraid to go on the warpath. If the hair of the image fell down over the face, it meant a natural death, while blood streaming down of course signified a violent end. In reply to the question whether he had ever used this form of divination himself, my informant, Bull-all-the-time, said that he was afraid of it (*bɑtsirik'*). Gray-bull said that this form of divination was not in vogue in his day, because people were afraid to use it. However, his grandfather had resorted to it and, having seen his reflection with white hair and wrinkled face, he became very brave and would thereafter dash into the midst of the enemy and wrest away their guns.

Wolf's-white-belly (*tsɛt-ɛ̃re-tsɪəc*) once went to herd horses. He watered them, took them out to the hills, and laid down a rope. Then he took his saddle and sat on it. While watching his horses, he felt something move under his seat. He thought he would go home, took off his blanket, and tried to take the rope, but it had turned into a snake. He had to leave the rope there and go home without it. Next morning he came where he had left it. The snake had turned back into a rope as before.

Scolds-the-bear was about fourteen years old when the Crow were camped fifteen miles above the site of Forsyth on the Yellowstone River. A boy about sixteen years old, being the oldest of the boys, had the rest gather round him for a leader. They played being on a war party and imitated warriors. They took bark and used it as a scalp. This boy's father saw them and said, "Two days from now I'll send my boy on a war party and all of you shall go with him." He was roused by the boy's playing and had this announced by the crier. After the boys had started and gone some distance they waited. Scolds-the-bear was in the party. The boy's father also went along, but his son was leader; he had two center tail feathers of a magpie tied to the back of his head and at the bottom there were red-dyed plumes. This was his medicine. Only one white man's hut was standing where we camped in the day. In the evening the boy's father had disappeared. At night he returned. "All you boys, saddle up, there's one enemy there whom we'll fight." In this basin they came upon a man in an Indian coat with a knife in his hand. This man ran after the boy. They could not kill him. The smallest boys got scared and merely watched. He chased one boy, when another ran behind him and shot him in the back. One boy hit him first, thus gaining a first coup. It was a long-haired man of about forty; they stripped off his clothing and scalped him. "All you boys, I'll give you a chance to look at it tomorrow; don't turn back to look at it," said the leader's father. They went home and after eating went to bed. The next morning they brought horses, which happened to go to the place of the killing. Scolds-the-bear chanced to go for horses. Though told not to look, he disobeyed. What they had killed was only a rotten piece of wood shaped like a man. The arms and legs were only of ground-cedar. The knife was a real knife, which like the clothing belonged to the man who made it. The scalp they took off was that of a former enemy and had been placed on the head of the manikin. When they scalped, the blood looked as if fresh; the next day it was dry like an old scalp. The leader of that boys' party is living still. There are many other witnesses to this *bakumbíriu* (p. 347).

Long ago the Crow suffered from a heavy storm in the early part of the spring; when the grass came up and colts were born, they had to fix blankets for the colts so as to protect them against dying from the cold. The people called the storm Dog's-vulva (*micg'e'-cirèc*). One spring the storm was especially violent and blankets were provided for all the newborn colts. One man coming home through the storm caught sight of a man wearing a hat, overcoat, and gloves. Putting down his load, the

Crow took his gun and killed the stranger. After returning he told the people he had killed Dog's-vulva. They would not believe it. He said he would prove it. All the people came out to see what he had killed, being very anxious about it. When they arrived, they found an old piece of wood. Since that time they never suffered from that storm.

Mr. Simms has described and figured a peculiar stone monument situated in the Big Horn range in Wyoming just across the Montana boundary. From a stone 'hub' about 3 feet high he found 27 spokes, i.e., lines of stones, radiating to a stone circle about 245 feet in diameter; at or near the periphery there were seven smaller stone structures.[1] According to Flat-dog this monument was regarded by the Crow as the Sun's lodge, i.e., as a lodge made for the Sun and used by him as a camping-place. As a boy Flat-dog walked through it, counting fifty steps. Many of the Crow would go there to fast; the structure has been there as long back as any period alluded to by previous generations. Those who fasted there would sometimes hear steps of some one walking, but looking up would see nothing. Of such a one the other people were wont to say, "He is a coward, that is why he did not see a vision." This meant that he had been terrified by the sound and had looked round, thus losing the vision he would otherwise have secured.

The High Lodge dance (*ac-hátsg'i-risùə*) was never performed by the Crow until about twenty-five years ago (in 1914), when they saw the Nez Percé dance it. A member of that tribe told Old-dog the following story. One very cold winter evening a young man fell sick and died as the darkness was setting in. The people cried all night. They said, "We'll dig a hole and bury him tomorrow." In the morning they built a fire. The dead man rose and said, "Cook, I want to eat." They cooked breakfast and he ate. He called for the Nez Percé chief and said to him, "I wish to talk with you." "All right." "I am talking with you now, but at noon my father will take me back. Bid all the young men in your tribe prepare a feast and bring it in." They did so. "Let all men come into the tent." When all were there and had sat down, he continued: "I am going to sing; learn my song." He had a bell in his hand, which he shook, singing his song till all inside the lodge knew it. "All shall sing it now." When he felt sure that all knew it, he rose and danced, singing at the same time. He told them he should die and was not to be buried at once. All were to stand in two rows facing each other and were to sing and dance to the song. During this performance he was to be washed and laid

---

[1] S. C. Simms, A Wheel-shaped Stone Monument in Wyoming, (*American Anthropologist*, N. S., vol. 5, 1903), 107 seq.

down. Then a hole was to be dug and he should be buried. "Hereafter, whenever any one dies in the winter, do exactly the same way." Thereafter they were to dance for four days and buffalo would flock from all directions so there would be no trouble about the meat supply. The young man did not order this of his own accord but for some being above. When the Nez Percé observed this ceremony they camped in a circle; not so the Crow, who did not regard it as sacred.

APPENDIX.

The Five Brothers.[1]

Once there was a big Crow camp on the Yellowstone belonging to the Many-lodges division. All the Indians were seized with cramps and died except five boys. These picked up their bows, arrows, and sinews, in search of other Indians. They had a flint to strike fire with, but it got worn out, so they were obliged to drill fire. They lived on birds and rabbits. In the season when the meadowlarks grow fat they sighted a big camp in the Big Horn Mountains. They said, "Let us wait before going in." On the side of a watering-place there was a thick brush, where they cooked and ate some meadowlarks late at night. They slept. The next day the men watering their horses saw the five boys. One man tending a herd turned them loose and entered the river to swim. He came out, carrying his clothes on his arm. The three older boys were asleep. Their birds and rabbits were cooking. The other men who were there did not invite the boys, but this man said, "Come with me to my tipi; wake up your brothers." These three were bashful at first. He said, "Come over and eat with me." "Wait till we have eaten our rabbits here." "Come, you will have a better meal there." When done, he took them to his camp. His first wife had died and his second wife's husband had fallen in battle. They had no children of their own and the woman's brothers had been killed by the enemy; her mother was living in another tipi. The man said to his wife: "You have been worrying about your brothers; I have brought you these to be your brothers." She sent the two youngest to her mother next door and said, "I am your sister, you are my brothers." She cooked a great deal of meat, giving them a better meal than they had had. "Have you enough?" "Yes." She made a bed for them.

The boys got fatter. They left, saying they were going to fast and he should not worry about them. Each chose a place of his own, the one a point, a second a knoll, and so on. One went to a gap and saw a snake fighting with a rock-lizard (*itārire* = *horned-toad*?). The snake had eaten up all its young. Where the boy was walking there was a slide and he followed the lizard to a cave, where it disappeared. It came out again with a male, hiding under a grass-grown knoll. The snake passed and the male caught it by its throat. It tried to wriggle loose. The female remained hidden, not knowing what to do. The snake could not

---

[1] This tale was found among my notes after the publication of other myths.

free itself and died.[1] The toad cut it open, and the little ones came out still alive. All the toads went where the parents had come from. The visionary as a result of his experience became a doctor.

The boy who was fasting on a point seated himself and looked down. He saw a light, but in the morning he could not find it. On the fourth morning he planted a stake in the spot where he thought the light might be. At night he saw the light and the stake a little above it. He went there and found a black *bacôritsi'tse* on top of some buffalo chips. This was the source of the light. The third boy saw a vision making him a good shot; he had four arrows. The two youngest boys did not fast but stayed at home.

A young man who had killed two deer passed the fasters. He said, "You must be hungry, pick out what you want to eat." They selected the hindquarters, front legs, and paunch, and asked him to build a fire for them. He did so; they cooked, ate, and went home. When they got home, the boy who had seen the sacred rock hung it up above his pillow. His brother-in-law was out hunting and killed a buffalo. His wife was going to make a parfleche but the boy said, "Make me a medicine bag (*bâcucè*)." They went to the river and painted the bag, dug up sweet-grass, dried it, smoked it and put it into the container on top of the medicine rock.

The boy who had seen the snake asked his brother-in-law, "What is a weasel-necklace (*â*ta-ware-âpia*)?" They did not know and sent for the older people, who said, "Our chief's son has one round his neck." It was made of the darkest part of an otter's skin decorated with weasel-skin and shells (*maxâxiə*); only well-to-do children wore it. The following morning the chief said, "Let us move camp to where there are buffalo." They moved. The boys left. The doctor could hear what was said at a great distance.   He heard his brother-in-law say, "I wish my brother-in-law were here to go with the hunters." The buffalo were chased and killed. The two younger boys got a man (?) and he gave them a buffalo to choose from, saying, "I'll carry it over to your grandmothers.' " The three older boys killed a fat buffalo with their medicine arrows. The young man took the two boys home. The three older boys butchered and divided their buffalo and got back late at night. They heard that the chief's son had been thrown from his horse and that his head was cracked. All night one could hear drums beating and the doctors' singing.

[1]Among the Paviotso of Nevada I discovered a strong belief in the power of the horned-toad to overcome a rattlesnake.

The young man said to the two boys, "You may keep the horse and saddle or bring it back as you please." The woman said, "Bring the horse back." They brought it back. The two boys told their three older brothers about it, and they said, "That is right, don't take what those people give you, we are orphans. We'll pay them back some time. The only ones we have anything to do with are our sister and our brother-in-law."

The doctor said to his brother-in-law, "Brother-in-law, tell the chief that we will doctor his boy." They wanted to get his necklace. Their sister said, "No, you are too young." Then they did not say anything. Their brother-in-law wanted to tell the chiefs, but his wife would not let him. He slipped out and told Cunning-man.[1] Cunning-man went to the chief and said, "Put all your presents together and go outside. The five boys over there want to doctor your son. Let no one pass in front of them. Have the door face the boys' tipi." Then it was announced that no one should cross the doctor's path. The five boys were glad. Four of them went ahead and the doctor came last. The two little ones sat down by their mother, the two older ones went to the foot of the bed, and the doctor stood by the door and stamped on the ground. The sick boy had been unconscious and was bleeding from the nose. When the doctor stamped on the ground, the patient groaned. The doctor came closer and stamped on the ground again. The boy sat up. A third time he did it, and the boy braced himself up. He went nearer and stamped the ground in front of the boy like a buffalo, turned back and ran for the door. The boy rose, followed him round and out of the tipi and came back again panting. He sat down and said, "Mother, I am hungry, give me something to eat." The chief was glad and gave them all presents and invited them to stay, but they would not do so. The boys said to their brother-in-law, "This is the first good thing we can do for you. You may keep these presents. The chief heard about the necklace and brought it to them. "That is what we wanted." They told their brother-in-law, "We are going on the warpath; do not tell anyone. If anyone asks, say 'They left me; I don't know where they have gone.'"

They started. The rock-visionary was leader. They had been gone two days when their brother-in-law was summoned to the council. "Where are your brothers-in-law?" "I don't know, they have left me." One man said in mockery, "If they should bring a big herd of horses, we should laugh." The doctor heard this from where they were and told

---

[1]This volume, 256.

his brothers. The rock-visionary said, "We'll see whether they are going to laugh." On the fifth day they saw an enemy with forty head of horses. They waited till he had halted. He did not go far. The horses were grazing. The rock-boy said, "Wait till he is asleep." He went up and blew out the enemy's brains. There were two especially fine horses, a pinto and a bay, the remainder were good too. It was a Piegan they had killed. The rock-visionary was leader, the arrow-owner killed the enemy, the doctor struck coups, the two little ones took the two best horses, the remainder were divided among them all. They returned. Before they got to the camp, the three older ones went ahead at night and got to their sister. They were hungry, and she cooked for them. She asked, "Where are your brothers?" "With the horses." She gave them breakfast for them. They told their brother-in-law to sing praise-songs. "If they ask you about it, say that you have had a good dream." So he acted accordingly, saying he had had a good dream about his brothers-in-law.

Soon the boys came into camp. Their brother-in-law took charge of their horses. The young man began to sing about the one who had mocked them, using the words he had uttered. After the horses had been corralled, they returned to the tipi. The women came and brought pemmican. "This is my sister's son." The leader of the war party threw their meat away. "When we were poor, they did nothing for us. We are going to deal only with our relatives and pay the two others who were kind to us." So they gave a horse to the man who had given them the deer and another to the man who had given meat to their younger brothers. "All the rest belong to you, brother-in-law and sister."

Not long after this the five boys were gone, no one knew where. The man said, "My brothers-in-law are gone." "You need not worry about them, they are men." They came back again with plenty of horses, all of which they gave to their brother-in-law. At this time the chief had a daughter. Young men wanted to buy her, but she refused their offers, though her father wished to own the horses offered. At last he said, "I want you to marry the doctor." So one night the girl came to where the three older boys were sleeping and lay down with the doctor. The following morning the brother-in-law roused his wife, saying "Your brothers are married." She looked and it was the chief's daughter. So she cooked for them and woke them up. "Which one have you come for?" she asked her sister-in-law. "I rejected all my suitors, and my father told me to come here, saying he would help me with property, so I have come to marry him." So they were married and after a while the young woman had her mother make moccasins for them and they went on the warpath.   They brought back seven head of horses, which they gave to the father-in-law.   The three older ones were named Medicine-stone, What-he-makes-is-medicine (the doctor), and Medicine-shot.

Some time after this the young woman invited them all to her tipi. The boys consulted with their sister, who said, "Yes, but don't go with him, he is married now." They went after buffalo, the people being short of meat. They shared the game and turned over the meat to the young woman's mother, who said to her daughter, "That is what I want. You refused your suitors but you met the right one."

The people moved. In the winter they camped. It snowed so they could not go hunting, and all their meat supply was consumed. If anyone killed a deer, his meat was soon gone. All the Crow were starving, so that they ate roseberries and boiled hair or deer hide for food.   The mother-in-law spoke to her daughter.   "Talk to your husband about this; see whether he can help us." She spoke to him, but he said nothing in reply. He saw his sister, returned and said, "I will get meat but they must get a beaver's castoreum."   The girl told her father and the crier announced it. Men asked to see the performance. "You may come in, but don't touch the door and don't go out." He got his medicine, which was hanging up, and they brought the castoreum. When all were in the tipi, the medicine rock was exposed; some of its sweetgrass covering was chopped fine and was smoked for incense. The stone was greased all over with the beaver musk, then it got smoky and foggy inside. All the smoke passed out óf the smoke-hole and as it did so the clouds outside began to part, the snowfall abated and it cleared up. When all the smoke had passed out of the lodge, there were no more clouds. The whole camp rejoiced and asked the young man to help them get meat. "I have done enough, the buffalo will come." He told the women not to chop wood. The men hunted buffalo for three days, killing plenty of them.   They were told not to break any buffalo backbones. They killed so many that each family had two rows of jerked meat about twenty feet long.

The shaman's wife told her father to tell the Indians to blacken their faces since some of the enemy were coming. It was in the spring of the year.   The enemies came; the Crow killed two Piegan and had a big round dance. The young men assembled and sang a song throughout the camp: "What I said is coming true, I am going." There was no more sickness, all people lived well since the coming of the boys.   The doctor had his wife decorated with elk teeth.

The three older brothers were married, only the two younger ones were still single. The rock-owner said, "I have been told to go over to One-tree (*mare-tát'*)[1] and live there." He was leader of the camp and everything was done in accordance with his commands. He went to the Yellowstone. All the country was covered with buffalo. The Crow kept in the woods out of sight of the game. They continued hunting buffalo, making two trips a day, and had an abundance of meat. This was in the winter time. It was so cold that the grease froze into solid condition in the morning. The rock-owner told his wife not to break any stones in their tipi. One day he went to his sister to sleep. He was told that his mother-in-law had cracked bones in the tipi. He told his wife about it. She went to her mother. "You broke a rock in here." "No, I never did." "How can my husband lie? Let me look." She saw that a rock had been cracked. She scolded her mother, "That's the worst thing you could have done." The mother went out crying. The herald announced that the enemy were stealing horses. "Get your best horses, we'll pursue them." They took the best horses. Four young men went along. One young man had no horse left and asked the shaman to help him recover his horses. "No, I did not go along because my mother-in-law broke the stone in my lodge." The young man went away. Another man whose son had been killed by the Piegan came to the shaman and asked him to help him get revenge, saying, "I have been mourning for a long time." But the shaman refused, giving the same reasons. This man cried. The war party was waiting for this shaman, but he sent a message that he was not going. However, when he heard the old man cry, he decided to go. He got two horses. "If I get killed, it will be well; you may have my horses." He followed and caught up with the party. He made medicine in the enemy's tracks. "I was not going to come, but since you asked me so hard, I came." He filled a pipe with tobacco and smoked on the buffalo chips lying on the tracks.

They started and sent scouts, who reported, "They are moving in a coulée." The warriors asked the rock-owner what to do. He told them to run immediately, not waiting for himself. His two young brothers were far in the lead, the elder one struck first-coup, the other dismounted and captured the enemy's gun. The Piegan ran into a wash, dug a pit and fought there. The rock-owner was far away, smoking. The man who had sought revenge said to him, "I asked for revenge. What are you doing here?" "I see I shall have to go no matter what comes of it." He ran into the thickest part of the fight and was wounded in the chest so that he was nearly dead when he was picked up. His four brothers

---

[1] A little above the site of Miles City.

were furious; they were going to kill the man who had asked him to go out. "It is as though you had killed him yourself; we'll kill you if he dies." He did not answer. They returned down-hearted because their leader was shot. He willed his rock to the brother who was a doctor. This one said, "I'll try to help you first, I don't know whether I can." He treated him and he improved, then he began to have faith again.

In the camp the people were down-hearted. The next day the doctor made them all stand toward the middle. There was no water to be seen in the river on account of the ice covering it. He went toward the river. A herald proclaimed that no one was to cross his tracks. The doctor made his patient dive into the water up to his neck four times. The river was covered with blood. He brought him back to the tipi, heated a stone, put cloth over it, and rubbed it over the sore part. Then the shaman was cured, and the people had a big dance.

The youngest of the brothers said, "As soon as the snow has disappeared, I am going to hunt medicine for myself." The oldest one answered: "You had better not go, you have all you want." "Something has always troubled me, I want to find out for myself." The boy left. The boys were the wealthiest people in camp and had everything they wished for. When this young boy left, he told his brother-in-law not to worry. He made his own arrows and killed meadowlarks, taking the first wing feathers to feather his arrows. He traveled about, trying to find out something. While walking he saw some cherry trees and among them some smoke. He sneaked up towards it and carefully approached. He saw a tipi with holes in it, and through one of them he saw a woman cutting lodge pegs (*t k'ace*). This woman was Hícictawìə. She had a kettle on the fire. He entered. "Well, well, my child, I am all alone. Where do you come from? Do you know me? Is that the reason you have come?" "I was traveling and saw the smoke, so I thought I should get something to eat." She had her tipi by the spring and she was sitting on one side. "Child, sit here." She spread something for him. She took out a parfleche of young buffalo skin and opened it. There were nice lumps of fat and pemmican in it. The boy ate the meal, then went and cut more cherry trees, got shafts for arrows, bit them with his teeth and stuck them all around. "Son, I'll tell you something. For a long time I have given you visions. You have not a strong will (*irðaxe*), that is why it has taken so long a time. I have been looking for you for a long time, but everything is the same to you (*dì xáxik*). Now I warn you not to go over there where the point of the hill is." (The tale here merges into a recital of Old-Woman's-Grandchild's adventures[1] with the snakes and the sucking monster.)

---

[1] This volume, 52 seq.

www.ingramcontent.com/pod-product-compliance
Lightning Source LLC
Chambersburg PA
CBHW072022080426
42733CB00010B/1788